EVERYDAY ACTIVISTS

Everyday Activists

*Undocumented Immigrants' Quest
for Justice and Well-Being*

Christina M. Getrich

NEW YORK UNIVERSITY PRESS
New York

NEW YORK UNIVERSITY PRESS
New York
www.nyupress.org

© 2025 by New York University
All rights reserved

Please contact the Library of Congress for Cataloging-in-Publication data.

ISBN: 9781479832224 (hardback)
ISBN: 9781479832231 (paperback)
ISBN: 9781479832255 (library ebook)
ISBN: 9781479832248 (consumer ebook)

This book is printed on acid-free paper, and its binding materials are chosen for strength and durability. We strive to use environmentally responsible suppliers and materials to the greatest extent possible in publishing our books.

Manufactured in the United States of America

10 9 8 7 6 5 4 3 2 1

Also available as an ebook

This book is dedicated to two of my most cherished teachers:

My father, Richard J. Getrich, who taught me the mechanics of writing, the importance of attending to detail, and how to find order amidst life's uncertanties.

My professor, Miguel Vásquez, who epitomized the scholar-activist with his dynamism, critical gaze, deep respect for community knowledge, and ethical mode of collaboration.

CONTENTS

LIST OF FIGURES AND TABLES

Introduction

Navigating Prolonged Policy Limbo in Everyday Life

Rebeca,[1] a thirty-two-year-old social worker originally from Peru, remembers vividly the Tuesday in September 2017 when her twin sister Yvette texted her with the update that the Deferred Action for Childhood Arrivals (DACA) program was going to be terminated. Created in 2012, DACA had provided the sisters, who came to the United States when they were fifteen and settled in suburban Maryland, with a temporary legal status that enabled them to work legally and protected them from deportation. As Rebeca explained, "[Yvette] checks the news almost every day. She's the one who texts me when anything [about DACA] happens. But I just don't like to think about it, to be honest, because I already have a lot going on and there's not much that I can do." Rebeca knew very well what life without DACA would be like since, as she noted, "we were already twenty-four when we got DACA. So we know that feeling of what it is like not having papers. I don't want to have to go through that again."

Rebeca recalled that when her family first migrated to join her maternal aunt in Maryland, "I didn't want to come. It was hard and we were mad at my parents that they brought us here. But then when we started school, it got better." When they turned seventeen, the girls started working at a national chain restaurant where they heard they could find work after they applied unsuccessfully to at least twenty other jobs; as Rebeca shared, "It was the only place where the owner was okay with taking us without papers." Rebeca described the working conditions as "stressful," recalling, "The manager kept changing our schedules. But we had to stay there because we had no choice and couldn't say anything." The sisters ultimately spent eight years working there while taking classes at a local community college, with Rebeca's interests gravitating toward health care and Yvette pursuing information technology. Rebeca remembers their manager telling them, "I don't know why you're studying, because you're never going to be able to work because you don't have papers."

President Obama introduced DACA to address the plight of some 2.1 million undocumented young adults like Rebeca and Yvette who migrated as children and came of age undocumented in U.S. schools and communities. Rebeca recalled the initial excitement she felt when she heard about DACA: "We filled out our applications right away, the same week we heard about it. We actually got the letter on the same day!" Once they received DACA status, Rebeca noticed that "the way our manager treated us was different right away because now we had papers. She was all nice, and then when we said we needed a day off, she said, 'Oh yeah, that's fine.'" Rebeca wrapped up her nursing program shortly thereafter and secured a far preferable and more lucrative job as a certified nursing assistant (CNA) in a safety-net hospital while she continued to work toward a bachelor's degree in psychology. Over the ten years it ultimately took her to finish her degree, she worked as a CNA and a Spanish-language interpreter. She was mostly uninsured while pursuing her bachelor's given that she worked part-time, which was quite ironic given that after receiving DACA she had always worked in the health care field. Rebeca then decided to pursue a master of social work (MSW), putting herself through school by working two jobs as an interpreter and family support worker.

Rebeca was barely into her MSW program when she received that text from Yvette that President Trump was attempting to rescind DACA. Rebeca took the news hard as she contemplated a potential return to not having the status that had facilitated her professional growth. Instead of cutting back her hours to focus on graduate school as she had planned, she actually took on more hours; as she told me in January 2018, "My plans changed since I had to save money because I don't know what's going to happen in a few months." Although many of her fellow DACA recipients took part in protests in nearby downtown Washington, D.C., Rebeca did not participate due to her insanely busy work schedule and because she had never taken part in any immigration-related protests before.

Instead, she channeled her anxieties about her future and used her voice in a different way. Though Rebeca had previously been guarded about sharing her status, the shift in political climate prompted her to be more open about it with friends and acquaintances, especially at work. As she explained, "Most of my coworkers at the hospital know that I have DACA because I posted something about DACA on Facebook. They asked me, 'So, tell me more about DACA' because many people didn't know much about it. I just want people to understand that there are so many young people going through this . . . this is our life. So, it was a way for me to bring awareness about DACA to people that didn't know." She quickly discovered that "everyone was really supportive. Some coworkers were like, 'Do you need anything? If you can't work for a few months and need money or anything, just let us know.' That was really nice." Instead of participating in mass mobilizations, Rebeca thus found her place in the immigrant justice movement through her everyday activism, by "representing DACA and being their source of information."

As she got deeper into her MSW program, Rebeca forged another node of everyday activism in 2020 through her work with immigrant high schoolers. Rebeca's MSW practicum took place at a large public high school with a sizable population of newly arrived immigrants. She felt particularly well suited for this position, based on her own background and experiences, and found it to be a good platform for sharing the navigational capital she had gained throughout her life as an undocumented and DACAmented immigrant. As she shared, "I've made good connections with the students. They're always asking me, 'How was it for you? How did you adapt?' I tell them, 'This is what worked for me and what didn't.' I share that with them and give them resources and help." Rebeca's navigational capital not only was useful for the students but also benefitted the teenagers' families and school staff. As she looked toward graduation and her social work licensure exam in the near future, Rebeca decided that her skill set would ultimately be best put to use in a career working with immigrant youth: "I wish I would have had a counselor or somebody to have done the same thing for me."

* * *

This book chronicles the lived experiences of DACA recipients like Rebeca as they have navigated prolonged policy limbo and grappled with deep uncertainty about their futures while also pursuing engaging and meaningful lives in the present. Like hundreds of thousands of other DACA recipients nationwide, Rebeca initially benefited immensely from receiving DACA, thriving professionally as she went from working in the informal economy, subject to the whims and scorn of her employer, to earning certifications and degrees that enabled her to serve in multiple professional roles as a CNA, interpreter, family support worker, and social worker. She specializes in serving immigrant clients and has been able to leverage her own life and work experiences in providing tailored care, which has benefited her clients but also the broader health care and educational systems within which she works. In spite of these positive incorporation strides, the DACA rescission announcement had an immediate effect on Rebeca's well-being. She took on extra hours to quell her anxieties about potentially losing status and no longer being able to work in the career field she had strived so hard to attain. Yet over the next few years, as the future of DACA grew ever-more uncertain, I also witnessed Rebeca flourishing as she discovered the power of her voice and the strength of the actions she takes in her everyday life in promoting well-being and justice for immigrants.

Rebeca's backstory is quite different from the typical DREAMer or DACA recipient as frequently represented in the media.[2] A basic internet search reveals how they are often portrayed in the public imagination: as youngsters who spent the majority of their childhoods in the United States and are "American" in every way but their legal status; as students who are unyielding in their pursuit of higher education and use symbols like graduation regalia and monarch butterflies to exemplify their dreams and right to move freely; and as dedicated activists staging mass mobilizations on their university campuses, at state legislature buildings, and in front of the Supreme Court, holding signs proclaiming, "We are all dreamers!" "DREAMers welcome!" and "Immigrants are #here to stay!" Indeed, these images convey the power and reach of the remarkable large-scale social movement that undocumented young adults have forged to fight tenaciously for policy reform to resolve their legal situation during the past nearly thirty years during which Congress has failed to pass major immigration reform.

Yet Rebeca does not identify as a DREAMer, and her life experiences vary considerably from these representations. Rebeca spent most of her childhood in Peru—a country not typically associated with DACA—

Figure I.1. A DREAMer sign at a Supreme Court protest, April 2016. Source: Christina M. Getrich.

before migrating to the United States as a high school student who had to quickly adapt to a new system and culture. She still identifies as Peruvian and maintains transnational connections via family members. She was already in her mid-twenties when DACA began, having negotiated many years of her adult life without a state-granted legal status, and has been doggedly focused on building her professional career over the past decade since receiving DACA. She has never participated in mass mobilizations related to immigration—nor has her twin sister or anyone in her immediate social circle. In fact, besides her sister, she knows very few other people who have DACA. Yet since I began conducting research with DACA recipients living in the Washington, D.C., Metropolitan region in 2016, I have found that Rebeca's experiences are not exceptional but rather resonate strongly with many other DACA recipients whose stories are not as well-known as they more quietly go about their adult lives. But to assert that these individuals are disinterested or disengaged from the immigrant justice struggle would be inaccurate. Instead, I have discovered that their political engagement strategies are rooted in everyday life and staged in more mundane locations like schools and workplaces, as Rebeca's actions underscore.

This book demonstrates that DACA recipients' legal status precarity produces forms of suffering that have tempered the program's beneficial impact.[3] Yet in response to this precarity, DACA recipients are forging political inclusion in the everyday by strategically deploying navigational capital and engaging in everyday activism in solidarity with other immigrants. This volume documents the harmful effects of precarious legal status on DACA recipients' health, but also how DACA recipients have cultivated resilience strategies for negotiating uncertainty and maintaining well-being. It highlights how DACA recipients gain access to resources within a complicated patchwork of local immigration-focused policies and leverage their navigational capital to provide critical forms of care to immigrants and advocate for their well-being. Further, it demonstrates that despite not identifying as activists, many DACA recipients channel their anguish about their legal situation into acts of everyday activism as they contribute to the larger immigrant justice project. This book thus demonstrates compellingly how political belonging is staked concertedly—and effectively—in the realm of everyday life. Activism itself is conventionally thought of as organized, collective, and public, set apart from the mundane, routine, and unnoticed aspects of the everyday.[4] However, as noted political scientist and anthropologist James C. Scott influentially argued, everyday forms of resistance are often effectively deployed by individuals in less visible ways to resist structures of power.[5] Indeed, everyday life is a productive site for locating resourceful political engagement strategies that work in conjunction with more conventional forms of activism as overlapping pathways for forging social change.[6]

The Establishment of DACA and the Ensuing Legal Roller Coaster

To contextualize DACA recipients' experiences over the last decade, it is important to understand the intricacies of the DACA program and how it became endangered. I have found from my own interactions with students, colleagues, friends, and even strangers that there are many misperceptions about DACA despite public awareness and support for DACA recipients growing tremendously after it came under attack during the first Trump administration. DACA was established by President Obama on June 15, 2012, to address the situation of undocumented young adults who arrived to the United States as young children but attended school and came of age in U.S. communities. Of the estimated 11+ million undocumented immigrants in the United States, at least 2.1 million have lived here since they were young children and spent much of their lives in the United States.[7]

DACA was created by executive order in the absence of immigration reform, which Congress has failed to pass since the mid-1990s despite numerous bipartisan attempts. The program was intended to be a stepping stone to provide qualifying undocumented young adults with legal work authorization and protection from deportation until Congress created a more permanent legalization pathway.[8] To qualify, applicants had to demonstrate that they possessed no lawful immigration status, were younger than thirty-one, came to the United States before age sixteen, had continuously resided in the United States since 2007, were enrolled in or graduated from high school, and had not been convicted of a felony or misdemeanor that "pose[d] a threat to national security or public safety."[9] These criteria meant that Rebeca and Yvette (who came at age fifteen) barely qualified; if they had been even just a little older—like their elder sister, who ultimately returned to Peru—they would have been ineligible. Since the program began, more than 825,000 individuals have received DACA.[10]

Provisional statuses like DACA have proliferated globally as a key feature of contemporary migration governance as states have become less likely to grant more permanent forms of status, instead intentionally crafting policies that render migrants legally precarious[11] and structurally vulnerable.[12] As one of many such statuses, DACA must be renewed every two years through an extensive and expensive application process. Because it was established by executive order instead of legislated through Congress, DACA has always had an uncertain future since incoming presidents may choose to retain, revoke, or replace their predecessors' orders. Indeed, the limitations of executive orders became quite clear when President Trump sought to revoke DACA five years into the program as part of his broader agenda of aggressively targeting immigrants. This move effectively turned DACA recipients into political pawns.

In the aftermath of the rescission, DACA recipients have been on "a non-stop roller coaster through the U.S. legal system," as public policy analyst Ewaoluwa Obatuase describes it, involving lawsuits and court decisions about the authority to create the program and seeking to determine its future.[13] The U.S. Supreme Court took up the case and ultimately blocked the Trump administration's attempt to dismantle the program in June 2020 on the grounds that the rescission was executed in an arbitrary and capricious manner. However, subsequent U.S. District Court and Fifth Circuit Court of Appeals rulings in 2021, 2022, and 2023 declared the program to be unlawful and dictated that renewals would be accepted but first-time applications would not, leaving thousands who might have benefited unable to apply. Indeed, some 1.16 million individuals could have been eligible for DACA based on the original criteria for the program, underscoring that there are ultimately fewer undocumented young adults nationwide with DACA than without it.[14] The program remains in legal peril, and if a court case seeking to end DACA goes to the U.S. Supreme Court once again as expected, the conservative-leaning court would likely not uphold it. These legal proceedings and the reelection of Trump have left the ultimate fate of DACA quite uncertain.

The DACA program is also emblematic of the phenomenon of Congress steadily delegating power regarding immigration policymaking to the executive branch, rendering the president "our immigration policymaker-in-chief."[15] While the structure of immigration law may appear to limit the president's policymaking discretion, in practice it has actually enabled the president to exert considerable control over the types and numbers of immigrants able to enter and reside in the United States. This trend is clear not only through actions like DACA that President Obama took to be more inclusionary but also the 472 more exclusionary immigration-related actions President Trump took during his first presidency, such as banning immigrants from several majority-Muslim nations, increasing immigration enforcement nationwide, making legal migration more challenging, and restricting humanitarian protection.[16] Though the actions related to DACA taken by Obama and Trump are starkly different in tenor, both administrations are part of a much longer period of immigrant exclusion stemming back to the 1990s, during which there has been no widespread mechanism for gaining legal status and immigrants have been increasingly and aggressively criminalized under both Democrats and Republicans.

Figure I.2. May Day immigrant rights protest in Washington, D.C., May 2017. Source: Christina M. Getrich.

Yet during this decades-long period without reform, immigrants have actively contested their exclusion and fought for policy change. In fact, DACA itself was created in direct response to more than a decade of undocumented young adults' tenacious organizing efforts and forging of the large-scale social movement initially known as the DREAMer movement. These young activists became a "politically identifiable group with a legitimate and identifiable voice," as sociologist Walter J. Nicholls describes them, which was noteworthy given their youth, their practice of making claims on the state despite not being official members, and the emergence of their movement in an exclusionary policy context.[17] Though President Obama is often credited with DACA, these activists' mobilizing served as the impetus behind the executive order, which clearly mirrored their language and arguments.[18] Although federal immigration reform has remained elusive, undocumented youth activism has yielded more than twenty state-level tuition equity laws, promoting greater access to higher education and improved career pathways. Their political engagement strategies have been facile and evolved to mesh with emerging sociopolitical developments, including the DACA rescission announcement in 2017 and subsequent court battles. Over time, youth activists have escalated their strategies to carry out staged and nonstaged acts of civil disobedience aimed at exposing the violence of the state, particularly in the first Trump era. In the aftermath of the attempted rescission, DACA recipients commanded increasing public attention and raised national awareness about their situation and the urgency of broader reform. As they became widely recognized and viewed as a legitimate political force, though, they have increasingly used their platform to advocate for policies that benefit *all* immigrants—not just undocumented youth, who are often perceived as the most "deserving" immigrants.[19]

Yet not all of the 825,000 DACA recipients—and the remaining million-plus undocumented young adults who did not receive DACA—actively participate in these mass mobilizations or regard themselves to be activists. Thus, if we are to understand the full impact of the DACA program, it is important to look beyond just the experiences of those who have been engaged in public, collective activism. Indeed, many immigrant young adults are deeply engaged in advocating for immigrant well-being and justice in their daily lives in ways that are less public and visible but still quite impactful. Many DACA recipients are also now deep into their adult lives and careers at this point—some even on the threshold of being "middle-aged"—and have found new outlets for engaging politically surrounding immigration. There is much more about DACA recipients' quotidian lives and long-term incorporation trajectories that has not yet been comprehensively captured but is essential for fully understanding the legacies of the DACA program.

DACA: Successful Immigrant Incorporation Policy or Abject Political Failure?

Social scientists have long been interested in the incorporation trajectories of undocumented young adults, who are members of what they refer to as the "1.5 generation," to distinguish them from first-generation immigrant adults and their second-generation U.S.-born children since their experiences are distinct from either group. DACA recipients among the 1.5 generation began arriving as children starting in the

1980s and came of age undocumented in the 1990s and early 2000s, when there was no widespread legal mechanism for them to gain formal status.[20] Undocumented children are guaranteed legal access to public school until high school graduation through the 1982 *Plyler v. Doe* U.S. Supreme Court decision, but they face "blocked paths" to higher education and the workforce into adulthood, placing them at greater risk for hardship and poverty.[21] DACA, which President Obama announced at the White House on the thirtieth anniversary of the *Plyler* decision, was created to address these "blocked paths" by opening up pathways for DACA recipients to legally participate in adult life.

Since DACA began in 2012, scholars have been tracking its impact on recipients' trajectories. Initial research that started coming out a year into the program provided an invaluable national demographic portrait of DACA recipients, and subsequent annual updates have captured recipients' evolving experiences under DACA. Sociologist Roberto G. Gonzales, who has led the mixed-method National UnDACAmented Research Project (NURP) since 2012,[22] has declared DACA indisputably the most successful policy of immigration integration since the 1980s.[23] Political scientist Tom K. Wong and his colleagues have likewise dubbed DACA "an integration success story" based on the results of their annual survey conducted since 2014 in collaboration with the Center for American Progress (CAP), United We Dream (UWD), and the National Immigration Law Center (NILC).[24] These leading scholars of DACA (and others) have lauded its benefits in peer-reviewed academic articles as well as in public-facing reports available via public policy research and advocacy organizations and through contributions to statements, memos, and amicus briefs highlighting scholarly research on DACA to advocate for its preservation and fortification.

Research has unequivocally demonstrated that one of the most impactful benefits of DACA is access to a legal work permit, which authorizes recipients' employment in the formal economy. Early on, scholars were quite focused on economic integration, finding that DACA served to increase high school completion and access to higher education and improved recipients' socioeconomic status and earnings while enabling them to secure jobs that better aligned with their professional goals. Beyond these economic gains, DACA was critical in opening recipients' access to driver's licenses, bank accounts, credit cards, and homeownership, all of which facilitated their incorporation. After a few cycles, the annual surveys directed by Gonzales and Wong also started demonstrating the positive impact that DACA had on family and community life, health and well-being, and belonging and civic participation, demonstrating that DACA recipients were able to achieve inclusion in much more than just economic terms. Into the first Trump era, however, the studies started tracking concerns about immigration enforcement and deportation risk, family vulnerability, and uncertainty of life with DACA, underscoring quite markedly the need to understand more than just DACA's benefits.

Scholars also started parsing out variability in DACA recipients' incorporation pathways stratified by gender, ethnic and national origin group, and age—key factors shaping transitions to adulthood.[25] For instance, females with DACA achieved higher educational attainment and secured employment in higher-skilled occupations than their male counterparts, while males were more likely to stay in school and delay labor force participation if they were eligible for DACA.[26] Males were also more likely than females to obtain credit cards and driver's licenses.[27] For Latinx men in particular, work authorization may have been particularly impactful in enabling them to better fulfill gendered expectations of being a financial provider, also influencing their decisions to get married and embark on parenthood.[28] Within the Latinx population, however, Mexicans were less likely than other Latinos/Caribbeans to increase their earnings, open a bank account, and obtain a driver's license, underscoring the importance of parsing out differences between national origin groups. Among both Mexican men and women, older recipients initially benefitted more from DACA, but the program was ultimately more impactful for younger recipients in terms of labor force participation and employment.[29] Younger recipients were also more likely initially to obtain driver's licenses and health care.[30]

Scholars have also demonstrated how DACA recipients' incorporation experiences vary considerably by geographic and socio-legal contexts.[31] Congressional inaction on federal immigration has devolved responsibility to states and localities, which became much more active in immigration policymaking starting in the early 2000s.[32] Statewide laws and local resolutions related to immigration and education, employment and workforce development, health, public benefits, identification and driver's licenses, and law enforcement have proliferated, varying considerably in their intent depending on the jurisdiction.[33] More integrative jurisdictions like California and New York have expanded rights and benefits accorded to immigrant young adults by enabling them to obtain driver's licenses, increasing access to health and social services, offering in-state college tuition, and curbing collaboration between local enforcement and federal agencies, while more exclusionary jurisdictions, by contrast, have attempted to reduce their rights and benefits.[34] The most exclusionary jurisdictions are found in new immigrant destinations like Indiana, Iowa, North Carolina, and South Carolina that are smaller, more geographically dispersed, and/or more politically conservative. Immigrants in new immigrant destinations confront weakened prospects for structural incorporation and upward economic mobility[35] and may experience racialized incorporation and rampant discrimination.[36]

Immigrants' incorporation trajectories are thus shaped not only by federal policymaking but also by variable and evolving state and local policies. Geographer Monica W. Varsanyi and her colleagues describe the "multi-layered jurisdictional patchwork" of overlapping and potentially conflicting immigration policies in the United States that produce uncertainty for immigrants as they must determine which policies prevail and attempt to navigate them.[37] Immigrants can also experience inclusion and exclusion simultaneously at federal, state, and local levels within what sociologists Tanya Golash-Boza and Zulema Valdez term "nested contexts of reception."[38] In more exclusionary contexts, immigrant young adults endure what sociologist Alexis Silver terms "tectonic incorporation" as they navigate political and institutional structures that are contradictory and move unpredictably.[39] These local contexts can also shift over time, which can potentially lead to what sociologist Jennifer Jones characterizes as "intragenerational reverse incorporation" through which immigrants see their social and economic gains reversed.[40]

The volatility and uncertainty surrounding DACA have fomented a much more pessimistic interpretation of the program's impact, often leveled by what sociologist Carlos Aguilar terms DACAdemics.[41] Legal studies scholar Joel Sati has deemed DACA to be an "abject political failure," noting that it exceptionalized "deserving" and "good" immigrants instead of acknowledging the humanity of all immigrants, ultimately compromising the end goal of securing citizenship for all twelve million undocumented immigrants.[42] He argues that DACA is a political tool used to pacify DREAMers and concludes that despite personally benefitting from the program, "it was a Faustian bargain that we never should have struck."[43] Sati also calls explicit attention to the violence of the state in politically, legally, and socially constructing illegalized persons,[44] further noting that "even if you *do* have the formal status of citizenship, that does not guarantee that the state will ensure your substantive enjoyment of the status and its benefits."[45]

Anthropologist Xitlalli Alvarez Almendariz likewise foregrounds state violence, arguing that DACA "entrenches young migrants' criminality by codifying border crossing at any age as a grave transgression that warrants indefinite surveillance. DACA recipients often find themselves closer to the grip of carceral systems, as this is the price of precarious and conditional 'protection.' Through the program's collection of personal information and close inspection of criminal history, the tentacles of federal and local law enforcement collude to ensure that DACA recipients are on the state's radar—an amplified concern during the Trump administrations."[46] Accordingly, these scholars argue for a shift in focus away from the "short-term success" of a program benefitting a small group of illegalized immigrants to the deeper structural context of policing. Such a shift foregrounds the state's active role in upholding illegalization and emphasizes that seeking "protection" under DACA is to accept the terms and legitimacy of one's own domination.[47]

Sati and Alvarez Almendariz's arguments sharpen the focus on state violence as a cornerstone of U.S. immigration policy and underscore that citizenship has always functioned through a logic of exclusion and legacy of violence. The United States was built on a foundation of settler colonialism, genocide, slavery, and white supremacy, which is often obscured by the pervasive myth about the country being a nation of immigrants.[48] The Naturalization Act of 1790 established that citizenship was to be the domain of free white men of good moral character, upholding prevailing racial, gendered, and class-based notions of belonging.[49] Immigrant incorporation has also been shaped by global capitalism, as migrants predominantly from the Global South who are largely racialized as nonwhite work in a labor market shaped by exploitation, oppression, and patriarchy.[50]

During some periods of the twentieth century, the pendulum of immigration policymaking swung more in the direction of inclusion—as evidenced, for example, by passage of the Immigration and Nationality Act of 1965, which eliminated discriminatory national origins quotas and majorly opened migratory pathways from around the world.[51] However, since the mid-1990s, federal immigration policymaking has taken a harder exclusionary turn through the passage of far-reaching and harsh anti-immigrant policies that have "erected needless and counterproductive barriers" to immigrant incorporation.[52] In 1996, for instance, the federal government passed three major policies with significant implications for immigrants: the Antiterrorism and Effective Death Penalty Act, the Illegal Immigration Reform and Immigrant Responsibility Act, and the Personal Responsibility and Work Opportunity Reconciliation Act. Together, these policies served to exclude and criminalize immigrants—notably, both undocumented immigrants and lawful permanent residents (LPRs; often referred to colloquially as "legal" immigrants). After September 11, 2001, immigrants were increasingly portrayed as a "threat" to the security of the nation and even more explicitly linked to criminality.[53]

Over the past three decades, increasingly aggressive policies passed at all levels of government have propagated state-sanctioned violence against immigrants with precarious legal status, LPRs, and even their U.S.-born children.[54] Starting in the mid-1990s, enforcement policies and practices implemented at the U.S.-Mexico border have subjected immigrants—and local residents of all statuses—to militarized violence, entrapping and immobilizing them and exposing them to extreme violence after deportation, with profound consequences for their health and well-being.[55] As techniques perfected at the border became a "mobile technology" exported to the U.S. interior in the first decade of the 2000s, subnational zones of confinement have emerged that resemble carceral spaces.[56] During that same period, enforcement activities also started devolving to nonfederal law enforcement agencies through the 287(g) waiver and Secure Communities programs.[57] The hyperfunded immigration enforcement machine has produced record numbers of deportations and removals—across both Republican and Democratic administrations and Congresses—and fueled the massive expansion of the immigrant detention system.[58] The immigration enforcement regime is militarized, traumatic, implicitly racist, and profoundly violent by design, with rippling effects on individuals, families, and entire communities.[59]

Beyond the direct violence of the state, critical migration scholars have started theorizing other more indirect forms of violence that manifest along what anthropologists Nancy Scheper-Hughes and Philippe Bourgois term the violence continuum to capture the range of forms and intensities that violence takes.[60] One such concept, sociologists Cecilia Menjívar and Leisy Abrego's influential legal violence, captures the normalized but cumulatively injurious effects of the law that manifest in work, school, and family life, shaping immigrants' everyday lives but also their longer-term incorporation.[61] Scholars have argued that DACA itself constitutes a form of legal violence since the status affords beneficiaries greater social inclusion, but simultaneous awareness that their gains are fragile and contested.[62] The state also enacts more subtle forms of violence through temporal governance, controlling immigrants' time through imposed periods of waiting in spaces like refugee camps and detention centers. Even outside of these controlled spaces, waiting functions as a means of dispossession as migrants experience detachment from the temporal rhythms of "normal" life.[63] Scholars have also described the violence of uncertainty, which is enacted through systematic personal, social, and institutional instability that injects fear into basic daily interactions and has a deleterious impact on immigrants' health.[64] Immigrants with precarious status may also encounter bureaucratic violence as they experience systematic harm through everyday bureaucratic processes and practices.[65] Collectively, these powerful forms of everyday violence[66] make a deep imprint on immigrants' quotidian lives and overall well-being.

Squarely naming the forms of state-sanctioned everyday violence to which DACA recipients are regularly subjected necessarily leads to a different focus on the "ugly underside of integration," as Alvarez Almendariz refers to it.[67] DACAdemics and allied scholars have thus reframed the end goal of immigration activism as something beyond just gaining formal legal recognition from the state. As Alvarez Almendariz explains, "Fighting for 'protection' under DACA is a strategy of recognition and inclusion, rather than an abolitionist endeavor that rejects the state's active role in upholding illegalization." Instead, they (with anthropologist Elizabeth Hanna Rubio) call for a different focus on alternative immigrant justice strategies illegalized activists pursue.[68] For many, these strategies involve community building with "other illegalized people to find ways to survive apart from hegemonic gazes and structures."[69] Some activists have become even more radical in their strategies, including DACA recipients who are electing to "self-deport" and leave the United States as a rebuke of the state's role in dictating how they live their lives.[70]

This book examines an alternative set of political engagement strategies carried out by nonactivists more quietly, on a smaller scale, and situated in the realm of everyday life. The strategies these DACA recipients are pursuing involve a different type of community building: deploying their navigational capital and providing support to other immigrants as well as engaging in everyday activism in the settings they regularly frequent. I argue that their actions, though unquestionably less radical than the political engagement strategies of many of their activist counterparts, enable them to wrest control over the state violence to which they are regularly subjected and serve as a complement to other, more visible critiques of the state as part of the larger immigrant justice project.

Investigating DACA Recipients' Experiences in the D.C. Metro Region

This book represents the culmination of a longitudinal, collaborative research project conducted between 2016 and 2021 with DACA recipients living in the Washington, D.C., Metropolitan region. The book's longitudinal approach provides an important temporal window into how changing policies shape immigrant young adults' lives over time and across the life course. It follows DACA recipients' lives across distinct periods, starting when DACA was fully intact under President Obama (in 2016; phase I), extending through the heightened targeting of immigrants and attempt to rescind the program during the first Trump administration (2017–18; phase II), and continuing into the Biden era during which DACA continued to languish with an uncertain future amid legal battles and congressional inaction (2020–21; phase III).[71] Briefly, the project's research design featured participant observation, semistructured interviews (79 total, with 30, 25, and 24 in each

Figure 1.3. The research team, March 2017. Source: Christina M. Getrich.

respective phase), a questionnaire, and regular engagement with a community advisory board (CAB) (see appendix A for more details about the research design and reflections on the evolving methodology).

As a critically engaged immigration scholar and medical anthropologist, I began this project curious to know about how gaining DACA status had impacted undocumented young adults' health and well-being. At the time—around DACA's three-year mark—the focus was more on tracking population-level trends in the realms in which DACA had the most measurable impact: educational attainment and labor force participation. While there was a general sense that DACA had improved recipients' access to health care and positively impacted their well-being, these realms were still relatively understudied. To explore them more concertedly, I formed a research team of student researchers—undergraduate students Alaska Burdette, Ana Ortez-Rivera, and Delmis Umanzor, who participated in the project for its duration and became invaluable long-term collaborators, and graduate students Kaelin Rapport and Umai Habibah, who participated through phase I. Phase I took place in 2016, during which the team recruited thirty local DACA recipients to participate. We discovered that DACA recipients' access to care was still quite constrained and that although DACA had positively impacted their well-being in some respects, they still experienced psychological distress due to the upcoming election and ongoing vulnerabilities of their legally precarious family members. Thus, I characterize this period as one of *tempered gains*.

I continued to adapt the project iteratively over the next few years in response to evolving sociopolitical developments and participants' preferences. After President Trump started aggressively targeting immigrants and DACA in early 2017, we held a community meeting to share findings and strategize about next steps. Stemming from that meeting, we formed a CAB of DACA recipients to guide the research, evolving into a more participatory structure as we began phase II in 2017. The CAB identified mental health as a critical concern, and the focus during this middle phase became how DACA recipients were, to quote anthropologist Anna L. Tsing, *"getting by* in terrifying times."[72] Given the constraints we previously identified, we became interested in how participants navigated access to resources and care. Though we (unsurprisingly) encountered profound psychological distress, participants were also building their knowledge of policies and services available to immigrants and navigating realms like employment, health care, and housing as they transitioned more deeply into adulthood. Although many DACA recipients nationwide became more involved in mass mobilizations given the urgency of their legal situation, our participants were instead cultivating more localized political engagement strategies rooted in the everyday.

We continued to follow participants' lives after another important DACA-related temporal marker: the June 2020 Supreme Court ruling temporarily upholding DACA. We chronicled the impact of prolonged policy limbo, though maintained our focus on the strategies DACA recipients used to get by. We expected to find DACA recipients grappling even more intensely with uncertainty and its impact on their adult lives, especially in the midst of the emerging COVID-19 pandemic. Yet participant after participant described their pursuit of "normal" lives and foregrounded affirmative developments about new career opportunities, evolving romantic relationships, homes they had purchased, trips they had taken (or were planning to take), and moves they had made. With the pandemic raging, they were deeply engaged in care work that they also increasingly framed as acts of political advocacy. This phase, then, ultimately coalesced around how participants were *flourishing*[73] as they actively pursued well-being and justice.

From the beginning of the project, I was struck by how different my participants' experiences were from those captured in the literature. One notable difference was rooted in local geography. Even by the two-year mark of the program,[74] scholars had started noting how DACA recipients' experiences varied immensely depending on the state where they lived and the local policies shaping everyday life for immigrants there. Yet the focus still remained largely on states as a unit of analysis—both traditional, immigrant-friendly settlement locations like California, Illinois, and New York as well as newer, more exclusionary rural destinations like Georgia, Indiana, and North and South Carolina.[75] My participants, however, lived in a very different type of place: a large, multijurisdictional metropolitan area consisting of multiple states (Maryland and Virginia) and the capital city of Washington, D.C., with local policies that varied considerably in their treatment of immigrants. Most also lived in suburbs—a typical settlement pattern for immigrants in the D.C. Metro region but one less commonly described. As participants talked about their lives, they drew distinctions between locations within the region, talked about moves between places, and described social networks dispersed throughout the region. Large, multijurisdictional metropolitan regions have largely been overlooked as distinct contexts of reception[76] but are nuanced local contexts that merit further attention, particularly since many immigrants nationwide move to and live in them.

The D.C. Metro region is also distinctive because of the composition and diversity of its immigrant population. Though not a classic immigrant gateway like other East Coast cities including Boston and New York, the D.C. Metro region has transformed over the past fifty years into a hyperdiverse gateway and preferred settlement destination for immigrants from a notably long list of countries.[77] Nearly a quarter of the region's population was foreign-born in 2021, with large numbers of Latinx, Asian, and African immigrants, though no single country of origin predominates, unlike other major cities like Chicago, Los Angeles, and Miami. DACA recipients in the D.C. Metro region mirror these local trends and diversity. Much of the scholarship on undocumented young adults is focused on Latinx immigrants—who indeed are the largest share of DACA recipients overall. However, DACA recipients are nationals of more than 195 different countries,[78] many of which are not captured at all in the public imagination or academic literature. This book highlights the experiences of DACA recipients from thirteen different countries of origin, spanning North America (Mexico), Central America (El Salvador, Honduras, and Nicaragua), and South America (Argentina, Bolivia, Brazil, Colombia, and Peru) as well as Africa (Liberia and Senegal) and Asia (Indonesia and South Korea). Beyond national origin, participants occupied other social locations, including race, ethnicity, age, gender, sexuality, and religion, that shaped how they experienced their precarious legal status, underscoring the importance of taking an intersectional approach[79] and highlighting the multidimensionality of undocumented young adults' life experiences.[80]

Another distinctive aspect of my participants' experiences is that they were largely not activists or engaged in the youth-led large-scale social movement. Quite a bit of research on undocumented young adults has focused on their political activism on university campuses and within community-based organizations (CBOs), particularly in immigrant-friendly cities with a large infrastructure of CBOs[81] such as Los Angeles and San Francisco,[82] Chicago,[83] and New York.[84] Only eight of my original thirty participants (27 percent) had participated in immigration activism during their lives, and only one identified as an activist by the end of the project. Some of this pattern is attributable to the fact that participants were not recruited on the basis of being activists or through their affiliation with campus organizations or CBOs, in contrast to the major national surveys on DACA.[85] Yet their experiences may actually be *more* reflective of the thousands of undocumented young adults nationwide who have never participated in immigration-related activism but are nonetheless engaging in the struggle for well-being and justice in less conventional—and immediately visible—ways.

Further, my participants' experiences underscore that they are not *merely* youth and indeed beg a larger question about how precisely to characterize them. Anthropologist Alyshia Gálvez has similarly wrestled with the appropriate terms to use to describe undocumented young adults, indicating that many have noted that "the term *youth* is infantilizing or maybe inaccurate" given that they are now in their twenties or even older.[86] When I first met participants in 2016, they ranged between eighteen and twenty-eight years old, placing them squarely in *early* or *young adulthood* in Erik Erikson's classic psychosocial development model.[87] Life course scholars conventionally describe the transition to adulthood in reference to five milestones or markers: completing school, moving out of the parental home, establishing employment, getting married, and becoming a parent.[88] These markers, however, are predicated on a normative U.S. early adulthood that does not account for cultural and religious practices, let alone structural influences on these milestones.[89] A newer category known as *emerging adulthood* more aptly captures the "winding road" to adulthood characteristic of contemporary industrialized societies in which young people are postponing typical life course transitions while living in a sustained sense of limbo.[90] Yet this sustained limbo does not reflect the existential challenges of undertaking these transitions while possessing precarious legal status. I ultimately use the term "undocumented young adults" in line with the literature, though I recognize quite clearly that adulthood is a slippery construct.

Despite these definitional challenges, Gálvez notes that there are a unique "set of characteristics, organizations, and moments conjuncturally shared by this particular subset of the larger population" that sets them apart experientially from other immigrants.[91] This book enhances our understanding of the everyday lives of this distinctive subset of the undocumented immigrant population by chronicling the lived experiences of a diverse set of DACA recipients in a large, multijurisdictional, hyperdiverse metropolitan region that is underrepresented in scholarly discussions about undocumented young adults. I follow developments in their lives over a five-year period during which they became adults, enduring prolonged policy limbo that produced deep uncertainty about their futures while they simultaneously pursued meaning and found order in their everyday lives.

Theoretical Frames for Contextualizing DACA Recipients' Incorporation Trajectories

In this book I argue that despite experiencing embodied distress due to their legal status precarity, DACA recipients are forging political inclusion through their deployment of navigational capital and engagement in everyday activism. I describe the structural forces that subject

DACA recipients to oppression and evoke very real anxieties, fears, and traumas, but also illuminate the ways in which they wrest control over insecurity and uncertainty by channeling their energies into the ordinary activities of everyday life where they make a deep and meaningful impact on their families and communities. In taking such an approach, I heed the appeals of DACAdemics to produce an account of DACA recipients' lives that does not "perpetuate a voyeuristic narrative of consistent suffering" but rather centers their agency and persistence by highlighting their navigational strategies and creative forms of resistance beyond political protest.[92] Indeed, my participants also shifted my analytic gaze in this direction as they focused less over time on the toll of possessing precarious legal status and more on the ways in which they were getting by and even flourishing—and sharing their knowledge, skills, and resources in solidarity with other immigrants in the process.

This book makes critical contributions to interdisciplinary theoretical debates about the embodiment of legal status precarity, the deployment of navigational capital, and engagement in everyday activism. The time period during which this project unfolded in the late 2010s mapped on to intensifying appeals to decolonize the social sciences and humanities as well as the research enterprise itself amid the first election of Donald Trump, national reckoning over racial injustice led by the Movement for Black Lives, and recognition of the myriad of social inequalities laid bare by the COVID-19 pandemic. These developments and currents influenced the research as I was conducting it and ultimately shaped my interpretations and the writing of this book.

Since the 1980s and 1990s, critical and Black feminist anthropologists have called for centering the theoretical contributions of nonwhite, female, and other minoritized scholars historically marginalized within the scholarly canon as a vision of how anthropology can reckon with its deeply colonial roots and instead be deployed as a tool of social change.[93] Carrying forward the charge of this "decolonizing generation" into the 2000s, Black and Indigenous scholars were at the forefront in theorizing about oppressive systems of knowledge production in novel ways while promoting a more deeply engaged mode of justice-oriented research practice deeply attentive to Indigenous ways of knowing and being.[94] Yet the election of Trump in 2016 activated critically engaged scholars to vociferously contest the overt racism, sexism, and xenophobia he fomented and enacted. Despite the widespread perception that the election represented some kind of marked shift in the national climate, anthropologists Jonathan Rosa and Yarimar Bonilla implored that the election of Trump not be exceptionalized but instead be properly situated within long-standing histories of domination and systems of inequality rooted in settler colonialism, chattel slavery, white supremacy, U.S. statehood, and global capitalism.[95] Further, their call to "unsettle anthropology" by interrogating these roots echoed and amplified the importance of attending to other ways of knowing, including those emerging from Black studies, ethnic studies, and Indigenous studies.[96]

In the late 2010s, several influential works from Latinx/Chicanx and immigration studies made important theoretical and methodological interventions and sharpened the theoretical frames through which I examine immigrant young adults' lives. Sociologist Leisy J. Abrego and education scholar Genevieve Negrón-Gonzales's pathbreaking *We Are Not Dreamers* showcases the contributions of currently or formerly undocumented immigrants as knowledge producers and central theorists of undocumented life in the United States. These scholars "speak back" to existing scholarship largely conducted by nonimmigrants and "remake the bodies of literature that speak to their experiences."[97]

Beyond this foundational volume, a cadre of currently or formerly undocumented scholars have also produced theoretically rich scholarship that is "about us, for us, by us," as articulated by anthropologist Argenis Hurtado Moreno.[98] Carlos Aguilar, for instance, articulates a novel theoretical framework, Undocumented Critical Theory (UndocuCrit), as "a new DACAdemic school of thought" that offers a roadmap for scholars through its enumeration of key tenets that honor the experiences of immigrant communities in negotiating fear and liminality and illuminate the importance of alternative forms of capital and centrality of relationships.[99] In *Decolonizing Ethnography*, women's and gender studies scholar Carolina Alonso Bejarano, anthropologist Daniel M. Goldstein, and activists Lucia López Juárez and Mirian A. Mijangos García present an innovative way of centering "alternative anthropologies."[100] Their emergent undocumented activist theory showcases how ethnography can serve as a tool for immigrants to theorize about their lives, in the process serving both academic and activist ends. Central to their framework is the affirmation that "all kinds of people—including ethnographers' collaborators—are theorists, often developing their own explanatory frames that make sense given their own knowledge and experience."[101]

Taking this assertion seriously, in this book I bring immigrant young adults' explanatory frames into direct conversation with academic ones. Indeed, there was convergence between these insider explanatory frames and analytic frames that conveyed very similar phenomena—albeit in quite different terms. Although I am a white nonimmigrant U.S. citizen professor in her forties who does not share many common bases of identity with my participants, I endeavor to do justice to the explanatory frames they shared with me and place them into appropriate context.[102] As I wrote the book, I also talked through these ideas with DACA recipient participants, CAB members, students, colleagues, and friends who have offered their feedback on—and ultimately overall endorsement of—my interpretations.

The Embodiment of Legal Status Precarity—"Living Life in Cycle"

The first major contribution of the book is its description of how legal status precarity is embodied by DACA recipients, impacting their mental health and overall well-being, but also deeper sense of time and space. In the decades-long period during which there has been no immigration reform or widespread mechanism for gaining more permanent status, scholars have theorized about the implications of being physically present in the nation-state but legally ambiguous in status.[103] Sociologist Cecilia Menjívar's foundational concept of liminal legality captures how immigrants with temporary status—like DACA and Temporary Protected Status (TPS)—occupy a unique legal position situated in the gray area between being documented and undocumented.[104] She argues that this in-between status penetrates different spheres of immigrants' everyday lives, influencing their educational and economic trajectories, disrupting participation in social life, impacting family relationships and social networks, and compromising emotional well-being.[105]

Indeed, scholars have tracked the implications of liminal legality on DACA recipients' emotional well-being over the life of the program. As sociologist Caitlin Patler and her colleagues demonstrated, initially,

DACA recipients experienced positive emotional effects from gaining status.[106] However, even with DACA fully intact, they still suffered psychological distress because of the temporary and politically contingent nature of their status.[107] DACA recipients experience temporal uncertainty as they are compelled to wait for years to find out their ultimate fate without a clear sense of when that will occur.[108] This uncertainty also serves as a threat to DACA recipients' deeper sense of ontological security—or the ability to count on the stability of the future.[109] Ontological insecurity can also be exacerbated by sudden and unexpected policy changes[110] and new stress events like threats to rights and discriminatory public sentiment.[111] During the years of appeals determining the future of the program after the rescission attempt, DACA recipients' health outcomes have worsened[112] as they have grappled with anticipatory loss and a range of emotions, including denial, sadness, disappointment, anger, resentment, and desperation about the potential end of DACA.[113] DACA recipients therefore experience their status not only as a positive force that facilitates their incorporation into U.S. society but also as a form of state discipline and even violence.[114]

There is growing attention to how precarious legal statuses shape immigrants' everyday, embodied experiences of being in the world in temporally and spatially uneven ways.[115] This book extends our understanding of how DACA recipients experience legal status precarity and the vulnerabilities associated with it at different time points and in distinct spaces. I argue that it is not merely temporal uncertainty and ontological insecurity that encroaches on DACA recipients' emotional well-being but also emerging forms of temporal dispossession they experience as they contend with lost or delayed documents, the existential fatigue of renewing their status at two-year intervals, and time they have "lost" from submitting renewals early due to fear about the program ending and anticipated bureaucratic delays. These experiences underscore the ways in which state-imposed uncertainty and waiting serve as forms of temporal governance, but also how bureaucratic violence can magnify psychological distress.[116] I also highlight strategies DACA recipients have cultivated for proactively wresting temporal control,[117] including their intentional focus on living "normal" lives in the present. I demonstrate how they enact this normalcy spatially by mapping out and navigating access to resources throughout the D.C.

Metro region, which they have then leveraged to help other immigrants in their personal and professional lives as forms of solidarity.

Of course, my participants did not use terms like "legal status precarity" or "bureaucratic violence" to describe their evolving legal situation or the structural forces enveloping their lives. Yet their insights about contending with the stresses associated with their status and intentional focus on pursuing normalcy in the everyday echo these academic constructs. Juan, who migrated to the United States from Mexico when he was two,[118] spoke powerfully about the anxiety inherent in possessing a temporary status. In August 2020, Juan reflected, "You live your life in an eighteen-month cycle, constantly. Right now I'm in like month four or five. I can breathe easy, right? But five months ago, it was all anxiety because I had to worry about renewing again. When you're in the middle of it, you try not to think of month seventeen or eighteen. You're like, 'I'm only in month five. I'm okay.' It never feels like it's enough time. It always feels like you blink and then you have to apply again." Juan proclaimed that the phenomenon of living "life in an eighteen-month cycle" was not at all unique to him but rather a defining characteristic of being a DACA recipient. He lamented, "No one is immune from that anxiety . . . everyone I talk to says the same thing."

Though they do not know each other, Madeline, who came from Senegal when she was five, had described the state-imposed temporal rhythm of her life in almost the exact same terms just a few weeks prior as she talked about "living life twenty months at time." She continued by saying, "It's like a pendulum or a weird seesaw where you're up and you're down for something that has a relatively quick turnaround. You just get tired, you know?" Juan and Madeline both effectively conveyed the specific anxiety and existential fatigue of "living life in cycle"—a phenomenon quite particular to immigrants with a temporary and endangered status.

Although participants detailed how their status negatively impacted their emotional well-being, they also described wresting control by focusing on normalcy and rechanneling their mental energies into the activities of everyday life. Camila, who came to the United States from El Salvador when she was thirteen, said that she felt like she was on "an emotional roller coaster" in May 2018 when she talked about her life in the period since the DACA rescission announcement. Yet she continued by sharing the strategy she uses to level herself out: "I do my best to have as normal a life as I can." Indeed, the term "normal" cropped up again and again as DACA recipients described their well-being strategies. In June 2021, Santiago, who came from Nicaragua when he was seven, similarly asserted, "I have to continue with my normal life . . . I can't let [DACA] control me," underscoring that the activities of normal life were precisely what allowed him to gain some control over his indeterminate situation. For both Camila and Santiago, a key component of their "normal" lives was working in the nonprofit sector, where they leveraged their navigational capital to help facilitate immigrants' access to education, employment, and affordable housing.

The Deployment of Navigational Capital—"Finding the Workarounds"

A second major contribution of this book is its novel elaboration of navigational capital to demonstrate how immigrant young adults navigate the multilayered jurisdictional patchwork of immigration policies and share their place-based knowledge to facilitate access not only to higher education but also to the health, labor, and housing sectors. Education scholar Tara J. Yosso originally introduced the concept of navigational capital as a component of the pathbreaking community cultural wealth (CCW) framework. Drawing from critical race theory, CCW is a corrective to deficit interpretations of cultural capital theory that regard immigrants as deficient in the forms of knowledge deemed valuable by dominant society. Instead, CCW centers the cultural knowledge, skills, and abilities that socially marginalized groups deploy to resist oppression. CCW encompasses six interconnected forms of alternative capital possessed by students of color, including navigational capital, which refers specifically to the skills of maneuvering through social institutions marked by inequality. Navigational capital validates experiential knowledge and reflects individual agency, but also foregrounds social networks and shared knowledge, highlighting collective capacity for coping and resilience.[119]

Navigational capital has most frequently been examined in higher education to illuminate how students of color persist and achieve.[120] Yet today undocumented young adults' experiences within higher education are fundamentally shaped by the state in which they are located and the state's evolving policies regarding immigrants' access to in-state tuition and state-based financial aid. Beyond higher education, states and localities have highly variable policies governing facets of everyday life including obtaining driver's licenses and accessing health care and social services. This book demonstrates how DACA recipients forge a nuanced legal-spatial consciousness[121] as they map out and navigate access to resources in differently configured socio-legal contexts in Maryland, Virginia, and Washington, D.C. I argue that into adulthood, they become quite adept at maneuvering between jurisdictions and strategically accessing resources. Thus, navigational capital is also an apt concept for examining how immigrants navigate the "multilayered jurisdictional patchwork."[122]

In her original formulation of the concept, Yosso acknowledges that navigational capital can also extend into other realms beyond higher education such as the labor market, judicial system, and health care system. Recently, scholars have started to describe how immigrants assert health-related navigational capital to negotiate constrained access to health care and forge alternative health care spaces[123] and organize to advocate for their health and well-being.[124] I expand the concept by demonstrating how immigrant young adults deploy navigational capital in the health, labor, and housing sectors—for themselves but also as intermediaries who broker immigrants' access.[125] Their brokerage is often undergirded by an ethic of care and enables them to address persistent forms of institutional exclusion for immigrants that the pandemic illuminated with stark clarity. I contend that their brokerage is also motivated by solidarity and serves as a mechanism through which they engage in everyday activism.

Notably, none of my participants used the term "navigational capital" to describe their burgeoning knowledge base, skills, abilities, and strategies. However, several used the term "workaround" repeatedly to describe how they learned to navigate immigration-related exclusions dictated by local policies. In June 2016, Juan's use of "workaround" stood out to me and my student collaborator Ana, and we made note of it in our interview debrief. But it was not until a few years later, as I thought about the conceptual utility of navigational capital, that the connection dawned on me. When he was twenty, Juan recounted how he had started realizing status-related limitations as a teenager: "I felt restricted to a certain point [because of my status], but it was more like a limitation. I couldn't do a certain thing, but I could always find a workaround. Because I didn't have that liberty of being able to drive at a young age, I learned how to use Metro very well. So now, I have every single station memorized backwards and forwards. I learned to be a little more independent early on. I just always found a workaround." Juan's use of "workaround" indexes it as a navigational strategy that he developed to literally get around the D.C. Metro region when he could not legally drive. However, he also indicates that figuring out these workarounds made him independent, and elsewhere he spoke of how it built his confidence and maturity. Juan mentioned "workaround" multiple times that day, including related to higher education: "I remember I had a conversation with my dad when I was transferring [from community college to a university]. His question to me was, 'if whoever the next president is turns away DACA, what are you going to do?' The way that I answered was, 'I'll just keep going.' I've never let my disadvantages get in the way of what I want to do. There's always a workaround, I've discovered." Juan discovered workarounds over the years related to transportation, higher education, and health care access. While he did not name policy explicitly, Juan was actually describing local policy exclusions and his way of navigating around them.

Juan was not the only participant to use the term "workaround"— Annisa also used the term regularly over the years. Annisa migrated to the United States from Indonesia when she was four. In August 2016, she reflected on how valuable it had been to meet other DACA recipients on her university campus since she did not know many others with her status in her community: "It's just nicer when you're around people who are in your same status. They understand what you've been through and they can help you too with the resources and how to work around them. Knowing the workarounds has really helped." While Annisa was initially focused on figuring out and leveraging workarounds in accessing higher education, she eventually applied this mindset to her work as a mental health technician. Four years later, in August 2020, she expressed that being a "resource person" was central to her identity: "I help people find support when they need it. If I've had a good experience with a resource, I share it with whoever needs it." Annisa is actively engaged in figuring out workarounds and sharing them not only with her clients at work but also with family and community members as part of her contribution to promoting immigrant well-being.

Engagement in Everyday Activism—"Showing Up in Different Ways"

A third major contribution of the book is its elaboration of immigrant young adults' everyday activism as a response to the hostile sociopolitical climate and immigrants' increased precarity, particularly in the first Trump era. The large-scale social movement forged by immigrant youth activists has been characterized by its overt and deliberate acts of political resistance and coordinated mass mobilizations that have garnered their cause greater social visibility and political legitimacy. However, much less is known about immigrant young adults who are no longer activists or never were in the first place, including the everyday activism in which they engage in support of immigrants through less conventional political registers. Political scientist Jane Mansbridge offers a useful definition of everyday activism as "talk and action in everyday life that is not consciously coordinated with the actions of others but is (i) to some degree caused (inspired, encouraged) by a social movement and (ii) consciously intended to change others' ideas or behavior in directions advocated by the movement."[126] Everyday activism offers an alternative way of thinking about activism, which is typically envisioned as being public, collective, explicit, and intentionally structured forms of collective action that are quite clearly distinguished from the more mundane, routine, and hidden aspects of everyday life.[127] The concept of everyday activism has been invoked by a wide range of scholars from distinct fields, typically to capture how marginalized residents within cities mobilize (outside of the political sphere) against poor living conditions and claim and construct their own counterspaces.[128]

This book traces DACA recipients' trajectories of political engagement and the emergence of everyday activism. Initially in 2016, surprisingly few of my participants had been involved in the organizing efforts of campus groups or CBOs or engaged in public immigrant rights activism. Yet their lack of public activism did not mean that they were politically disengaged or disconnected from the immigrant justice movement overall. As education scholars Júlia Mendes and Aurora Chang underscore, a lack of publicness does not necessarily equate to a lack of activism, as many immigrant young adults manifest their activism in less obvious ways.[129] DACA recipients are engaged in everyday activism to contest immigrants' social exclusion by seizing opportunities to educate about DACA and immigration in everyday interactions with friends, peers, coworkers, and even strangers. These smaller-scale actions in everyday spaces have allowed some undocumented young adults to engage politically surrounding immigration for the first time. Meanwhile others who work in service settings are involved in advocacy efforts that include and extend beyond their primary professional responsibilities to provide services to immigrant community members. Indeed, even those who work outside of service settings are also taking such actions. In these encounters, DACA recipients leverage their navigational capital as brokers in service to their communities who help members access resources and assert rights.[130] These actions ultimately serve as a complement to more public and collective forms of collective action like protests in contributing to the larger political project of fighting for immigrant well-being and justice.

Given that my participants did not largely identify as activists, they did not label the actions they took in support of immigrants in their everyday lives as "activism." Yet they *did* speak evocatively about the phenomenon of everyday activism in more vernacular terms. For instance, Nayeli, who migrated from El Salvador when she was seven, expressed feelings of guilt about not participating in immigration protests in February 2018—a common sentiment during the first Trump era. Nayeli had previously done public media interviews, though she had a negative experience with a reporter aggressively contacting her to confirm her identity that led her to stop sharing her immigration story. As she reflected, "People show up in different ways. That's what my boyfriend said. He's like, 'A lot of people are protesting on your behalf right now. Don't feel bad about it.' He was like, 'Just keep doing what you're doing. That's how you're fighting your battle.'" Nayeli's boyfriend—a citizen within an immigrant family—not only sought to assuage her guilt but also conveyed that there were different ways of "showing up" for immigrant justice. A few months later, in June 2018, Nayeli's older sister Angélica expressed a similar sentiment: "I'm doing more of the hands-on work, directly providing services and bringing resources. That's been my method of activism. It's so much better because I feel I'm directly able to impact versus if I go to a rally, I'm just one more person in a big group."

Indeed, Nayeli's and Angélica's comments index important questions about what constitutes activism and what roles they should play in promoting immigrant well-being and justice. While both participated in more conventional (immigrant young adult) political actions like strategically sharing their stories, they have both concluded that there are other ways of "showing up" for immigrants, including by doing "hands-on work" as a "method of activism." Yet Nayeli's boyfriend also clearly notes that "showing up" is a relational act as people show up in different ways to support one another—both when they do and do not share common bases of identity. Angélica is unquestionably showing up for her fellow immigrants by providing direct services. This book portrays the novel ways in which immigrant young adults show up for each other and their communities and forge new political registers for fighting for immigrant well-being and justice.

Overview of the Book

This book bridges these academic and insider explanatory frameworks to present how DACA recipients have reckoned with their prolonged legal status precarity by forging political inclusion in their "normal" lives through the deployment of navigational capital and engagement in everyday activism. Chapter 1 sets the stage by describing the Washington, D.C., Metropolitan region as a dynamic yet understudied context of reception. I highlight relevant historical and contemporary features of this unique hyperdiverse metropolitan region, including the variegated landscape of local immigration policies. I also present a national profile of DACA recipients before painting an overall portrait of my research participants that describes how they mesh with these larger national trends and reflect region-specific dynamics.

In the subsequent chapters, I describe research participants in more specific detail and delve more deeply into their individual and collective experiences. Chapter 2 provides a temporal analysis of DACA recipients' shifting emotional well-being during different chapters of the DACA program. I begin by highlighting the tempered gains DACA recipients experienced early the program while it was still fully intact under

Obama and continue by chronicling the embodied distress that the rescission and its immediate aftermath evoked under Trump as they were compelled to "live their lives in cycle." However, I also demonstrate how they increasingly pursued normalcy in their daily lives as a well-being strategy for wresting control of their lives in the present and ultimately flourishing into the Biden era.

In chapter 3, I add a spatial dimension to the analysis by describing how DACA recipients learn about and navigate the patchwork of local immigration policies in the multijurisdictional D.C. Metro region. I first describe how DACA recipients forge a nuanced legal-spatial consciousness as they discern differences in local jurisdictions' treatment of immigrants and then demonstrate how they assert navigational capital—and deploy savvy "workarounds"—in their everyday lives to strategically access distinct yet interconnected educational, labor, and housing sectors.

The examination of DACA recipients' pursuit of normalcy continues in chapter 4 with a description of their evolving trajectories of political engagement spanning the period before DACA existed, once the program was established, and after it became endangered. I argue that against the backdrop of the repressive state and racist political discourse about immigrants in the first Trump era, DACA recipients cultivated new forms of everyday activism—"showing up in different ways"—that served as a complement to more conventional forms of collective action. Given the pandemic-related constraints on gathering in large crowds, participants' everyday activism was particularly well suited for the times—and has the potential to shape how immigrants continue to fight for social justice.

Finally, in chapter 5 I describe another mode of DACA recipients' everyday activism: deploying their navigational capital to broker care for more economically, socially, and legally precarious family and community members. I describe the configurations of care within which DACA recipients are embedded, demonstrating how their care practices—and the "workarounds" they deploy for others—promote immigrants' access to resources, security and stability, and overall well-being. DACA recipients' everyday care practices can be read as political acts of solidarity meant to tackle the deeply entrenched inequalities faced by structurally marginalized communities that were particularly pronounced during the height of the COVID-19 pandemic.

The conclusion considers the future trajectories of DACA recipients more than a decade after the program began and amid its highly uncertain future. I briefly discuss the potential impact of policy change at multiple levels, though I do not merely offer policy recommendations, in line with anthropologist Gabrielle Cabrera's charge to researchers writing about undocumented young adults to do something more and different.[131] Instead, I adopt everyday activism as a larger frame for thinking about different ways of showing up for immigrants and the immigrant justice movement. Everyday activism has great potential as a broader political engagement strategy that extends beyond DACA and immigrant justice in contesting other forms of structural marginalization produced by neoliberal global capitalism. In addition, I argue in appendix A that it is an instructive frame for thinking through how critically engaged scholars can and should show up for their collaborators as part of their scholarly praxis. Collectively, these chapters capture how DACA recipients in the D.C. Metro region have cultivated practices for getting by and flourishing despite their pronounced legal status precarity and ongoing threats to their health and well-being.

Additional Notes on Terminology

Thus far, I have included notes clarifying my reasoned usage of terms like "undocumented immigrant" and "legal status precarity." Though I briefly referenced my choice to use "DACA recipient" over "DREAMer," a few additional clarifying comments are in order. I most frequently use the term "DACA recipient" in this book, though I acknowledge from the outset that it is not an ideal one. "DACA recipient" is not a label with which most participants squarely and comfortably identify, and it is not one of the aspects of their identities that matters most to them. In fact, all of my research participants actively aspire to no longer have DACA and to possess a more permanent legal status.

Throughout my research, I paid close attention to how DACA recipients referred to themselves as they spoke about their legal status. Early on, I noticed that some did not use "DACA recipient" at all to refer to themselves or others with the same status. For instance, Madeline talked about how she and her sister were "on DACA," while Mae (originally from South Korea) and Elena (originally from Honduras) described themselves as being "under DACA." Notably, none of these three women ever referred to herself as a DACA recipient. I asked Madeline directly about how she regarded the term "DACA recipient" in 2020, and she shared, "I think I connect more with just being an immigrant since DACA has always felt temporary. It's not like something you could really hold onto, almost. During the Obama administration, it would make more sense or I would feel more comfortable saying I am on DACA. But now, it's just like 'I'm just an immigrant.'" Madeline thus preferred a more general label that did not signal anything about legal status. Madeline's comments also indicate that her preferences have shifted across administrations, which others noted as well. Some participants stopped calling themselves DACA recipients and just referred to themselves as immigrants (like Madeline) or, even more commonly, as being undocumented. Some participants had always referred to themselves as undocumented, underscoring the instability and temporary nature of their status. Scholars have also noted immigrant young adults' preferred usage of undocumented as revelatory of their "durably embodied undocumented subjectivities,"[132] acknowledging that even with DACA, many recipients still feel, or have always felt, undocumented as they maneuver around the world.

Of course, the "DACA recipient" label—as well as the terms "immigrant" and "undocumented"—gloss over a vast range of different immigrant experiences. DACA recipients came from quite distinct countries of origin through different migration channels, including crossing the border and arriving by plane. Some of them arrived without status, though others lost it by overstaying a tourist visa or having but then losing another state-sanctioned legal status. Even as I recognize the homogenizing nature of these labels, I actively attempt to represent a diversity of undocumented immigrant young adult experiences and attend to intersectional dimensions of their experiences.[133] It is also the case that several participants featured in the pages to come ceased being DACA recipients altogether—indeed, five of them would now be more accurately described as LPRs, or "legal" immigrants, in more vernacular terms. Despite my acknowledgment that "DACA recipient" is a problematic label for multiple reasons, I use it because it is analytically useful in speaking to the common bases of experience of immigrant young adults who possess a uniquely politicized status that was always fundamentally temporary and unstable.

1

"I Have a Strong Sense of Identity Tied to This Place"

DACAmented in the D.C. Metropolitan Region

I consider myself a proud Marylander. I live in Maryland
and mostly grew up here. Maryland is where my heart
lies, as corny as that sounds. I feel like I belong here, and I
have a strong sense of identity tied to this place. But I see
that Maryland is a little more fragmented than D.C. when it
comes to social services. It definitely shows me that there's
work to be done in Maryland.
—Lucas, twenty-seven-year-old Mexican DACA recipient,
December 14, 2021

Lucas's comments illuminate that immigrant young adults are incor-
porating not merely into U.S. society but also into different local
communities nationwide, in the process forging connections to those
places. In fact, Lucas more strongly asserted his identity as a Marylander
than an American during our interviews spanning several years, culminating in these reflections in 2021. He has strong affective ties to the state
and, because of that, is also critical of its treatment of immigrants, comparing it (less favorably) to nearby Washington, D.C., where he works as
a community health worker providing expansive health care services to
undocumented immigrants—a rare situation nationwide, as most jurisdictions have status-related restrictions. Lucas's comments also index
what scholars have increasingly been recognizing: that precarious legal
statuses are experienced quite differently depending on where in the
United States an immigrant lives and the immigration-focused policies
shaping everyday life there.[1]

The Washington D.C. Metropolitan region offers a unique and understudied context of reception from which to observe the incorporation trajectories of immigrant young adults. In their seminal volume on

U.S. immigration, sociologists Alejandro Portes and Rubén G. Rumbaut highlight that immigrant incorporation is shaped by how open and accepting a community is to immigrants—otherwise known as the context of reception. Contexts of reception are formed by a constellation of structural features including government policies, local labor market conditions, social institutions, public attitudes, and the demographic composition of the community, including existing ethnic communities.[2] As immigration policymaking has stalled at the federal level and devolved to states and localities into the 2000s, immigrants confront significantly different socio-legal contexts within the multilayered jurisdictional patchwork.[3] Sociologist Laura E. Enriquez uses the term "context of illegality" to underscore that these distinct socio-legal contexts are intentionally created by laws and policies that produce immigrants' vulnerabilities within them.[4] Thus, is it no mere coincidence that Lucas has discovered that Washington, D.C., invests more deeply in the health of its undocumented residents than Maryland does; rather, this situation is reflective of intentional policy decisions made by each jurisdiction. Socio-legal contexts are classified based on their treatment of immigrants and range from more inclusionary/integrative/hospitable/accommodating to exclusionary/hostile/restrictive.[5]

Large, multijurisdictional metropolitan regions have largely been overlooked in the literature on contexts of reception, which has focused more on newer exclusionary rural destinations and classic inclusive gateway cities like Chicago, Los Angeles, and New York.[6] However, even the quintessential gateway city—New York—is officially identified by the U.S. Census Bureau as the New York-Newark-Jersey City, NY-NJ-PA metropolitan region and spans three states.[7] Other multijurisdictional metropolitan regions along the Eastern Seaboard include Boston (Boston-Cambridge-Newton, MA-NH), Philadelphia (Philadelphia-Camden-Wilmington, PA-NJ-DE-MD), Baltimore (Baltimore-Columbia-Towson, MD), and Washington D.C. (Washington-Arlington-Alexandria, DC-MD-VA-WV). These metropolitan regions merit further attention because of their large share of immigrant residents overall, but also because their residents regularly move through multiple jurisdictions, in the process encountering different socio-legal contexts, as Lucas does every day as he shuttles between where he lives in Maryland and works in next-door Washington, D.C.

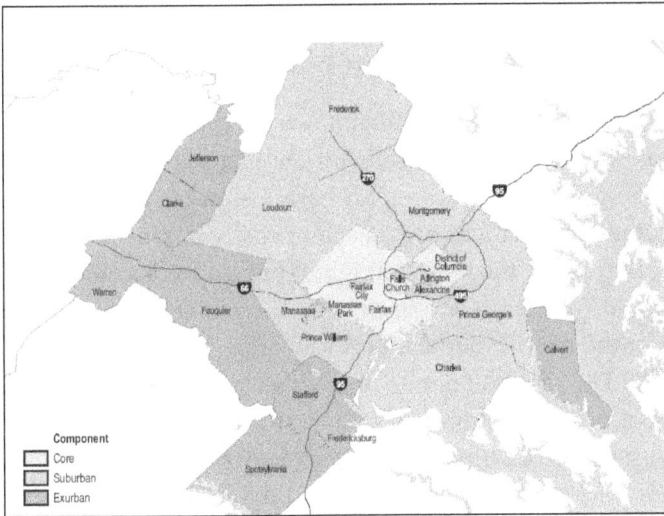

Figure 1.1. The Washington, D.C., Metropolitan region. Source: U.S. Bureau of Labor Statistics.

The U.S. Census Bureau–designated Washington-Arlington-Alexandria, DC-MD-VA-WV Metropolitan area includes twenty-two separate jurisdictions and is politically complex because it includes counties in three states and the capital city of Washington, D.C.—a uniquely configured jurisdiction that is neither a state nor a city located within a state. Slightly narrower than the census designation, the National Capital Region is another U.S. government designation codified by the National Capital Planning Act of 1952, consisting of D.C., Montgomery and Prince George's Counties of Maryland, and Arlington, Fairfax, Loudon, and Prince William Counties of Virginia. The Washington Metropolitan region and D.C. Metro region are also commonly used labels, though less clearly defined. Most residents of the region refer to it as "the DMV," in reference to Washington, D.C., Maryland, and Virginia. This commonly used local term underscores the perceived interconnectedness of these jurisdictions and is revelatory of a shared place-based identity rooted in geographic proximity and historical connections. Hereafter, I refer to the region as the D.C. Metro region, unless participants refer to it specifically as the DMV.

The D.C. Metro Region's Transformation into a Newly Emerged Gateway and Shifting Settlement Patterns

Though Washington, D.C., is not known for being an archetypal immigrant gateway city like New York City or Chicago, the capital city and surrounding metropolitan region have a sizeable and diverse immigrant population that has grown substantially in recent decades. Over the past fifty years, the total immigrant population has increased more than tenfold—from 130,000 in 1970[8] to 1.4 million in 2021.[9] By 2021, 23 percent of the region's population was foreign-born.[10] One notable feature of the D.C. Metro region's immigrant population is that no single country of origin predominates, in contrast to cities like Los Angeles (with 41 percent of immigrants from Mexico), Chicago (with 40 percent from Mexico), and Miami (with 32 percent from Cuba).[11] In fact, as the city and surrounding area solidified into a newly emerged gateway in the early 1990s, admissions data reflected that local immigrant residents came from 193 different countries of origin.[12] In 2021, 39 percent of foreign-born residents were from Latin America, 36 percent from Asia, 16 percent from Africa, 8 percent from Europe, and 1 percent from North America.[13] The D.C. Metro region has joined the ranks of hyperdiverse immigrant gateways nationwide[14] and has become a top destination for immigrant newcomers, with the seventh largest metropolitan concentration of immigrants.[15]

The history of migration to the D.C. Metro region is quite distinct from other major East Coast metropolitan areas. During the third wave of immigration in the late 1800s and early 1900s, European immigrants fueled the growth of many rapidly urbanizing East Coast cities like Boston, New York, and Philadelphia; Washington, D.C., which was never a major industrial or commercial center, was largely bypassed as a settlement destination during this wave of migration. Instead, newcomers to D.C. in the early twentieth century were largely internal migrants, particularly African Americans who had migrated from the rural South during the Great Migration.[16]

By the 1950s, however, D.C. began a process of internationalization as the major organizations representing the postwar economic order, including the International Monetary Fund, the World Bank, the Inter-American Development Bank, embassies and other international institutions, and nongovernmental organizations, set up in the nation's capital.[17] In addition to foreign nationals working for those entities, women from Caribbean and Central and South American countries were actively recruited to work in the domestic, care, and service sectors, making them early pioneers in the gendered reproductive labor force and paving the way for future migration from those regions.[18] In this era, the largest migratory flows from Latin America were from Cuba and the Dominican Republic in the Caribbean and Peru and Bolivia in South America.[19] Black Africans also started settling in the region in the late 1950s and early 1960s as diplomats of newly independent African countries settled and students enrolled in local universities, most especially at historically Black Howard University in D.C.[20]

In the late 1970s and 1980s, D.C. became a major settlement destination for migrants fleeing civil war, repression, and economic hardship in El Salvador, Guatemala, and Nicaragua. Despite the passage of the Refugee Act of 1980, the U.S. government deemed that these Central American migrants fell outside of the refugee category (due to the U.S. government's complicity in the conflicts that displaced them), instead designating them as voluntary economic migrants.[21] Consequently, these Central American migrants were unauthorized and endured long periods of family separation as parents often had to leave their children at home under the extended care of family. Even after peace agreements were signed, economic crises and natural disasters in these countries perpetuated further migration. Latina migrants with ties to the region acted as labor mediators for relatives and acquaintances, who worked in the gendered, low-paid labor market in care and domestic sectors (women), construction and related sectors (men), and food and cleaning services in the city and surrounding suburbs (both women and men).[22] By the late 1990s, some 150,000 Salvadorans lived in the D.C. Metro region. They manifested a strong cultural presence in D.C. neighborhoods like Adams Morgan and Mount Pleasant, where they established businesses, health clinics, service providers, community centers, and churches.[23]

As the refugee resettlement program solidified, those who had been officially recognized by the government as refugees also started arriving to and transforming the region; the largest initial refugee groups in the D.C. region were from Southeast Asia and Africa.[24] Among the earliest arrivals were Vietnamese and Korean refugees who were displaced by the U.S. wars and their aftermath, dating back to the mid-1970s as the resettlement program formed.[25] The D.C. Metro region eventually became the third largest resettlement destination for Vietnamese refugees, after California and Texas, and the third largest metropolitan region of residence for Koreans (both refugees and immigrants), after Los Angeles and New York by 2019.[26] The region also became a hub for sub-Saharan African refugees, initially from Ethiopia and Eritrea and then from Somalia and Sudan.[27] More than 12,000 Africans were resettled between 1983 and 2004, progressively composing two-thirds (67 percent) of all refugees resettled in the region overall by the early 2000s.[28]

By the 1990s, the D.C. Metro region was a "newly emerged immigrant gateway" (per sociologist and demographer Audrey Singer's typology) and the fifth most common destination nationwide for those who were legally admitted to the United States.[29] The Immigration Act of 1990—the first major overhaul of the U.S. immigration system in a quarter century—greatly increased the number of legal immigrants admitted annually and also introduced the diversity visa program, designed to admit and provide permanent residency to immigrants from "low admittance" countries. African migrants became the dominant recipient of this program by 2014, receiving nearly half of available visas annually. The Immigration Act also created Temporary Protected Status (TPS), a temporary status (as opposed to permanent residency) allowing citizens of specific countries facing ongoing armed conflict (such as civil war) or environmental disasters (such as an earthquake or hurricane) to temporarily live and work in the United States; El Salvador was the first country whose nationals could seek TPS, though it was subsequently expanded to twelve others including other Latin American (Haiti, Honduras, and Nicaragua) and African (Guinea, Liberia, Sierra Leone, Somalia, South Sudan, and Sudan) nations.[30] Many TPS holders, most notably Salvadorans and Hondurans, live in the D.C. Metro region. The D.C. Metro region has been an attractive destination for these and other immigrants due to its relatively stable economy, owing to the presence of the federal government and associated institutions. The knowledge industries that form the base of the economy have also attracted large numbers of highly skilled laborers, and the rapid population growth bolstered robust construction and service sectors.[31]

By 2010, Latinos/Hispanics were the largest foreign-born group in the D.C. Metro region. El Salvador was the top country of origin of the foreign-born population overall (13.7 percent), with Mexico (4 percent), Guatemala (3.2 percent), and Peru (3.1 percent) also represented in the top ten. Indians were the second largest national origin group overall and largest Asian national origin group (6.4 percent), with Korea (4.9 percent), Vietnam (3.9 percent), the Philippines (3.8 percent), and China (3.8 percent) also among the top ten.[32] The largest African national origin group was Ethiopians (3 percent), though the region also became a preferred settlement destination for West Africans from Nigeria, Sierra Leone, Ghana, and Cameroon.[33] Though smaller in overall size, the D.C. Metro region became home to the second largest African immigrant population nationally (167,000 individuals by 2011–15), second only to the New York Metropolitan area.[34] The D.C. Metro region also has a sizeable Caribbean immigrant population (83,400 in 2016), with the largest numbers from Jamaica, followed by Trinidad and Tobago, the Dominican Republic, Haiti, and Cuba.[35] Immigrants within all of these national origin groups are quite diverse by racial/ethnic background, language, religion, and economic status and have a mixture of economic, political, religious, and academic motivations for migrating.[36]

Another notable feature of the D.C. Metro region is the predominant pattern of suburban dispersal and presence of multiethnic neighborhoods instead of ethnically homogenous residential enclaves.[37] These settlement patterns track with the transformation of the U.S. economy toward the end of the twentieth century that led to the decentralization of economic activity away from cities into suburbs, facilitated by the extensive development of highways and the suburban construction boom.[38] Indeed, less than 10 percent of the region's immigrants settle in D.C., with the vast majority settling in the suburbs of Maryland and Virginia, where there are more jobs, access to excellent public education, and affordable housing.[39] Initially, immigrants settled in the residentially dense "inner" or "urban" core (consisting of D.C., Arlington County, Virginia, and Alexandria City, Virginia) and "inner" suburbs (consisting of Montgomery and Prince George's Counties in Maryland and Fairfax County, Fairfax City, and Falls Church City in Virginia).

This suburban settlement pattern also bears out by specific regions of origin. When Central Americans first arrived in the 1950s, they settled in northwestern D.C. in the neighborhoods of Adams Morgan, Mount Pleasant, and Columbia Heights. The area came to be known as the Latino *barrio* of D.C. and developed major infrastructure and services. Though the barrio is still thriving in many respects, gentrification has also pushed out Latinx immigrants to inner and increasingly outer suburbs in Maryland and Virginia, where they were highly concentrated by 2010.[40] As the Asian and Pacific Islander population started growing substantially in the 1990s—getting closer in size to the longer established Latinx population—the majority (95 percent) settled in the inner suburbs of Fairfax (Virginia) and Montgomery (Maryland) Counties.[41] The region's Black African immigrants also clustered in the inner Maryland suburbs (60 percent lived in Montgomery and Prince George's Counties by 2000), with large pockets also living in Arlington and Alexandria (Virginia) as well as neighborhoods in central and northeastern D.C.[42] Similarly, Caribbean immigrants also clustered in the inner suburbs of Maryland (47.5 percent lived in in Montgomery and Prince George's Counties by 2016), with smaller pockets in D.C. (10 percent).[43]

Into the 2000s, immigrants started settling even further away from the urban core and inner suburbs in "outer" (Calvert, Charles, and Frederick Counties in Maryland and Loudoun, Prince William, and Stafford Counties in Virginia) and "far" exurban counties (Clark, Fauquier, Spotsylvania, Warren Counties and Fredericksburg City in Virginia and Jefferson County in West Virginia). The immigrant population is growing most rapidly in these exurban areas, though these jurisdictions are historically much less accustomed to immigrant newcomers.[44] In the twenty-first century, the immigrant population in the D.C. Metro region is quite regionally dispersed, living in very different types of jurisdictions.

The D.C. Metro Region's Variegated Policy Landscape

The D.C. Metro region features a variegated policy landscape; indeed, everyday life is quite different for immigrants depending specifically on *where* within the region they live.[45] The region is politically complex, spanning twenty-two separate jurisdictions, including counties in three states (Maryland, Virginia, and West Virginia) as well as the capital city of Washington, D.C. The heart of the region—the inner/urban core and inner suburbs—long ago developed the infrastructure and capacity to smoothly integrate immigrants with broad public support. The city of Takoma Park in Montgomery County (Maryland), for instance, became one of the first jurisdictions nationwide to pass a "Sanctuary City" ordinance in 1985, as local churches provided sanctuary to Salvadorans and Guatemalans denied refugee status by the government. However, the rapidly growing outer and far exurban areas did not have experience or infrastructure for integrating immigrants and even started aggressively targeting them, fueled in part by media attention and local electoral politics. One such jurisdiction, Prince William County (Virginia), became infamous for passing an unusually tough ordinance in 2007 requiring the police to check the immigration status of anyone detained for violating a state or local law, presaging restrictive state-level policies passed in Arizona in 2010 and then Alabama in 2011.[46]

This variegated policy landscape is quite apparent in examining state- and local-level policies related to immigrant incorporation on issues like education, employment, health, identification and driver's licenses, law enforcement, public benefits, resolutions, and voting.[47] Comparing the largest three units of the MSA designation—the three states (Maryland, Virginia, and West Virginia) and the district (D.C.)—D.C. is the most integrative local jurisdiction (see table 1.1). In 2011, the district enacted a long-standing policy (General Order 201.26) prohibiting district government agents, agencies, officers, or employees from making inquiries about citizenship or residency status; more recently in 2020, the district passed a bill (B486) limiting the district's cooperation with federal immigration agencies, including by complying with detainer requests, absent a judicial warrant or order. The district started extending health care coverage to undocumented immigrants through the D.C. Alliance Program in 2011, has allowed them access to driver's licenses since 2014 (B812), and has enabled them to access in-state tuition and some state financial aid (D.C. Act 21–650) since 2017. Also in 2017, the district passed a resolution declaring D.C.'s commitment to its status as a Sanctuary City (R75). In 2020 in the height of the pandemic, the district launched an excluded worker fund (the D.C. Cares Program) to assist workers like undocumented residents, returning citizens, and workers in the informal economy who were otherwise ineligible for government assistance like expanded unemployment and stimulus payments; this program has continued as advocates have argued that these workers continue to bear the effects of the pandemic.[48]

TABLE 1.1. D.C. Metropolitan region jurisdictions and select immigration-related policies

Jurisdiction	Inclusionary policies	Exclusionary policies
Washington, D.C.	• Prohibiting district employees from inquiring about citizenship or residency status (2011) • Health care coverage (D.C. Health Care Alliance) (2011) • Driver's licenses for undocumented immigrants (2014) • Tuition equity and local financial aid (2017) • Sanctuary City status (2017) • Limiting cooperation with federal immigration agencies (2020) • Excluded worker fund (D.C. Cares Program) (2020)	
Maryland	• Establishment of Maryland Council for New Americans (2008) [state level] • Resolution expressing concern over Secure Communities (2011) [county level; Montgomery] • Tuition equity (2012) [state level] • Driver's licenses for undocumented immigrants (2013) [state level] • Bar on local agencies working with federal immigration enforcement (2018) [county level; Prince George's] • Bar on local agencies working with federal immigration enforcement (2018) [county level; Montgomery] • State financial aid (2019) [state level] • Health care coverage for pregnant noncitizens and their babies (2022) [state level] • Professional health care licensure or certification regardless of status (2023) [state level] • Removal of immigration status as eligibility requirement for purchasing a health plan (2024) [state level] • Health care coverage for minors (Care for Kids) [county level; Montgomery and Prince George's] • Noncitizen voting [city level; various jurisdictions in Montgomery and Prince George's Counties]	• Restrictions on health care coverage for adults (Maryland Health Connection) [state level] • Participation in 287(g) agreements [county level; Cecil, Frederick, Harford]
Virginia	• Establishment of Office of New Americans (2020) [state level] • Tuition equity for undocumented, refugees, and special immigrant visa holders (2020) [state level] • State financial aid (2021) [state level] • Driver's licenses for undocumented immigrants (2021) [state level] • Limit on release of Department of Motor Vehicle data for immigration purposes (2021) [state level] • Bar on local agencies working with federal immigration enforcement (2021) [county level; Fairfax]	• Restrictions on health care coverage (Virginia Marketplace) [state level] • Participation in 287(g) agreement [county and city level; Culpeper County and cities of Herndon and Manassas]
West Virginia	• Teaching certificate eligibility for work-authorized noncitizens (2020) [state level]	• Restrictions on health care coverage for adults through West Virginia Medicaid (2011) [state level] • Collaboration between municipalities and counties and ICE (2023) [state level] • Prohibiting sanctuary cities (2023) [state level]

Maryland has been characterized as an immigrant- and particularly DACA-"friendly" state,[49] due to its passage of a state DREAM Act in 2012 (S167) and opening up state financial aid for undocumented students in 2018 (S532). Maryland has also allowed undocumented immigrants to obtain driver's licenses since 2013 (S715) and in 2023 passed a law (S187/H454) allowing immigrants (regardless of status) to apply for health care licensure/certification. Activists have campaigned for expanded access to health care for immigrants, resulting in the passage of the Health Babies Equity Act (S778) in 2022, extending Medicaid coverage to undocumented pregnant women. However, more broadly, Maryland maintains immigration-related health care restrictions (enacted in 2011 through S182 and H166). Three Maryland counties (Cecil, Frederick, and Harford) also maintain 287(g) agreements with Immigration and Customs Enforcement (ICE).[50]

Indeed, the county level is an important unit to examine within Maryland, with the inner suburbs actively passing inclusive policies. The Montgomery County Council passed a resolution in May 2011 expressing concern about the implementation of the Secure Communities program. Subsequently, Prince George's County passed the Community Inclusiveness Act in 2018 and Montgomery County passed the Promoting Community Trust Executive Order in 2019 barring local agencies from working with federal immigration authorities. Both counties (Montgomery first, followed by Prince George's) have also invested in the Care for Kids program, which provides primary, specialty, behavioral health, and dental care to children until age eighteen regardless of immigration status. Both counties also have municipalities (including Chevy Chase and Takoma Park in Montgomery and Hyattsville and Mount Rainer in Prince George's) that have allowed noncitizens to vote in local elections since the state constitution gives them the authority to change voter criteria without seeking state approval.

Virginia has historically been more exclusionary, though more recently has adopted state policies more in line with its northern neighbor. In 2020, the state established the Office of New Americans and bills allowing undocumented immigrants and refugees and special immigrant visa holders to access in-state tuition went into effect (HB1547 and HB1179). In 2021, the state legislature passed a bill (HB2123 and SB1387) expanding access to state financial aid for undocumented students. Likewise in 2021, undocumented immigrants living in Virginia became eligible to obtain a driver's license (through SB34) and the General Assembly passed a measure (HB2163) limiting the release and dissemination of data from the Department of Motor Vehicles for civil immigration purposes. However, like Maryland, the state has status-related restrictions for accessing health care and public benefits and has one county (Culpeper) with an active 287(g) agreement, with two other northern Virginia jurisdictions (Herndon in Fairfax County and Manassas in Prince William County) holding them until recently.[51] As in Maryland, the inner suburb counties have passed more inclusive policies, such as Fairfax County's Public Trust and Confidentiality Policy (passed in 2021) to ensure that local employees do not voluntarily cooperate with enforcement of federal civil immigration laws.

West Virginia, which has a substantially smaller immigrant population than other D.C. jurisdictions, has the most markedly exclusionary policies. Most recently, in 2023, the state passed HB2008, which "protects taxpayers" by requiring that West Virginia municipalities and counties contact ICE to identify where noncitizen residents are residing and prohibits sanctuary cities in West Virginia. In 2019, the state had introduced a bill (that did not pass) requiring local police to enforce federal immigration law as well as another (that likewise did not pass) that would have permitted the governor to prohibit refugees from resettling in the state. Like Maryland and Virginia, West Virginia has immigration-status-related restrictions for West Virginia Medicaid (codified in SB408 in 2011), though unlike both of those states, it has not yet passed policies on access to in-state tuition or state financial aid or undocumented immigrants' access to driver's licenses. Somewhat surprisingly, however, the state did pass a bill in 2020 (CB623) allowing noncitizens with valid employment authorization to be eligible for teaching certificates.

The D.C. Metro region overall trends more integrative; glancing at table 1.1, the tally of integrative policies outweighs the exclusionary ones. Some state, county, and even municipal policies are model local policies for promoting immigrant inclusion and have been recognized nationally as such. It is also worth noting, however, that the table does not include bills that ultimately failed to pass—both more integrative and exclusionary in intent. These local policies have not emerged in a vacuum but rather are highly responsive to developments at the federal level. For instance, on the more integrative side, D.C.'s affirmation of Sanctuary City status in 2017 was a rebuke to President Trump's 2017 executive order withholding federal funding from sanctuary cities and was meant to signal support for D.C.'s immigrant residents. On the more exclusionary side, West Virginia's attempt to permit the governor to prohibit refugees from resettling in the state was in direct response to President Trump's gutting of the national refugee resettlement program and 2019 executive order requiring states and local governments to provide consent authorizing the resettlement of refugees in their communities.

It is also important to note that socio-legal contexts are not static and indeed may even be unstable.[52] While California is often held up as a model of immigrant inclusion in the twenty-first century, anti-immigrant sentiment was pervasive there in the 1990s, culminating in the passage of Propositions 187, 209, and 227, targeting immigrants' access to publicly funded services, affirmative action, and bilingual education, respectively.[53] Pockets of anti-immigrant sentiment still exist at the county and municipal levels, despite the state's overall receptivity to immigrants and supportive policies. More locally, Virginia is an interesting case study in shifting local policies—even during the time frame of this research. In 2016, when I started my research, none of the inclusive policies enumerated in table 1.1 had yet passed and the state was known within the D.C. Metro region to be less welcoming (with the inner suburbs as a notable exception). Yet in part in response to tireless legislative advocacy by local immigrant rights organizations, several major inclusive laws passed in a short time frame (2020–21), extending driver's license eligibility, limiting the release of Department of Motor Vehicles data, and ensuring tuition equity and access to state financial aid. However, Virginia is still quite contested, as evidenced by the shift from a Democratic to a Republican governor and the return of the House to Republicans in 2022. Thus, these gains are slightly tempered by the possibility of markedly different new policies being introduced and passed.

In examining immigrants' experiences within these local socio-legal contexts, it is also important to recognize that perceptions of places matter and that legacies of exclusion may lag behind policymaking and the social change it seeks to usher in. My participants, who overall had the strongest ties to Maryland, frequently shared that they felt less safe in Virginia, where they described being more likely to encounter problems with racist policing and immigration enforcement; indeed, their concerns are revelatory of the enduring legacy of racism and exclusion in the state.[54] Their perception in fact bore out in the 2021 election when the state elected an ultraconservative governor, threatening the gains made for undocumented immigrants in 2020 and underscoring the instability of this socio-legal context.[55] Geographers Marie Price and Giancarla Rojas, who carried out research with DACA recipients living in the suburbs of Virginia, acknowledge the impact of the state's "mixed record" and the fact that the supportive institutional structures found in more traditional immigrant gateways were still developing there.[56] Even so, their participants felt that the D.C. Metro region—and northern Virginia in particular—was a safe space for undocumented people. Thus, it is entirely possible that their research participants expressed feelings of safety and security in their Virginia neighborhoods while mine simultaneously felt amplified anxiety in those same places. Our participants' mutual place-based perceptions and experiences also underscore the importance of identifying what sociologists Laura E. Enriquez and Daniel Millán refer to as "protective locations" within larger jurisdictions, where anti-immigrant sentiment is less pervasive, serving to moderate immigrants' fear and sense of perceived risk.[57] Indeed, over time, several participants who had previously identified concerns about Virginia actually moved there, clearly staking out protective locations as they settled into new communities.

DACAmented in DC: Social Movement Locations, Overall Demographic Profile, and a Portrait of Research Participants

Despite being a primary metropolitan settlement destination and hyperdiverse gateway, the D.C. Metro region has not received as much scholarly attention in the literature on DACA.[58] Yet D.C. is an important geographic site within the undocumented young adult movement and in the creation of DACA itself. California is the location most prominently featured, particularly given that many scholars of DACA (including DACAdemics) have lived, worked, and conducted research there and because of the significant position the state has occupied in the national undocumented youth movement.[59] Indeed, the roots of the undocumented youth movement were in campaigns forged at the state level in California (Assembly Bill 540) and Texas (House Bill 1403) in 2001 to allow undocumented students to be classified as state residents for tuition purposes.[60] Both of these states became important locations for understanding the impact of state policies on undocumented immigrant young adults' access to higher education. The mobilization for AB 540 also created a network of undocumented student organizations and paved the way for subsequent community-based organizing in Los Angeles and Orange County.[61]

This local and regionally based organizing was complemented by national-level campaigns to pass the DREAM Act launched in 2001 by prominent immigrant rights organizations like the L.A.-based National Immigration Law Center and D.C.-based Center for Community Change. These organizations responded to a niche opening created by the rise in immigration enforcement in the late 1990s and the practical need to prioritize resources only on the most dangerous cases. DREAMers were thought to be the ideal group of highly assimilated and well-integrated undocumented immigrants to put forward for legalization on moral and humanitarian grounds.[62] Despite being introduced multiple times over the next few years, the DREAM Act continued to stall. By mid-decade, the immigrant rights movement was propelled forward by the nationwide protests that emerged in spring 2006 in response to the passage of HR 4437 in December 2005, not only in gateway cities like Chicago, Los Angeles, and New York but also in places not conventionally associated with the immigrant rights movement like Columbus, Nashville, and Las Vegas. An estimated 3.5 to 5.1 million people nationwide participated in these protests, which also served as a crystallizing moment in the political socialization of a million youth from immigrant families.[63]

After comprehensive reform failed to pass in 2006 and yet again in 2007, national immigrant rights organizations helped form a network of DREAMer-friendly associations initially called the United We Dream Coalition, ultimately leading to the establishment of the permanent nonprofit advocacy organization United We Dream in 2008, with its home in D.C. Young activists from throughout the country regularly came to D.C. for internships and workshops to learn how to produce effective messages and run campaigns and then took these skills back to their home organizations.[64] Thus, D.C. emerged as an increasingly important site within the movement as an incubator of youth activism. Over time, other emerging national organizations—like FWD.us and the UndocuBlack Network—set up D.C. offices or chapters, further cementing the city's place in the movement. Meanwhile, regional networks of CBOs solidified in the late 2000s, including in immigrant gateways like Chicago, another important place within the movement.[65]

The combination of new locations hosting immigrant rights actions, state and local organizing, and national infrastructure expanded DREAMers' networks, which also flourished due to the proliferation of social media, an increasingly critical platform for the movement.[66] Given the movement's focus on federal reform and the fact that D.C. is home to the federal government and its three branches of government, the city has remained a central location for staging in-person political actions, with groups and organizations nationwide often sending delegations to D.C., despite the logistical barriers involved (for instance, traveling without possessing a valid driver's license). These actions, however, have evolved and become higher risk and more diversified in terms of where they are staged. Initially, DREAMers came to D.C. to more peacefully lobby, meet with members of Congress, and stage teach-ins and protests. By 2010, they started more strongly asserting control over their place in the immigrant rights movement and escalating their tactics.[67] For instance, in early 2010, four immigrant young adults undertook the Trail of Dreams, a fifteen-hundred-mile walk from Miami, Florida, to Washington, D.C., to advocate for the passage of the DREAM Act. The activists' journey culminated in a civil disobedience action that ended in the arrest of a hundred individuals, including members of Congress.[68] Youth activists started explicitly risking deportation as a political strategy, including by staging a sit-in at Senator John McCain's Arizona office and occupying a downtown intersection in Georgia.[69] Notably, these actions were staged in more exclusionary socio-legal contexts that had not traditionally been notable places within the movement.

During this time, United We Dream and local affiliates also started targeting the executive branch of government, pushing for "administrative relief" for "low-priority" immigrants and demanding that President Obama use his authority to address their legal situation. Though Obama had already issued an executive memo in June 2011 directing Department of Homeland Security (DHS) field officers to use their discretion for "low-priority immigrants," the memo was ambiguous and not clearly enforceable. DREAMers—who increasingly eschewed that label—launched a wave of coordinated civil disobedience actions aimed at DHS and ICE offices to push the administration to take a stronger stance. By 2012, they launched another wave of actions, occupying President Obama's campaign offices nationwide, designed to ratchet up pressure on him before the election. Soon after, he signed a memo creating DACA.[70] During the decade subsequent to the creation of DACA, D.C. has remained an important location for staging political actions as activists have participated in regular and targeted actions focused on securing a more permanent solution for DACA recipients and fighting for broader immigrant rights. After the 2017 rescission and court battle when DACA became an issue heard by the U.S. Supreme Court, DACA recipients' mass mobilizations have also taken place there, involving the third branch of government infrastructure in D.C.

Indeed, as the nation's capital city, D.C. occupies a central place within the larger undocumented youth movement and has been a regular site of political action over the past fifteen years. However, it is also worth noting that not all (or even the majority of) undocumented young adults nationwide are activists who participate in the larger social movement. While undocumented young adults in the D.C. Metro region theoretically do not face the same logistical barriers to participating in D.C.-based national actions as others throughout the country, the majority of my participants had never done so. Thus, it is important to capture the experiences of these undocumented young adults as well.

As DACA went into effect in 2012, scholars shifted from chronicling the experiences of youth activists in particular locales to tracking the impact of DACA on a national level to gain a bigger picture of who was benefitting from it and how. Since DACA was created, 825,998 individuals nationwide have applied for and received it; 86,139 individuals also applied but were not granted approval, and uncounted thousands more never applied and/or were ineligible. The vast majority of DACA recipients are originally from Latin America (772,516; 93.5 percent). Mexico is by far the leading country of origin (650,353; 78.7 percent), with El Salvador (29,777; 3.6 percent), Guatemala (20,981; 2.5 percent), Honduras (19,175; 2.3 percent), Peru (9,299; 1.1 percent), Brazil (7,650; 1 percent), Ecuador (6,897; 0.8 percent), and Colombia (6,757; 0.8 percent) all among the top ten countries. Yet South Korea is the country of origin with the fifth largest share of DACA recipients (9,011; 1 percent), clearly signaling that DACA recipients are from countries well beyond Latin America; in fact, the top twenty nations also include the Philippines, India, Jamaica, and Trinidad and Tobago. Overall, DACA recipients are nationals of more than 195 different countries.[71]

Beyond national origin, more DACA recipients were female (54 percent) than male (46 percent) in 2022. In 2002, the median age of DACA recipients was twenty-eight years, with an increasing share (35 percent) over the age of thirty.[72] The average DACA recipient arrived at age seven and has lived in the United States for more than twenty years. As DACA recipients have gotten older, more have become parents, to some 256,000 U.S. citizen children.[73] In 2022, the majority were single (69 percent), though more than 30 percent were married, divorced, or widowed.[74] There are an estimated 39,000 LGBTQ+ DACA recipients, the majority of whom live in the states with the most DACA recipients. The states with the largest concentrations of DACA recipients are California, Texas, Illinois, New York, and Florida, with almost half (45 percent) in California and Texas.[75] Not coincidentally, these states have historically had the highest concentration of immigrants and contain traditional gateway cities like Chicago and New York, post–World War II gateways like Los Angeles and Miami, and emerging gateways like Dallas–Fort Worth.[76] The Washington-Arlington-Alexandria, DC-VA-MD-WV Metro region has the tenth largest population of DACA recipients (12,060), behind Los Angeles, New York, Dallas–Fort Worth, Houston, Chicago, Riverside, Phoenix, Atlanta, and San Francisco.[77]

With an ongoing sense of the national picture, provided by U.S. Citizenship and Immigration Services (USCIS) enrollment data and the annual National UnDACAmented Research Project (NURP) and the CAP/UWD/NILC surveys, scholars also started documenting differences in DACA recipients' incorporation trajectories in different socio-legal contexts.[78] Yet studies on different socio-legal contexts have tended to capture more integrative or exclusionary socio-legal contexts (in the singular) or compared them in rather static terms, instead of describing multijurisdictional metropolitan regions that are mixed in their treatment of immigrants, with differently configured urban, suburban, and rural contexts existing in relation to each other.[79]

As we sought to recruit DACA recipients in the D.C. Metro region, my student collaborators and I used a convenience sample, meaning that we did not seek to represent the overall demographic profile of D.C. Metro region DACA recipients. Even if we had wished to compose a representative sample, granular demographic data on local DACA recipients were not accessible. Instead, we deliberately sought to recruit a broad set of D.C. Metro region DACA recipients to capture a wide range of identities and experiences. Given what I know about D.C. Metro region immigrants from published scholarship and my own experiences having grown up and residing in Montgomery County at the time, and as a professor at a state university with a high proportion of immigrants and children of immigrants in Prince George's County, I anticipated that participants would be from many different national origin groups—and ones not commonly found in the DACA literature. Unlike the NURP and the CAP/UWD/NILC surveys that recruit principally from within CBOs or educational settings, we explicitly sought to reach individuals who were not activists or students. Even as we conducted research with individuals who fell into either or both categories, we also connected with their friends and family members who did not. Ultimately, the demographics and experiences of the thirty participants both mirror and are distinct from the macro-level regional and DACA-specific trends presented thus far (see table 1.2). Here I paint a general portrait of participants' collective experiences, though in the chapters to come I present more individualized stories, observations, and reflections. Appendix B also provides demographic details about each participant.

Not surprisingly, participants' countries of origin reflected regional demographics. Half were Central American (Salvadoran, Honduran, and Nicaraguan), with the majority (nine; 30 percent) being Salvadoran—the leading national origin group in the D.C. Metro region and the second largest national origin group of DACA recipients nationwide. The Central American participants' families had lived in the region for the longest period of time, with parents often arriving before their children and then reuniting with them once they became more established. These participants were also more likely to have been involved in immigrant rights activism in Latinx-focused CBOs, many having participated in youth development programming as high school students and recent graduates in the period before the passage of DACA in 2012.

TABLE 1.2. Demographic profile of participants (n=30)

Birthplace (by region and country of origin)	Central America (15; 50%)	El Salvador	9 (30%)
		Honduras	5 (17%)
		Nicaragua	1 (3%)
	South America (7; 23%)	Peru	3 (10%)
		Argentina	1 (3%)
		Bolivia	1 (3%)
		Brazil	1 (3%)
		Colombia	1 (3%)
	North America (3; 10%)	Mexico	3 (10%)
	Asia (3; 10%)	South Korea	2 (7%)
		Indonesia	1 (3%)
	Africa (2; 7%)	Liberia	1 (3%)
		Senegal	1 (3%)
Gender	Female		21 (70%)
	Male		9 (30%)
Age (in 2016)	Range		18–28
	Median		21
Age of arrival to the United States	Range		2–15
	Median		8

The next largest region of origin was South America (Peru, Argentina, Bolivia, Brazil, and Colombia). Peruvians are among the top five D.C. Metro national origins groups and sixth on the list of DACA national origin groups, so it was not surprising that they were the largest South American group. There was one participant each from Argentina, Bolivia, and Brazil. These South American participants described robust family networks in the region but did not report regularly interacting with conationals, instead living in the multiethnic inner suburbs of Montgomery County. Three Mexican nationals participated—fewer than in many states and metropolitan regions, including those prominently featured in the DACA literature. However, these smaller numbers reflect their smaller representation in the D.C. Latinx population and relatively newer migratory flows.

The final five participants were from Asian or African countries of origin, which are quite underrepresented in the DACA literature. Two participants were from South Korea—a national origin group strongly represented in the D.C. Metro region and among the ranks of DACA recipients overall. I also had an Indonesian participant, whose experiences as an "Asian" immigrant were quite distinct from the South Korean participants. Though Indonesians do not show up in the macro-level regional population data, her description of her tight-knit community signals that the Indonesian presence in the D.C. Metro region is much stronger than numbers might indicate. Her Muslim religion also grounded her locally and factored in significantly during the study period as she reflected on the negative impact of President Trump's anti-Muslim immigrant agenda. The final pair of participants were from West African countries of origin (Liberia and Senegal)—in line with the patterns of African migration to and settlement in the D.C. region. The DACA recipient from Senegal was also Muslim and spoke powerfully to the exclusion she experienced along multiple axes of identity (e.g., being an immigrant, Black, Muslim, and female).

Though several participants crossed the U.S.-Mexico border without authorization (including participants from Mexico, El Salvador, Honduras, and Peru), the majority traveled by plane and arrived with valid visas, which subsequently expired. Two Salvadoran participants were caught while crossing the border and spent their first one and three months in the United States in detention facilities in Illinois and Texas, respectively; they were both eight years old when this happened and described this formative experience with incredibly specific and painful detail. Many of the Central American children, including these two individuals, migrated to reunite with parents who had already been living and working in the United States for years while they lived back in their countries of origin with relatives. These individuals spoke of the challenges of adjusting to life in a new country but also adapting to new family configurations with parents and even U.S.-born siblings who were effectively strangers to them. Five participants (from El Salvadoran and Honduras) had fathers who had TPS, which gave their families much greater stability (in terms of employment and residence) and access to resources (like health insurance and scholarships) than their counterparts with undocumented parents. However, their mothers did not have TPS, meaning that they grew up acutely aware of the difference having even a temporary status made.

All participants were from mixed-status families—families in which members hold different statuses, including being U.S. citizens, being lawful permanent residents, having temporary statuses like TPS or DACA, and/or being undocumented. Aside from the five participants whose fathers had TPS, most of the remaining parents were undocumented. The vast majority (twenty-one) had siblings who also had DACA, though six had siblings who were ineligible for the program (three because they arrived when they were too old and three who would have qualified under the original criteria but were unable to apply after the 2017 rescission and subsequent freeze on new applications). Five had siblings who had returned to their countries of origin (Bolivia, Colombia, and Peru) or settled in a new country (Canada) as they were ineligible for the program and/or were not readmitted to the United States. Ten individuals had younger siblings who were born in the United States and were therefore citizens; they observed major differences in these siblings' incorporation trajectories and access to social resources, including health care and federal financial aid.

In terms of gender, all participants identified as female (twenty-one; 70 percent) or male (nine; 30 percent); it ultimately proved more challenging to find and recruit males. Participants were born between 1988 and 1998, and ranged between the ages of eighteen and twenty-eight in 2016. They migrated to the United States between the ages of two and fifteen, at a median age of eight, during the mid-1990s to the mid-2000s (although before the DACA cutoff date of June 15, 2007). They arrived as the D.C. Metropolitan region was rapidly transforming into a newly emerged/hyperdiverse gateway, with growing Central, North, and South American, Asian, and African populations that were increasingly dispersing throughout the suburbs, where the majority of them grew up.

Though they were not recruited based on where within the D.C. Metro region they lived, participants were initially more Maryland-based—reflecting where the research team lived and worked and our personal networks (rooted more in Montgomery and Princes George's Counties in Maryland and D.C. than in Virginia). Participants migrated directly to Maryland (twenty-two), Virginia (four), or D.C. (two), largely joining family and friends who were already established there, though several initially lived in other states, including Arizona and Florida (one) and Michigan (one). The two participants who initially lived in D.C. subsequently moved to the inner suburbs, while most (twenty-six) settled directly in the inner suburbs (Montgomery and Prince George's Counties in Maryland and Fairfax County in Virginia)—consistent with the emerging pattern of suburban settlement in the 1990s and early 2000s. Several families moved to different jurisdictions within the D.C. Metro region within their first few years; these moves had significant implications for their access to social resources depending on where they moved. These regular moves—both within the region and between states—underscore that immigrant settlement patterns are not as static as often portrayed in the literature. Indeed, as I followed participants over time into phases II and III, their spatial mobility expanded even more as they moved to new places, including outer suburb counties (including Howard and Frederick Counties in Maryland and Prince William County in Virginia) and even other states (including California, Michigan, and Texas).

In 2016, the majority of participants were students; however, many of them attended college on a part-time basis as they worked (frequently multiple jobs) to pay for their schooling. The majority (eighteen; 60 percent) were enrolled in a four-year university in 2016, with another nine (30 percent) enrolled in a community college. Many enrolled in universities had gone through community college, since the 2012 Maryland DREAM Act dictated that they attend community college first. Two individuals were not enrolled and had no plans to be after graduating from high school and with an associate's degree. Finally, one completed a BS degree; into the subsequent phases, many more (twenty) completed BS/BA degrees and three enrolled in graduate programs in social work, information management, and accounting. Over time and as participants got further into adulthood, their and my focus became much less on their educational experiences and more on their work and everyday adult lives. Many are now deep into their twenties and thirties, building careers, forging relationships and partnerships, having families, buying homes, and pursuing opportunities in all of these realms that take them to new places beyond the D.C. Metro region.

Conclusion

As Sarah Bruhn and Roberto G. Gonzales emphasize, "*Place* matters deeply in the lives of immigrant young people and their efforts to belong."[80] The D.C. Metro region is an intriguing yet understudied place for examining the incorporation trajectories of undocumented immigrant young adults. The region is notable for its hyperdiversity, suburban settlement patterns (with immigrants living in multiethnic neighborhoods), variegated policy landscape, and prominence within the immigrant rights movement. Yet DACA recipients' experiences in diverse, multijurisdictional metropolitan regions like the D.C. Metro region have not yet been adequately captured in the scholarly literature, even though they reveal a more complete picture of DACA recipients' lives overall. The chapters ahead describe how DACA recipients living within this dynamic region have cultivated practices for flourishing in their daily lives despite their precarious legal status and ongoing threats to their health and well-being.

2

"I Have to Continue with My Normal Life"

Embodying Status Precarity and Controlling Uncertainty

Juan first came to the United States from Mexico when he was one year old, though he noted, "I was a toddler, so I don't remember crossing over. My earliest memory is just being here." After living in Arizona and then Florida, his family settled in Maryland when he was twelve, and they have lived there ever since. Juan reported that as a child "I always knew I was in some kind of danger. I remember having thoughts that 'if ICE was to come to my home today, I would not be here tomorrow.' But I had never seen an ICE car, so it was almost like an urban legend, a myth. I did know of the danger, it just never became real for me."

By 2016, when he was twenty, there had been an uptick in immigration enforcement in Maryland, making the "urban legend" much more real. Juan recounted his first encounter with ICE that past January: "My mom was going shopping for food on Sunday morning. When she got to the grocery store, ICE was there, so she didn't stop . . . she just came back home and made me go buy the food we needed instead." Juan's mother asked him to go to the store for her because DACA provided him a layer of protection that she, as an undocumented person, lacked. Juan dutifully obliged, relating, "I was like, 'Okay,' and then I got out my work permit to take with me." Once he got to the store, he recalled, "ICE was in the parking lot, asking people questions. I had my work permit in my pocket. An agent came up to me and I just pulled out my permit and showed him and kept walking without saying a word. I felt like I was controlling the situation to a certain point, and it made me feel secure." After that, Juan explained, "I started carrying my work permit with me everywhere I go. I see clearly the danger of not having it. I make sure that if I go outside the house, I have it with me. If I had to boil it down, it gives me security wherever I am. It gives me assurance, and makes me feel like I belong in the grand scheme of things."

Whenever the topic of Juan's work permit came up during the interview—which it did multiple times—he subconsciously tapped his wallet pocket, as if to reassure himself that the permit was still there, a visceral reminder of the importance of the prized document and the weight that it carried in his life. When Ana and I debriefed about the interview afterward, we both made note of Juan's subconscious wallet tapping. Though other participants had reflected on the importance of their documents, his embodied response was particularly telling. Also interesting were the words he used to describe what these documents provided him—control, security, assurance, and belonging. Juan's focus was not merely on the practical utility of his documents in enabling him to get a job in the formal economy. Though these documents held a specific bureaucratic purpose, it was clear that possessing them also impacted Juan's mental health and overall state of being.

During a subsequent interview in November 2017, Juan was once again subconsciously tapping his wallet, and I decided to ask him directly about it. He actually laughed in response, saying, "My mom made a joke that I must have some kind of itch, because I'm touching my wallet all the time. It's a compulsion—like every five minutes, I'm touching my wallet area just to make sure that it's there." However, Juan shared that the practice of always carrying his documents had backfired:

I was working with my dad, and we were throwing out trash from a construction site at a public dump. You drive your car up to this disgusting-smelling building and put down the latch to the truck to push everything to the floor, and then this big machine comes and scrapes the ground and pushes everything into this pit of fire. Somehow my wallet, which is black, fell on the ground, which is black because it's so filthy. I didn't realize it, so we left. It had my Social Security, my DACA, and my license. Once we realized it an hour later, my dad and I were both freaking out, trying to figure out what happened. I was thinking, "My documents are in there. If they fall into the raging pit of death, I'm never going to get them back!" Luckily my dad's business card was in my wallet, and we got a call that they had found it. We had like a little party in the car, so excited, because we thought it was lost.

Though it had a positive resolution, "because of that incident," Juan explained, "I don't carry them around anymore. It really freaked me out. So, yeah, having them on me stresses me out, and not having them on me stresses me out too. I'm just going to be stressed out either way." While he shared that "the actual documents are at home, locked up, just in case," he noted, "I do carry around a copy, folded up, to ease my mind." This incident took place around the time of the DACA rescission announcement in September 2017, so Juan was extra attuned to the implications of losing his documents. As he noted ominously in November 2017, "In the back of my mind, it's still there . . . an aura of danger, that something could go wrong. If I don't have papers in the future, all I'm going to think about is, 'How can I obtain some kind of security?'"

For Juan—and as I came to find out, numerous other participants as well—control and security were common idioms through which they described their mental health. Yet Juan's lost documents also underscore the turmoil associated with not possessing them, even temporarily. Every time I saw Juan thereafter—both for formal interviews and informally—I would inquire about his documents, which in many ways became a gauge of the state of his mental health during what turned out to be a prolonged period of instability. When I interviewed him in August 2020 and checked in about the status of his documents, Juan reported a marked change in his behavior: "I don't carry around my papers and I don't even carry around copies anymore . . . I feel much more in control and confident now." Initially, I was surprised at Juan's comments, given that his documents had been so critical to his previous feelings of security and control. However, as he continued to tell me more about recent developments in his adult life, I gained much more insight into the confidence he now projected.

This chapter describes the impact of prolonged policy instability on DACA recipients' well-being by chronicling DACA recipients' mental health at three distinct time points: when DACA was still intact (2016), when it initially came under threat (2017–18), and as DACA continued to languish with an uncertain future amid legal battles and congressional inaction (2020–21). It describes how DACA recipients have embodied their status precarity and managed their ontological security[1]—the ability to count on the stability of the future—across time and amid destabilizing developments related to DACA. Undocumented young adults face unique stressors and vulnerabilities and are known to exhibit high levels of depression and anxiety. Initially, transitioning to possessing status through the DACA program diminished their psychological distress; Juan's story about his ICE encounter demonstrates that possessing bureaucratic documents gave him a sense of control, security, assurance, and even belonging. However, it is also clear from Juan's practice of obsessively carrying his documents and compulsively checking his pocket that even as he felt more "in control" of his legal situation, he still experienced distress due to the temporary nature of DACA status, surging immigration enforcement, and his undocumented parents' continued vulnerability.

Also evident from Juan's experiences is that his psychological distress heightened considerably during the first Trump era when DACA came under threat in 2017. Juan reported being anxious whether he had his documents on him or not and started carrying around a copy of his documents (that most definitely would not have held up to ICE agents' scrutiny) just to ease his mind. In the aftermath of the rescission, DACA recipients like Juan exhibited clear signs of psychological distress because of their endangered status; indeed, DACA itself became a chronic stressor and also became tied to anticipatory stresses rooted in having only a temporary form of status.[2] Scholars have described temporal uncertainty as a defining feature of life for those with precarious legal status like DACA recipients who are forced to endure directionless stasis as they wait to find out their ultimate fate without knowing when it might be decided.[3] Indeed, the state controls migrants' time and imposes periods of waiting as a form of temporal governance through which migrants experience detachment from the temporal rhythms of "normal" life.[4] Yet it was not only uncertainty but also emerging forms of bureaucratic violence[5] like inexplicably delayed documents, new steps to the renewal process, and time "lost" submitting reapprovals in anticipation of bureaucratic challenges that magnified DACA recipients' psychological distress as they awaited news on DACA.

Even as they contended with heightened distress, though, participants actively cultivated resilience strategies that allowed them to wrest a modicum of control over their lives. In 2020–21, despite DACA's future being less clear than ever as it wound its way through the courts and the new challenges introduced by the raging COVID-19 pandemic, participants gained temporal control[6] over their indeterminate situation by focusing on normalcy and rechanneling their energies into the activities of everyday life in the D.C. Metro region. As I spoke to participant after participant in this period, they were flourishing as they pursued normalcy instead of focusing on the ongoing threats to their mental health that dominated previous phases. Thus it became clear that as they got more deeply into their adult lives, they moderated their enduring legal precarity by finding meaning in the activities of everyday life.

The Impact of Precarious Legal Status on Mental Health and Well-Being

Precarious legal status—produced by the state via intentional policymaking—has a profound impact on immigrants' overall health status and emotional well-being.[7] Legal status precarity penetrates different spheres of immigrants' everyday lives, impacting family relationships and social networks, disrupting participation in social life, and influencing educational and economic trajectories.[8] Yet it is experienced quite differently depending on immigrants' generation and life cycle stage.[9] Some undocumented youth are not fully aware of their status during childhood but then later face the legal repercussions of it as teenagers when they miss out on important rites of passage like obtaining driver's licenses, getting first jobs, and planning for college.[10] Roberto G. Gonzales and anthropologist Leo R. Chavez liken this process to "awakening to a nightmare" as their abject status bears a deep imprint on their subjectivities.[11] As they fully grasp the magnitude of the limitations they face, many undocumented youth exhibit high levels of depression and anxiety stemming from chronic stress and fear of deportation.[12] They also must manage complex emotions like shame and exclusion as they navigate their status against the backdrop of a hostile sociopolitical climate.[13]

Transitioning from undocumented status to lawful presence initially led to meaningful reductions in DACA recipients' symptoms of psychological distress,[14] particularly by reducing or relieving two primary stressors—deportation threat and exclusion from the formal labor market.[15] In more affective terms, psychologist Basia D. Ellis, Roberto

G. Gonzales, and human development scholar Sarah A. Rendón García highlight the profound shift from hopelessness to hopefulness that DACA recipients underwent, while sociologist Tara Fiorito describes the newfound joy, calmness, and normalcy that many DACA recipients experienced.[16] Leisy Abrego argues that DACA gave immigrant young adults renewed optimism but also benefitted their families as they navigated family needs better and felt a sense of collective optimism about their place in U.S. society.[17] DACA has also helped improve the mental health of recipients' children, demonstrating a powerful intergenerational effect.[18] Beyond family, DACA also enabled recipients to gain broader social support and build more authentic social lives.[19]

Yet DACA recipients' mental health continues to be shaped by the temporary and politically contingent nature of their status.[20] DACA recipients exhibit clear signs of psychological distress, manifested as symptoms like stress, nervousness, and anxiety.[21] Many also lack access to both employer-based and publicly funded health coverage to help manage these symptoms and encounter gaps in mental health services and a lack of culturally competent providers.[22] Although social support can contribute positively to lowering mental health symptomology, scholars have found that it ultimately cannot buffer structural-based stressors.[23] DACA recipients' mental health is also shaped by ongoing concerns over family members' continued legal vulnerability, underscoring how legal status is experienced intersubjectively and relationally.[24] Many DACA recipients experience "survivor's guilt" and distress about the position of privilege they occupy relative to family members still subject to detention, deportation, exploitation, and denial of health care.[25] Thus the experience of gaining status for many DACA recipients is actually "bittersweet" and filled with emotional complexity.[26]

Further, even with DACA, recipients are still subject to the legal violence of the citizenship regime[27]—and face new stressors in being known to the state. As they undergo the bureaucratic inscription process,[28] immigrants reluctantly and fearfully submit to state scrutiny. Being on the radar of formal recordkeeping institutions like the immigration bureaucracy can heighten immigrants' sense of risk and unsafety.[29] Indeed, since the beginning of DACA, many applicants harbored concerns about USCIS possessing their personal information, and many otherwise-eligible youth elected not to apply for that very reason. Trump's plans to end DACA and increase deportations in his second term underscore the justifiability of these concerns. Even with legal protections, DACA recipients still experience new or renewed stressors. In fact, DACA itself has become a chronic stressor linked to anticipatory stresses rooted in the experience of having been granted some rights but not full inclusion.[30] The accumulation of chronic stressors is associated with higher allostatic load, which over time can adversely impact health.[31]

The shifting national policy climate has also undermined DACA recipients' mental health gains. Many DACA recipients returned to pre-DACA levels of distress even by 2015 as then-candidate Trump started expressing his intent to end DACA.[32] Once Trump became president, they were forced to prepare mentally for another four years without any possibility of immigration relief.[33] The Trump administration's jarring attempt to terminate DACA in September 2017 and the lengthy appeals regarding the future of the program have led to worsening health outcomes.[34] Recipients have described increased stress and depression, reported that their social networks have grown smaller, experienced greater barriers to health care, and confronted episodes of discrimination due to DACA-related social stigma.[35] DACA recipients have experienced anticipatory loss as they grapple with a range of emotions about the potential end of DACA including denial, sadness, disappointment, anger, resentment, and desperation.[36] Uncertainty about the program's fate post-rescission may even be eroding the positive gains to DACA recipients' U.S.-born children's health.[37] DACA recipients now face the distinct possibility of being stripped of their protected status, having already experienced the enhanced opportunities associated with being legally present.

In her original formulation of liminal legality, Cecilia Menjívar notes that it is not merely the temporary status itself but also long-term uncertainty that shape immigrants' well-being.[38] DACA recipients exist in a heightened state of temporal uncertainty as they endure directionless stasis as they wait to find out their ultimate fate without knowing when it might happen.[39] Indeed, the state controls migrants' time and imposes periods of waiting as a form of temporal governance.[40] Waiting is enacted as a means of dispossession through which migrants experience the slowing and accelerating of time frames and detachment from the temporal rhythms of "normal" life.[41] Social work scholars Breanne

Grace and Benjamin J. Roth and physician Rajeev Bais describe the violence of uncertainty to which immigrants with precarious legal status are subjected as they wait, arguing that such violence is enacted through systematic personal, social, and institutional instability that injects fear into basic daily interactions.[42] As anthropologist Lauren Heidbrink argues, immigrants who are ultimately deported experience temporal violence as their past and present collide with devastating impacts on their health and well-being.[43] As immigrants navigate a complex bureaucratic system while seeking to gain status, they also experience new forms of suffering.[44] The immigration bureaucracy itself produces barriers and harm as it exerts force through processes of decision making, paperwork, knowledge production, inaction, and exclusion.[45]

Chronic temporal uncertainty also serves as a threat to immigrants' deeper ontological security—or the ability to count on the stability of the future—that compromises their well-being.[46] Ontological insecurity can also be exacerbated by policy changes happening suddenly and without advance warning[47] and new stress events like threats to rights and discriminatory public sentiment.[48] A lack of ontological security can disorder individual subjectivity, but also generate a collective sense of risk and vulnerability.[49] This lack of ontological security also shapes migrants' everyday, embodied experiences of being in the world, deeply affecting their sense of space and time.[50] They must constantly be on alert[51] and make "embodied alterations"[52] to manage their fears and accomplish the necessary routines of everyday life.[53] As anthropologist Andrea Flores points out, these actions are reactive to the work of the state.[54]

Possessing state-issued bureaucratic documents makes carrying out these daily routines easier and facilitates a sense of security for DACA recipients; it also allows them to increase their spatial mobility, which can also benefit other family members.[55] Yet it is not merely possessing documents and being able to furnish them on demand that ultimately enables immigrant young adults to bring order to their lives; immigrants also wrest temporal control of their lives through other more proactive means.[56] I argue that DACA recipients gain temporal control over their indeterminate situation by rechanneling their energies toward pursuing normalcy in their everyday lives, outside of the purview of the state. Indeed, I have found that DACA recipients have cultivated a range of resilience strategies[57] that have enabled them to even flourish as they pursue meaningful lives despite their enduring legal status precarity and the multiple forms of state violence to which they are regularly subjected.

Embodying and Managing Legal Status Precarity during Different Phases of DACA

By chronicling how DACA recipients embody their legal status precarity and manage the ontological insecurity that accompanies their status during three time periods of particular DACA significance—when DACA was still intact (2016), when DACA initially came under threat (2017–18), and when DACA languished with an uncertain future amid legal battles and congressional inaction (2020–21)—we can see that, across time, not merely insecurity and uncertainty but also temporal dispossession adversely impact DACA recipients' mental health as they contend with missing or lost documents, the existential fatigue of living life in renewal cycles, and lost time due to fear and anticipated bureaucratic delays. However, they have also cultivated strategies for gaining temporal control in the everyday, culminating in their pursuit of normalcy in the present.

"I'm Still No One Here without My Papers": Persistent Distress Even with DACA

In 2016 when I first met them, participants reported that overall receiving DACA had positively impacted their health and well-being. Nancy, who came from Argentina at age eleven, shared that before receiving DACA she was "completely depressed" in high school as she realized that it would be difficult to afford college: "I saw my future, and it was like, 'I want to be over there, but there's a curtain that's covering what I'm going to be.' I felt like I had no control over it whatsoever." She heard about DACA on the news during her senior year and obtained application assistance at a CBO, noting the burdensome process of collecting documents to verify her identity and continuous physical presence.[58] Nancy was pleasantly surprised to hear back quickly: "That was a moment that was very emotional for me. Getting my Social Security card gave me a sense of, 'I'm actually someone here. I'm recognized here.'

In high school, I felt totally fake in the sense that I'm here, but I'm not. It is something that I battle with a lot—that I don't belong here. Getting that card made me feel legitimate." Indeed, DACA afforded recipients like Nancy a greater sense of social legitimacy and belonging. Nancy recounted that her mental health improved as she was able to take more control over her life; like Juan, she always kept her documents on her to feel more secure. She began taking classes at a community college, graduating with an associate's degree within a year since she took many Advanced Placement classes in high school.

Beyond the Social Security card and work permit, DACA also enabled recipients to get more "normal" Maryland driver's licenses. Although Maryland passed a bill in 2013 enabling undocumented immigrants to get state licenses, the license itself bears an imprint that specifies that it is not valid for federal identification purposes.[59] DACA recipients' licenses do not have that imprint, so there is no indication of immigration status. Elena, who had come to the United States from Honduras with her mother and two older sisters when she was eight, was highly attuned to this difference. She was fortunate to get DACA and an unmarked driver's license when she was sixteen, but she explained, "The MVA [Motor Vehicle Association] puts a stamp on people's licenses when you don't have papers. My mom's has it but we don't have that on ours." Reflecting on the benefits of an unmarked license, Elena noted, "It does make you feel more, American [Laughs]." Her comment underscores that possessing an unmarked license also was tied to incorporation. Elena also shared that her unmarked license opened up travel opportunities: "If you have that stamp on your license, you can't really risk being on a plane or at an airport. I went to California last summer with my sister . . . that was our first time flying, and it was a great feeling. It was something that we didn't have to worry about anymore. We were safe." DACA recipients can move more "safely" without the fear of being stopped by police and deported, greatly facilitating their spatial mobility.[60] Elena's father is a TPS holder and also has an unmarked license, though she lamented, "it just sucks for my mom. Whenever we think about taking a trip, all four of us can do it. But what about my mom? I'm like, 'I wish we could all go to Cali,' but we just go to Virginia instead because we can drive instead of fly."

Elena's eldest sister, Sara, also noted that the unmarked license provided an additional layer of safety: "Before I had DACA, I was scared of police officers, worried about an encounter where they would call immigration just for speeding. Every time a police officer was behind me, I would get really nervous." Sara also noted that since she migrated when she was older, her slight accent would make her more vulnerable. Sara's nervousness was justified, as she recounted that a member of her congregation was stopped en route to church and ultimately detained and taken to a detention center. Because of that, Sara noted, "DACA gives me peace of mind, because I don't have to worry. I can just show my license. It's not marked or anything. I can pass with it. And if they ask for my social, I have a copy of it too, just in case." Sara's comments underscore the importance of compellingly performing belonging in these power-laden interactions ("passing" in her words), including by furnishing copies of documents that officers likely would not accept anyway.

Despite these enhanced feelings of legitimacy and belonging, and assurance and safety, participants still contended with stressors that negatively impacted their mental health.[61] Verónica, originally from El Salvador, became visibly emotional when I first interviewed her in August 2016. She had been detained at age eight while trying to reunite with her father: "We got caught while we crossed the border in Texas. We stayed [in a detention center] for three months and I remember crying all of the time because I didn't like it and was separated from my brother. It changed a lot for us, because my dad was actually in the process of getting his papers and they took that away from him because of us." Her father picked them up and brought them to Maryland, where he was living, though Verónica reflected, "That experience changed me in a lot of ways. I remember being more social back home. It was a struggle . . . I still struggle with it." Verónica noted that before DACA

fear was always there. We were always hiding from everything. The little things that could have maybe exposed us, we didn't do. My brother didn't drive even though he was old enough, because my dad was like, "If you get caught, then you'll get deported." I'm a sports-type person, but we couldn't do them because my dad would say, "They ask for a Social Security, you guys don't have one." Or, "they're going to tell someone and we might get deported." I couldn't go out late with my friends—"late" being like after 5:00 p.m. We were always "afraid of getting deported."

Verónica received DACA at age sixteen and noted its immediate impact: "I didn't struggle as much when I was in high school—those were my years! I felt like everyone else for once. While everybody was getting their driver's permit, I was getting it too. That's why I felt like I was part of this country and not just someone who's not. Because sometimes I feel like I'm nothing here."

Since she received DACA as soon as she was eligible, Verónica had never had to navigate the adult world without documents. However, she had a very rude awakening when she was eighteen: "I had my DACA card in my wallet because I was going to [name of restaurant] because I got a job there. I went in for the interview and was going to fill out all my paperwork." While in the restaurant, she realized she had forgotten her wallet, so "I ran out to my car and when I got there, I saw someone broke into it and stole it. It was a big deal for me. That's when everything started hitting again, where I started realizing that I'm still no one here without my papers. I can say my Social Security number, but they won't believe me if I don't have the card." Verónica experienced the loss of her card as a costly inconvenience (as she had just renewed and had to pay the fees to replace her card), but also as a deeper form of ontological insecurity. Verónica's insecurity is also fueled by her previous experiences contending with direct state violence when she was forced to spend months alone in immigrant detention.

Stolen or lost documents were not the only document-related stressors participants described. In fact, several experienced administrative snafus even though they had submitted their paperwork on time. Laura, who came from Mexico at age fourteen, also became quite emotional as she talked about being overwhelmed juggling full-time employment, college, a husband and a child, and the needs of her extended family. Before DACA, Laura worked a full-time night shift for a cleaning company while taking college classes during the day. Since she could not (yet) work legally, Laura noted, "I did a lot of internships during my four years of trying to get my associate's degree!" With DACA, Laura noted, "many opportunities opened for me." She was offered a full-time position with benefits at a CBO where one of her internships was based. As she recalled, "I was like, 'What? Me? Like, for real? How am I going to do it with my night time job?' That's when my supervisor said, 'I'm offering you this position so you can quit the night time job!' I was just so thrilled!" Laura then told me the exact date that she started her position two years prior; when I commented that she had a good memory for dates, she said, "Yeah, I always thought that it was very important for me to know my dates."

Yet when Laura renewed DACA for the first time in 2014, her new documents did not arrive before the original documents expired.[62] "I was out of status for two weeks," Laura recalled. "There was a concern in the office, 'we can hold your position for so long, but it can't be like a month or two.'" Laura's hard-earned position was endangered as she checked the mail each day to see if the USCIS envelope had arrived. Even more, she noted, "At that point I was pregnant, so I was like, 'Oh my God, if I lose my job, I lose health care.' It was completely overwhelming waiting." The waiting caused Laura obvious distress, but luckily her employers understood her situation; she noted, "The director spoke to my supervisor and was like, 'It's okay, we're not going to freak out.' So having that support in the organization put me at ease and gave me that security."

Annisa (originally from Indonesia) was also quite forthcoming about her mental health struggles. Prior to DACA, she recalled that "I had so much anxiety based on my status," leading her to see multiple specialists. "When I was in high school," she noted, "I got check-ups for a lot of things because I was having physical symptoms. I remember having an ultrasound around this area [points to midsection] because I'd been reporting cramping. We thought it might be a cyst, but they didn't find anything and concluded it was just stress related." Scholars have noted the range of somatic symptoms that immigrants with precarious status report, such as stomach pains, diminished appetite, headaches, and poor sleep,[63] which are often exacerbated by difficulties in accessing medical care.[64] Even after she got DACA as a high school junior, Annisa continued to have health issues, noting in 2016, "Just last year I went to urgent care because I was having heart problems. But it turns out that it was just a physiological response to my anxiety, the physical symptoms. They said there's nothing wrong with my heart and I'm just being paranoid."

Annisa noted that DACA had not actually alleviated much of her anxiety—especially since she had been contending with new stressors. For one, she lost health insurance once she became an adult and was no longer eligible for the county program that allowed her to get specialty care as a teenager. By college, she no longer had insurance and tried to see a therapist on campus but had to wait a really long time. Once she finally got an appointment, she recalled, "a lot of my anxiety was financially based at that time. She was like, 'well, why don't you do work study?' and I told her I wasn't eligible. She was like, 'why not?' and I told her it was because I was under the [state] DREAM Act. She didn't know what that was. So it was hard for her to help me." Annisa was not alone in struggling to access care, let alone mental health services; more than half of the participants (sixteen, or 53 percent) were uninsured or underinsured in 2016.[65]

Annisa had also grown more concerned about her parents: "As I get older, I understand my parents' struggle more. Now I also have deportation anxiety because my parents don't have this status, so they could be deported any time." Even as Annisa had become more legally secure, she simultaneously realized the depth and implications of her parents' legal vulnerability. Echoing Juan, she noted the uptick in immigration enforcement in the D.C. Metro region that aggravated her deportation fear. This fear was not just abstract, either—members of her aunt's family had recently been deported. As she lamented, "It was devastating for them to have to move back to Indonesia. We were really close, so it was hard for us too." She also connected her anxiety to the upcoming election: "With Trump as a candidate, that's put a lot of anxiety on my family. We just know that if he wins, he'll maybe stop DACA [since] it's a temporary program. The Islamophobia has also been hard, and just doubled that anxiety too."

In 2016, participants clearly indicated how receiving DACA had improved their mental health as they gained a greater sense of social legitimacy and belonging and felt more secure and safe. Possessing bureaucratic documents fostered a deeper sense of ontological security, yet episodes of stolen and delayed documents revealed the distress participants experienced when they no longer possessed their physical documents (even temporarily). Lapses in documentation represented threats to their livelihoods and health, but also rapidly intensified their ontological insecurity. These experiences underscored the fragility of their DACAmented existences and help to explain why some participants continued to experience somatic forms of distress like stomach aches and heart problems even after receiving DACA. Their psychological well-being was also impacted by the ongoing—and heightened—legal vulnerability of family members. Participants' accounts are peppered with the violence of the state, through direct mechanisms like detainment and family members' deportation, but also indirectly as they contended with unexplainable bureaucratic challenges and delays that provoked distress. Though DACA had improved participants' mental health in some aspects, these ongoing and new stressors very much tempered these gains.

"There's All These What-Ifs . . . It's Just Exhausting": Getting By in the First Trump Era with DACA under Threat

After the DACA rescission announcement, participants' psychological distress intensified immensely.[66] As Elena reflected during a follow-up interview, "I've definitely been more anxious. I thought about that when I was filling out the survey. The last time you interviewed me I had never had any mental health issues. But I have found myself being more anxious and noticing things a lot more." Elena shared that she dealt with her anxiety by "stress eating," admitting, "It's been so bad. I literally probably ate fast food every single day during this last semester. I can tell when my cholesterol is increasing again because I can't breathe normally. I've noticed that when I go up the stairs, like when I go to the gym, I get dizzy sometimes and have to hold onto something and breathe." DACA uncertainty adversely impacted Elena's health as she contended with anxiety for the first time and exacerbated a condition that was previously under control. Several participants had anxiety attacks for the first time, including Elena's sister Pau, who, in January 2018, shared, "I've been very depressed and stressed out. Just today, I had an anxiety attack. That's never happened to me before. All of this just bottles up and then little things trigger it." Those who had chronic anxiety, like Nancy and Annisa, shared that it ramped up and compounded with other stressors related to "adulting," like graduating, navigating the job market, and negotiating long-term relationships, in their cases.

Participants also reported other somatic manifestations of distress. Marcela, who migrated from Honduras when she was eight, started experiencing mysterious symptoms in early 2018 that interfered with her job at a local grocery chain where she had worked for four years: "I started having a lot of physical symptoms, and the main concern was the hand tremors since I couldn't use my hands when it happened. I went to a neurologist but the tests didn't show anything. They were just like, 'Maybe it's anxiety.'" As her provider continued to try to figure out what was wrong, she recalled, "I was supposed to have MRIs done to get a concrete answer, but I didn't have insurance. They were very expensive, and I was like, 'I just can't get them.' So she said that I should try therapy." Marcela tried therapy, though she noted, "Every time I went, I would have to pay forty dollars. The counselor wanted me to come every week, but it was too much. So, I would do every two weeks and then it became like two months. Since it was so spaced out, I don't think it really helped." She also wondered if the sessions really addressed the root cause of her anxiety—her legal status: "I understand what she was trying to say . . . that it's normal that I'm feeling anxiety. But I was like, if things were normal for me immigration-wise, I wouldn't be here!"[67]

Even after taking a position with a corporate food and beverage organization—which thankfully offered health insurance—Marcela still experienced crippling anxiety: "There were sometimes when I couldn't go to work because it was so bad. It was like that for about three months. I ended up going to the hospital three times during that time. I finally decided to tell my supervisor because I didn't want him to think I was lying or a bad employee. He told me that the company had a lot of benefits, including short-term disability." Marcela followed her supervisor's advice and took three months of disability. During that time, she tried therapy once again since she had coverage through her insurance and felt like "it definitely helped a lot. But one of the biggest things was I just wanted the symptoms to be over with . . . but apparently it's not like these [immigration-related symptoms] are ever really over." So Marcela returned to work, with her anxiety slightly better in check, but still deeply concerned about how to manage it.

With DACA under threat, recipients experienced intense distress about their renewals, which they had to stage well in advance of the expiration date on their documents. As first revealed in the introduction, Juan described the temporal rhythm of the renewal process and the mental health impact of being compelled to "live your life in an eighteen-month cycle." Juan asserted that all DACA recipients could relate, saying, "No one is immune from that anxiety . . . everyone I talk to says the same thing." He identified the waiting period after submitting the application to USCIS as the most stressful point in the cycle: "It's like, 'I just applied a week ago.' I'm like, 'What if it got lost in the mail? What if it spontaneously combusted? What if it got, you know, eaten by a bear?' There's all of these what-ifs. It's exhausting. Everyone's going through the same exact anxiety and it's different from any other kind of worry in life."

Juan's "exhaustion" indexes a deeper existential fatigue that set in for DACA recipients as they were subjected to increasingly stressful renewal processes. Several participants actually started talking about their DACA expiration dates as if they were a terminal diagnosis. Pau, for instance, said, "I feel sort of like a have a terminal illness. I've never traveled, and if I have the opportunity to, I probably have the means to do it right now. I'm looking into going to Texas with a church group and am really pushing toward that because it's one of the things that's like, 'If I don't do this, I'm probably never going to get to do this. I've never been on a plane before and this is my chance.'" For Pau and others, their documents shifted from having a legitimizing and security-inducing effect to being material evidence of their enduring legal status precarity.

Due to uncertainty about DACA, many participants started submitting their applications even further in advance, in the process "losing" time. Elena lost a month when she applied early, noting frustratedly that "[USCIS] cut another month on top of it." That particular renewal process also came with an unexpected outcome: "I only got it for a year, unfortunately. Technically, it's supposed to be valid for two years, but the card only says a year. I've been checking the website and there aren't any updates if they're going to issue new cards. It's nerve-wracking, because my work is already requesting the new one." Though this was not her first renewal, Elena lamented, "it's been a new experience every single time, which is annoying. For me, I'm a planner. I like to have a plan for everything I do, and come up with contingency plans. But every single time I go for a DACA renewal, it's like, 'What if it doesn't happen? What if it doesn't get approved because of whatever the hell is happening with the government at that point?'"

Santiago, originally from Nicaragua, had lost even more time: "I just renewed and lost four months. It was a risk that I had to take. I could have waited a little longer to renew but then maybe things could've gone sideways. They did tell me that since we were applying ahead of the 180 days, they could potentially turn it away or deny it. But I was like, 'That's a risk I'm taking.' Thankfully everything went through." Santiago had previously shared in 2016 that he suffered from chronic anxiety and had ended up seeing a cardiologist for what he thought was a heart problem: "I felt like I was having a heart attack but it wasn't one. I was so stressed out it was causing me to have heart palpitations." By 2018, he noted, "I've been struggling a lot with anxiety and stress this last year. There's just so much uncertainty about what's going to happen." This time, however, he reported, "I started therapy to try to learn to cope with my anxiety. She helped me try to manage things beyond my control. I haven't had anything serious physical health-wise since." Though I had expected Santiago to dwell on the stress of renewal and time he lost, he surprised me slightly by saying, "My mentality is that if things are going to happen, there's nothing I can do. It's beyond my power. My whole legal status, I try to keep it in the back of my head. I put it in the back, and I just keep moving. I know it's there, and sometimes it comes out. But at the end of the day, I'm like, 'I can't let that control me.'"

Although more participants like Marcela and Santiago reported seeking therapy for the first time during this period, they more commonly described informal coping strategies that allowed them to gain a sense of control and moderate their intensifying ontological insecurity. Sociologists Elizabeth Vaquera, Elizabeth Aranda, and Isabel Sousa-Rodriguez indicate that coping strategies can be both negative, like taking part in behaviors that result in self-harm like drinking, using drugs, or ideating or attempting suicide, and positive, including engaging in activities like listening to music or playing sports, turning to family members and friends for support, or participating in advocacy organizations.[68] Positive emotional well-being is connected to the development of resilience strategies that enable individuals to overcome hardship.[69] Though these strategies are certainly not stand-ins for regular access to care and mental health services, they nevertheless demonstrate that DACA recipients "keep moving" and are actively pursuing strategies to promote their well-being.

Some participants like Pau described deliberately keeping busy: "Being busy is one of my coping skills. I keep myself busy and try not to think about [DACA]." Marcela likewise reflected, "For me, my mind races a lot, so it's just always having something to do. . . . I have work, and then after work, I go to school. After school, I go to church. I always have something to do. The only way is to keep busy to distract me from thinking too much."[70] Many participants talked about exercising, like Camila, who noted, "I go to my Zumba class at least four times a week and am part of a salsa team. It gets my mind distracted and I don't think about those other things." John, who migrated from South Korea when he was ten, sought out new activities to keep himself occupied, playing ultimate frisbee in a weekend league and taking up rock climbing, with his shoes clipped to his bag when we had our interview in 2018. Others mentioned such activities as cooking, playing computer or video games, and playing or listening to music. Juan talked about "making sure that I'm in the present, enjoying all of the little facets of life and not let it creep into present-day enjoyment. I'm not going to go to a concert and think about DACA. That would ruin the night." Annisa likewise noted, "My mental health now is trying to live in the moment."

Others, like Emine, who migrated from Liberia when she was four, described taking an opposite approach by completely disconnecting; she shared, "I can get overwhelmed really easily and feel like everything is crashing down. So I take what I call my 'mental days,' where I'll disconnect from everything. I just kind of relax and do nothing. I let my friends and boyfriend know and they're good about giving me that space." Madeline also talked about disconnecting, especially from politics. As a political science major in college and self-described political junkie, she noted in our first interview, "I watch politics a lot. That's my life, 24/7." By November 2017, though, Madeline noted, "Now, I don't really watch the news anymore, following the [rescission] decision and things like that because there's no coherence in what's being done. I'm not on CNN anymore, and I used to be all day, every day. Now I'm on Netflix."

John noted that he leaned on reason to make sense of what was happening with DACA, since "I have a very unemotional mind." He explained, "I like to think of things very logically. I try to logically reason myself out of the situation basically. I just cut it off. So I was basically telling my sister, 'If you look at the numbers and everything, it's just very improbable that we will be physically kicked out. They don't have the money to come to every one of our houses, drag us out, and send us on planes.'" Antônia, who came from Brazil when she was eight, described going inward by relying on her faith, which she had also emphasized in

2016. In February 2018, she showed off a new tattoo, meant to encapsulate the power of her faith, saying, "My faith is what really helps me cope with everything. Sometimes I'm talking to my friends about my frustrations, but they can only understand so much, or give me so much support. So I have my own time in my room, and lock myself in there and pray and open the Bible. That restores everything. I got a tattoo last year to represent and help me remember how tremendous it was that God took care of me in every single way in 2017."

While Emine and Antônia described their social supports as being limited in mitigating DACA distress, numerous others leaned on their religious leaders and congregations during this uncertain time; as Madeline noted, "I've been talking to the imam and he has been very helpful in just helping me tap into coping methods and also just to be more positive." Others reported getting support from significant others and trusted friends. On the day of the rescission announcement, I was texting with Pau and we ended up getting together. She told me that although she was feeling quite emotional, she also felt reassured by the messages of support she received from her cohort of fellow scholarship recipients and showed me their GroupMe thread (which was full of compassion and humor). John's younger sister Mae (who came from South Korea at age six) reported in February 2018 that she was "definitely more anxious and stressed. I'm not exactly where I want to be mentally. DACA is definitely lying there in the back of my mind." She had just made an appointment at the student counseling center, the first time she had sought such care. But in the meantime, she also shared that she had been keeping busy by training a service dog for the blind and visually impaired. She found that the dog was also lending her support in the process: "We all love my guide dog in training. It's been helping a lot with life in general. He's almost turned into my emotional support dog."

The DACA rescission unquestionably intensified DACA recipients' temporal uncertainty, ushering in compounded mental distress for some and resulting in new forms of embodied distress for others.[71] Juan evocatively described how DACA recipients were compelled to live life in eighteen-month cycles, with anxiety at its pinnacle during renewal, resulting in a cumulative existential exhaustion fairly unique to DACA recipients. Because of concerns about the instability and unpredictability of DACA, participants like Pau talked about taking advantage of the limited time before her expiration date and Elena and Santiago "lost time" by completing their applications earlier than typical, shortening the window during which they had relative peace of mind even more. Yet despite these wrenching experiences of temporal dispossession, DACA recipients also consciously decided to "keep moving" (as Santiago phrased it) and sought to wrest control over the uncertainty through deliberate strategies meant to ground them in the present and promote their well-being.

"I Can't Let DACA Control Me . . . I Have to Continue with My Life": Finding Normalcy Even amid DACA Limbo and Pandemic Pressures

As the ongoing lack of certainty about DACA's future continued with each new court case, participants also contended with additional stressors related to the emerging COVID-19 pandemic. While the pandemic introduced a proliferation of new stressors for everyone, there were unique aspects of these stressors for immigrants with legal vulnerabilities,[72] including that they and their families were disproportionately impacted by systemic factors including employment in high-risk-exposure environments, financial strain and unemployment, exclusion from pandemic economic relief, substandard housing conditions and housing instability, and food insecurity.[73]

The pandemic presented clear new challenges for participants. Annisa, Emine, and Camila all contracted COVID early on, very likely at work. Annisa had just started a new job as a hospital-based mental health technician early in 2020 and was initially concerned that she would not yet have enough paid time off; thankfully, her new coworkers shared their paid time off with her and her health care coverage included a behavioral therapist to help manage what turned out to be long COVID. Even as she felt grateful for her situation, though, she also worried tremendously about her parents and two younger siblings since she could not see them and none of them had insurance. Emine got COVID almost immediately at the coffee shop where she worked and was fairly quickly furloughed as the pandemic set in. Shortly thereafter, her roommate, who was still a student, vacated their apartment when the university went online and she moved back home. As she struggled financially and emotionally, Emine begrudgingly had to move back home with her parents out of state in May 2020, feeling that she had no other option.

Given that she had just purchased a home for her family and was able to successfully isolate (see chapter 5), Camila was able to manage COVID without transmitting it to her family members.[74] Yet even after she recovered, she worried about her parents' ongoing exposure working in landscaping and the restaurant industry since they did not have access to health care as she did. Many participants were also quite impacted by their family members' vulnerabilities. Juan was incredibly worried about his parents; his father was working in person at several restaurants, while his mother had unchecked pandemic-related anxiety, to the point where she was bleaching produce, which he found quite a challenge to manage. Meanwhile Nancy's boyfriend and parents had to move in with her when they lost their jobs in catering and tourism.[75]

Consequently, Camila described her mental health in this period as "all over the place. It was just an emotional roller coaster for me with DACA, the pandemic, and work, and trying to keep myself and my family safe." Madeline described how her pandemic-era distress was also compounded by "my different identities always being under attack. I wake up, and see police brutality and Islamophobia on the news, but then am still undocumented with the election coming up and the inability to vote. And as a woman, you don't ever get a break. I don't ever get to wake up and not be one of those things. It's always something." Emine also talked about how the George Floyd murder in May 2020 and protests for racial justice that followed throughout the summer impacted her as a Black immigrant: "I felt like I went even more inward. That was just really tough. There's so much collective pain and suffering. Half of me is like, 'Live your best life, do everything to the fullest.' But the other half of me is like, 'There are constant reminders that you can't live your best life.' It definitely plays into me even wanting to become a citizen here."

The pandemic also exacerbated and introduced new bureaucratic stressors for participants as they processed yet another round of renewals. Madeline had reported fairly smooth renewal processes previously, she though found it more stressful this time around:

> Every time that it's time to renew again, they've added new things . . . like
> the section asking how you got here and asking for a copy of the passport

that you used to travel. That never used to be in there, which made me wonder what the ulterior motive was. I don't have my passport, so I had to provide alternate documentation and get it notarized. They don't realize that if my documents are in French, it's difficult to do. It's not even so much the cost, but the mental energy it takes to put everything together. And this was a renewal application, not even an initial application! That really got under my skin.

In addition to the existential angst of submitting her renewal application in twenty-month cycles (which, similar to Juan, is how she described it), Madeline also noted the extra "emotional labor."

Participants also worried immensely about the impact of pandemic-related USCIS delays and office closures.[76] Nayeli concurred that her most recent renewal was her most stressful one: "My renewal was coming up in August [2020], but everything was so delayed. I was freaking out, especially since there was a pandemic going on. I sent it in like the second week of April. I had a friend who has literally the same expiration day, and he sent it back in March." Already feeling like she was behind, Nayeli found assembling the application to be stressful: "I went to take the pictures, but they weren't taking pictures because of COVID. I had to call three different pharmacies to figure that out. One I called said 'Yes, we're doing them,' but then I get there and they're like, 'No, we're not doing them.'" From there, she had trouble securing the money order: "Then I went to the bank to get the money order, and they're like, 'No, we're not doing them right now.' So I went to the post office and spent thirty to forty minutes waiting in line before I realized that I needed to go home to get my documents to make a copy. It was ridiculous, and I spent my entire day sweating and freaking out from the stress." Lucas also noted how social media served only to fuel this renewal-related anxiety: "Unfortunately, there were a lot of horror stories on Twitter of people waiting and waiting for a long time or losing their work permit or not being able to work because their permits got lost."

Because of ongoing uncertainty about DACA and pandemic processing fears, participants started "losing" even more time. Sara, for instance, lost six months because she had to strategize her renewal in relation to her upcoming move to California to start graduate school. Her expiration date (and her driver's license expiration date synched to correspond to the work authorization card) was in October 2021, but she had to submit her renewal in May to "take off the pressure" and ensure that everything was in place for her cross-country move later that summer. Nayeli's sister, Angélica, experienced COVID-related delays that prevented her from renewing her driver's license. As she shared in August 2020, "My license is actually expired right now. I couldn't get an appointment until [later in the month] because of COVID so I'm just hoping something doesn't happen. I'm thankful I still have my job. But that expiring is obviously a big challenge for me." Her younger brother Juan recalled the stress this delay caused his sister: "I still remember the morning she realized the trouble she was in. I remember hearing her going through her papers in a panic. [Nayeli] just stayed with her for like an hour, and they were going back and forth online until they found information. And then there was the sudden realization of 'I should not be driving but I need to for work.'" These renewal challenges definitely magnified participants' already-heightened anxiety.

Nayeli's anxiety became much more pronounced, and not just because of renewal stress. Nayeli is one of the participants whom I know the best, as a member of the CAB whom I see and am in touch with fairly regularly. When I first met her as a twenty-one-year-old in 2016, she was energetic and confident and had a clear plan for her future. She had gotten DACA before graduating high school and therefore could work legally from an early age while attending community college, unlike Angélica. By February 2018, she was still thriving despite the DACA rescission and uncertainty; she had continued on to a university and was about to graduate with a bachelor's degree in business and had lined up a job as an executive team manager at a major corporate store. Though she definitely felt the impact of the DACA uncertainty, she noted at the time, "You know my personality—I don't like anything getting to me."

Yet when I saw her in January 2020 at our CAB meeting, Nayeli's affect was very different—she was visibly anxious and said so to the group as we did our usual initial check-ins. When I interviewed her a few months later in August, I shared my observation with her. She agreed, and said, "It's just getting so tiring, like how many more times will I have to renew? When is that ever going to change? I have so much anxiety from just . . . life." She shared how stressful the early summer had been as she awaited the decision about DACA: "I was an anxiety ball the whole month of

June. The decisions were coming from the Supreme Court, and I was on my phone at like 7:00 a.m. every day just refreshing and refreshing." Nayeli's anxiety was also fueled by the realization that as an adult, she now knew more about what she stood to lose. As she reflected, "Since I was seventeen when DACA came out, I was perfectly ready to enter work and be an adult. But now I'm a fully functioning adult and I have all of these responsibilities. If DACA's taken away, I don't know how to be."

As I began phase III in 2020, I anticipated that I would be continuing to hear about profound suffering and vulnerability as participants described their everyday lives during the pandemic, tempered only slightly by the affirmative Supreme Court decision leaving DACA fragilely and temporarily in place. Indeed, participants were contending with a range of new stressors, particularly their renewal processes, which produced new forms of temporal disorientation. These stressors compounded the mental distress some participants like Madeline and Emine were simultaneously experiencing related to new incidents of racial injustice and intensified it for participants like Nayeli who had previously been less affected but increasingly felt the weight of insecurity.

However, as I talked with participants about their lives since I had last been in touch with them, they more commonly foregrounded affirmative developments rooted in the present, in the more mundane and ordinary aspects of their everyday lives. As Camila noted, "I do my best to have as normal a life as I can." Given that participants ranged in age between twenty-two and thirty-two at this point, these developments were oriented toward their careers, romantic relationships and growing families, moves and home purchases, and travel (for both work and leisure). Many, including Camila, had switched jobs, gotten promotions, and found satisfying careers that also offered them economic stability; three had continued on to graduate school (in accounting, information sciences, and social work) to further their careers. Of the twenty-four participants from this phase, seven (29 percent) had gotten married and several more were engaged or in long-term relationships—albeit others had also been through major breakups. Three participants had children, and numerous others talked of their desire to start families in the near future. One of the more surprising developments that came up repeatedly was buying a home; nine participants (38 percent) had become homeowners, with a few more thinking seriously about doing so. They were also on the move locally, with nine (38 percent) moving to new neighborhoods, cities, counties, and states in the D.C. Metro region and others moving out of the region to California, Massachusetts, Michigan, and Texas. Participants described the "bucket-list" trips they had taken as they explored new places like California, Hawaii, Montana, and Puerto Rico.

The way in which participants actively pursued "normal" lives stood in distinct contrast to the anything-but-normal state of ontological insecurity that was previously so pronounced. As Santiago asserted, "I have to continue with my normal life . . . I can't let [DACA] control me," underscoring that the activities of normal, everyday life were precisely what allowed him to bring a sense of temporal order to his life. Scholars have chronicled how people contending with chronic illness and debilitating health conditions "get on with life" as a way of finding meaning and regaining a sense of control over their lives.[77] DACA recipients likewise are finding meaning and control in their everyday lives even amid chronic temporal uncertainty. Price and Rojas similarly have found that ordinariness—and specifically engaging in everyday practices located in local communities—is a deliberate response DACA recipients have deployed as a means of negotiating precarity.[78] I have found that channeling their energies into the everyday is precisely what is enabling DACA recipients to flourish, which anthropologist Sarah S. Willen and her colleagues recognize not merely as a state or condition but as a dynamic, ongoing pursuit.[79]

In this phase, participants most strongly emphasized their pursuit of normalcy and the resilience they had cultivated to navigate the challenges inherent in their situation. In this vein, in August 2020 Juan reflected,

> Certain life challenges are constantly present . . . they're still there. And there's been so much up and down of DACA—whether it's going to go, or whether it's going stay. You just kind of learn to take the news, process it, and then go about your day anyway. That's the resilience that you have to develop to survive, but also to thrive. And I don't know a single person that has DACA that isn't extra resilient, extra resourceful. I've learned to appreciate the resilience and the motivation that I've developed. It makes me more confident to tackle bigger challenges than I thought that I could.

After all of our discussion about his documents and mental health woes over the years, I was heartened to hear about how Juan described his pursuit of flourishing, even against the backdrop of great uncertainty. During an interview in 2021, Nancy described a similar shift: "I'm in a much better place, and feel like I have better control of my life. Before, I used to exist in the *being* part of well-being, but now I'm closer to the *well* side."

Conclusion

It is, perhaps, easy to surmise that DACA recipients' emotional well-being was majorly compromised by the DACA rescission attempt in 2017 and subsequent years of uncertainty they endured as DACA wound its way through the judicial system. As the program became and remained endangered, DACA recipients unquestionably experienced chronic and new stressors that profoundly impacted how they functioned in their everyday lives. What is more surprising, though, is how DACA recipients responded to these destabilizing developments over time—by cultivating resilience strategies that allowed them to achieve greater control in the present and even flourish amid great uncertainty and deep insecurity. DACA recipients are deliberately pursuing and managing to attain surprisingly normal adult lives and find order and meaning in the everyday—even during the most intense period of the pandemic, when everyday life was anything but normal. The chapters to come highlight different aspects of DACA recipients' pursuit of normalcy by examining their everyday lives as the site where they pursue well-being and justice. The next chapter continues to explore how DACA recipients contend with policy exclusions by describing how they negotiate differently configured state and local immigration-focused policies in the D.C. Metro region.

3

"D.C. Has More Benefits for Immigrants Than Maryland"

Maneuvering within the Policy Patchwork

Lucas migrated from Mexico to Washington, D.C., when he was ten years old to join relatives and friends in the area; he explained, "My father's brother lived in Maryland, and a really good friend who's almost like a brother lived in D.C. We lived in D.C. when we first arrived and stayed there for some time. We had people we could rely on." Lucas recalled it being a fairly easy transition initially: "There's a lot of Latino kids in D.C., and my principal and lots of teachers also spoke Spanish." Lucas also noted that his family had good access to health care: "We decided to get health insurance within the first year that we were here. We were advised by the friends we were staying with to do . . . to have it for the records—something to show that we lived here." Enrolling in insurance was not merely to document their physical presence, though—Lucas remembered that he and his mother went to the doctor regularly during those years.

After they had lived in D.C. for about six years, though, Lucas's family moved "just two blocks away from D.C." over the line into Prince George's County in Maryland. Despite living essentially in the same neighborhood, his family discovered that resources for undocumented immigrants were quite different there. "D.C. has more benefits for immigrants than Maryland," Lucas explained. "We had insurance from D.C. Alliance for years, but lost it after we moved to Maryland when I was seventeen. Maryland doesn't provide insurance to those who are undocumented. If you're living in Maryland, you're out of luck." Indeed, Lucas had been "out of luck" since moving to Maryland, lacking access to health care as he worked and attended school, both on a part-time basis. "I just try not to get sick now," Lucas remarked. "I take over-the-counter stuff. I try to eat healthy, drink plenty of water, and exercise."

While these strategies "mostly worked out okay," Lucas needed emergency care when he got jumped at a Maryland shopping mall when he was twenty-two:

> I was walking outside the mall during the day, at like 5:00 p.m. A group of aggressors came and started to punch me in the face and hit me in the head. I was all bloody . . . but one of the things I knew was that I didn't want to go to the hospital. An ambulance came and cleaned me up. They said, "We'll have to take you to emergency room because you have head trauma." I'm like, "No, I'll go myself" because I know if the ambulance takes you, it's going to be an extra bill that you have to pay. I didn't want to go at all, to be honest . . . because I knew it was going to be a lot of money.

Instead, Lucas got his mother to drive him to the hospital, where staff ran a number of tests. If Lucas had still been a D.C. resident, he would have had very different access to care and perhaps been able to make decisions that were more responsive to his medical needs than the cost of care. He would likely have incurred substantially less medical debt, too, since he ended up with sizeable bills (in the thousands of dollars) that he steadily paid off over the next few years through a monthly payment plan. His lack of access to care was particularly notable given that Lucas had worked in health care settings since he was a teenager when he started volunteering in a hospital as a health advocate even when he was unable to work legally and was passionate about increasing immigrants' access to care.

As he settled into his public health career, Lucas pursued employment opportunities in both Maryland and D.C. When I met him in 2016, he was working for a community health clinic (CHC) with sites in D.C. and Maryland. From there, he worked for a faith-based nonprofit organization in D.C., the D.C. Department of Health, and another CHC with sites in D.C. and Maryland. These clinics served clients from throughout the region, meaning that Lucas regularly had to discern and tailor services depending on where people lived. Over time, Lucas preferred working in D.C.: "D.C. has more money when it comes to HIV prevention. Maryland's much bigger and blue but it really doesn't. That's why there aren't as many community-based organizations in Maryland as in D.C. Many organizations in D.C. offer free HIV testing for STIs and

STDs regardless of status. They have so much more information and access to services for sexual health. And that's what we tell people—that they shouldn't miss out." Yet despite his preference for working in D.C., as we saw earlier, Lucas still considered himself a "proud Marylander" and continues to live there, underscoring his nuanced connections to both places.

By 2018, Lucas had started attending national trainings and conferences in other cities, including Los Angeles, which, he noted, "was amazing and a great networking opportunity." During the conference, Lucas learned about HIV/AIDS prevention work in San Francisco, noting, "Since 2012 when it was approved, San Francisco was one of the very first ones to jump into PrEP [preexposure prophylaxis] as a method of prevention. San Francisco is way more open and progressive when it comes to that." Beyond learning more about local initiatives in a city even more progressive than D.C., Lucas reflected, "I was not prepared for meeting such a large Mexican community there! There were taco trucks on every street and the food was *real* Mexican food." Around this same time, Lucas also took his first out-of-town vacation to celebrate Atlanta Pride, recalling, "My trip was amazing! There were lots of firsts. It was exciting being by myself as a complete stranger in an entirely new different city and not really knowing anyone." Lucas's travels—which he can undertake since he has an unmarked driver's license issued by the state of Maryland that enables him to travel freely—have allowed him to venture to new places and learn more about how they compare to the D.C. region and have also been identity-affirming.

The scholarship on undocumented immigrant young adults has evocatively captured how they come to learn about their marginalized status and the immigration policies that structure their lives. Leisy Abrego has described how undocumented immigrants—and young adults in particular—articulate legal consciousness, or commonsense understandings and interpretations of the law used in everyday life.[1] Earlier we saw how DACA recipients' legal consciousness has been shaped by policy instability and prolonged uncertainty. Yet as Andrea Flores, American studies scholar Kevin Escudero, and sociologist Edelina Burciaga point out, immigrants also develop awareness of how law and space are mutually formed and influence their lives as they cultivate legal-spatial consciousness in different communities throughout the United States.[2] Indeed, precarious legal status is experienced quite differently depending on where one lives within the policy patchwork and whether that jurisdiction is more integrative like D.C. or less so, as with some D.C. Metro region jurisdictions described earlier. Lucas's experiences underscore that socio-legal contexts with important policy differences sometimes coexist in close geographic proximity and exist in relation to each other.

Despite increased attention to the nuances of everyday life in distinct socio-legal contexts, there has been less attention to immigrants' lives situated within large, multijurisdictional metropolitan regions like the D.C. Metro region and their regular movement between jurisdictions. The immigration literature elaborates the phenomenon of secondary migration—when migrants elect to move to new geographic locations, often motivated by social networks, the presence of ethnic communities, and/or greater potential compatibility with the local climate and culture.[3] Secondary migration underscores that settlement is not a permanent or static process and that migrants make active decisions about their quality of life in different locales. Once they move, though, immigrants must rapidly adjust to the new jurisdiction's receptivity to immigrants and accompanying local policies. After moving, Lucas's family experienced firsthand how different the allocation of social resources was in Maryland with clear implications for his family's well-being.

Yet the immigration literature does not capture how immigrants negotiate multiple jurisdictions simultaneously. As an adult, Lucas lives and works in one place and lives in another, moving between them on a daily basis. His work as a public health advocate also involves understanding the nuances of additional socio-legal contexts—Virginia—to be able to best advise his clients about accessing services, which he does by building on his own experiences and knowledge. Such frequent movement and local variability is not unusual in large metropolitan regions like the D.C. Metro region. In these large, multijurisdictional metropolitan regions that are often home to a large share of immigrant residents, immigrants confront differently configured socio-legal contexts as they go to school and work, interface with social institutions like health clinics and schools, and visit family and friends, in the process discerning consequential differences between them.

This chapter demonstrates how DACA recipients in the D.C. Metro region have forged a nuanced legal-spatial consciousness as they have mapped out and made sense of immigrants' access to resources in differently configured local socio-legal contexts.[4] It argues that as DACA recipients refine their legal-spatial consciousness, they simultaneously forge and assert place-based navigational capital[5] that enables them to adeptly maneuver between contexts and strategically develop "work-arounds" to access distinct yet interconnected educational, occupational, and housing sectors. With DACA status and its accompanying bureaucratic documents (e.g., work permits, driver's licenses), participants have also become emboldened to move more freely within the region and expand their spatial mobility to new places beyond the D.C. Metro region. Instead of viewing immigrant young adults as immobilized and passively subject to the policy contexts in which they live, I demonstrate the agency they assert in navigating them and cultivating practices for thriving within and across them despite their precarious legal status.

Building Socio-legal Consciousness and Asserting Navigational Capital in Differently Configured Social-Legal Contexts

Scholars have compellingly demonstrated that precarious legal status is experienced differently depending on the local context of reception and accompanying policies shaping everyday life there.[6] As immigration policymaking has stalled at the federal level and devolved to states and localities over the past three decades, immigrants encounter radically different local policy contexts in distinct states, counties, and cities, making them important sites for understanding more localized incorporation experiences.[7] Socio-legal contexts have been characterized along a continuum, ranging from integrative/hospitable/accommodating to more exclusionary/restrictive/hostile.[8]

California is portrayed as an exemplary integrative context, given its large overall share of the immigrant population and its reputation for having the most pro-immigrant state policies nationwide, particularly for immigrant young adults, resulting from two decades of activism.[9] Passed in the early 2000s, Assembly Bills 540, 130, and 131 granted undocumented young adults in-state tuition, opened up private scholarships to them, and allowed them to apply for state financial aid, respectively.[10] Immigrant students have benefitted from a university system characterized by targeted policies, university resources, and supportive institutional agents.[11] Yet sociologist Angela S. García emphasizes that anti-immigrant sentiment was quite pervasive in California in the 1990s, culminating in the passage of Propositions 187, 209, and 227, targeting immigrants' access to publicly funded services, affirmative action, and bilingual education, respectively.[12] Shifts like these make it clear that socio-legal contexts are not static but rather can change over time and indeed may even be unstable.[13] Such rapid shifts and instability are more common in new immigrant destinations like North Carolina, South Carolina, Iowa, Indiana, and Colorado that are more exclusionary contexts overall.[14]

A growing body of scholarship compares immigrants' experiences across contexts—typically by directly contrasting more integrative and exclusionary jurisdictions. Sociologists Kara Cebulko and Alexis Silver, for instance, compared DACA recipients' experiences in Massachusetts and North Carolina, finding that the more inclusive policies in the former state led to DACA recipients' enhanced feelings of legitimacy.[15] García adopted a matched-pair comparison approach to tease apart strikingly divergent socio-legal contexts found in Southern California in Santa Ana (Orange County) and Escondido (San Diego County). She found that the threat of deportation was amplified in more restrictive Escondido, influencing how immigrants conceptualized physical space and their relation to law enforcement.[16] Yet she also noted that more accommodating contexts like Santa Ana could not ultimately insulate immigrants from the threat of deportation emanating from federal immigration enforcement.[17] Flores, Escudero, and Burciaga compared young adults' experiences in Los Angeles and Atlanta and discovered that they diverged in predictable areas like access to higher education, which was more restricted in Atlanta than in more integrative Los Angeles. However, they found that young adults in both states shared a sense of "stuckness" due to the temporariness of DACA at the federal level.[18] Scholars have only begun to consider how integrative and exclusionary contexts exist side by side and in relation to each other in large metropolitan regions. For instance, political scientist Els de Graauw and sociologist Shannon Gleeson discovered that while the urban core of metropolitan Houston was more welcoming to DACA recipients and featured supportive local actors and institutions, those who lived in the less diverse and more heavily policed suburbs and rural areas surrounding the city felt more insecure and limited in their educational pathways and professional aspirations.[19]

These studies make it clear that even immigrants who live in more integrative local contexts are still constrained by the intensity of federal immigration enforcement and the lack of federal reform, underscoring that their lives are situated in nested contexts of reception.[20] Given their ongoing legal vulnerability, scholars have sought to make sense of how undocumented young adults carve out and occupy local geographies of belonging, including at even more micro community and family levels.[21] Highlighting the experiences of undocumented young adults living in California, Laura E. Enriquez and Daniel Millán posit that deportability is not always an ever-present fear but rather can be situationally triggered or reduced when individuals occupy protective spatial and social locations that limit exposure to enforcement.[22] Looking across both more integrative (California, Illinois, and New York) and more exclusionary (Arizona, Georgia, and South Carolina) socio-legal contexts, Roberto G. Gonzales, sociologist Kristina Brant, and Benjamin Roth likewise contend that DACA beneficiaries cultivate protective personal and social spheres in their everyday lives that allow them to assert belonging.[23] They note, however, that cultivating these spheres is much more challenging in exclusionary contexts that function as spaces of vulnerability. As immigrants with precarious legal statuses venture beyond these protective locations or spheres, though, their concerns about enforcement intensify and impact their spatial mobility.[24] They— and even their citizen children—may limit time spent outside the home, shop only at night, and/or withdraw from community events as strategies to minimize risk. They may also avoid highways and routes that they perceive to be dangerous or even driving altogether.[25] These "embodied alterations," as García refers to them, are made to accomplish the necessary routines of everyday life.[26]

Immigrants' experiences within local socio-legal contexts are also shaped by social locations like race, ethnicity, class, gender, and sexuality, leading scholars to call for a more nuanced and intersectional approach.[27] Recent scholars use have racialized illegality as a frame to foreground how immigrants experience their precarious status differently depending on how they are racialized.[28] For instance, Cebulko demonstrates how white-passing Brazilians in Massachusetts experienced racial and class-based privilege, enabling them to navigate public space without being stopped, questioned, detained, and/or deported.[29] By contrast, geographer Juan Herrera illuminates particular forms of discrimination experienced by Mayan Guatemalan migrants in California based on indigeneity, language use, and skin color.[30] Enriquez and sociologist Caitlin Patler examine racialization relationally, demonstrating how Latina/os in California were more likely to be stereotyped as undocumented than Asian Pacific Islander and Black undocumented youth.[31] These studies collectively demonstrate how the state produces illegality but how it is also shaped by racialization processes within more local institutional sites like workplaces and educational institutions and through quotidian interactions with a range of actors.[32]

Immigrants also build keen awareness of different socio-legal contexts as they maneuver between them. Legal consciousness captures people's commonsense understandings and interpretations of the law used in everyday life.[33] Applying sociologists Patricia Ewick and Susan S. Silbey's foundational concept to immigrants, Abrego elaborates how immigrants in Los Angeles made sense of their legal situation, finding that while fear predominated the legal consciousness of older first-generation immigrants, immigrant young adults' was more heavily infused by stigma.[34] Several years later after the DACA program was created, Abrego chronicled changes to the legal consciousness of DACA recipients living in greater Los Angeles. She discovered that DACA enabled them to achieve a stronger sense of pride and belonging in the United States but that their legal consciousness was also relational, rooted in how members of their social networks experienced legal vulnerability. Therefore, she found that their shifting legal consciousness was also rooted in insecurity due to growing awareness of the expanding system of immigrant detention and deportation.[35] Scholars have also noted how legal consciousness shifts through interactions with legal services and the immigration bureaucracy. Chicano/a/x studies scholar Lucía León, for instance, examines how Los Angeles–based Latinx young adults' legal consciousness intersects with social and cultural norms about marriage to inform their decisions about legalization. She demonstrates that undocumented young adults find themselves in a catch-22 situation: they risk accusations of marriage fraud and must prove that their marriages are "for love" and not just "for papers," while the bureaucratic and invasive legalization process simultaneously pushes their relationships in directions that feel inauthentic.[36]

Flores, Escudero, and Burciaga expand legal consciousness to include a spatial dimension, arguing that immigrants also develop awareness of how law and space are mutually formed and influence their lives.[37] Their concept of legal-spatial consciousness captures not only how undocumented youth understand and experience their status but also how it is continually reproduced as they move through differently configured legal spaces in their everyday lives. Specifically, they highlight how undocumented youth are made more "illegal" through harsh educational limits in Atlanta and through 287(g) agreements (through which state and local law enforcement collaborate with the federal government to enforce immigration laws) and the inability to obtain driver's licenses in Nashville, while their counterparts' negotiations of their precarious legal status in Los Angeles and Chicago (both sanctuary cities in sanctuary counties) are vastly different. Yet they find that the legal-spatial consciousness of even those who live within those more integrative jurisdictions is shaped by experiences with or knowledge of more hostile contexts.[38] Cebulko and Silver similarly demonstrate that even immigrants living in integrative contexts like Massachusetts hold a keen awareness of other states' more exclusionary policies.[39] This more expansive legal-spatial consciousness is facilitated by the increased spatial mobility that bureaucratic documents enable for immigrants, allowing some undocumented and DACAmented young adults to travel into different jurisdictions without the fear of being stopped and deported.[40] As Escudero notes, this burgeoning cross-jurisdictional awareness can "create unexpected openings for solidarity and activism."[41] While he refers to activism as more conventional forms of political mobilization, I posit that DACA recipients' everyday activism is also enhanced by this cross-jurisdictional awareness within multijurisdictional metropolitan regions.

Immigrant young adults also apply their legal-spatial consciousness as they cultivate and deploy place-based navigational capital and interface with local social institutions.[42] While navigational capital has most commonly been applied in educational settings, it also extends to other sectors like the health care system, labor market, judicial system, and health care system.[43] As DACA recipients have transitioned deeper into adulthood, these other sectors are increasingly the places where they exert their navigational capital, including for the benefit of others. Navigational capital is a particularly apt concept for understanding how immigrants navigate differential access to social resources within the "multilayered jurisdictional patchwork"[44] and devise workarounds rooted in their experiential and collective knowledge of local socio-legal contexts.

Maneuvering through the Multilayered Jurisdictional Policy Patchwork

As DACA recipients maneuvered throughout the D.C. Metro region's different socio-legal contexts during their childhood and early adulthoods, they refined their legal-spatial consciousness as they mapped out different jurisdictions' receptivity toward immigrants. As they got older, they forged navigational capital that they have leveraged to effectively negotiate distinct yet interconnected educational, employment, and housing sectors within the local policy landscape. Though many had already moved with their families beyond their initial settlement location into their twenties, many expanded their spatial mobility even further by moving to and visiting new jurisdictions within and outside of the D.C. Metro region, continuing to refine their proficiencies for safely maneuvering through different places.

"I Lost My Insurance When We Moved": Mapping Socio-legal Contexts and Cultivating Legal-Spatial Consciousness

As I first got to know them in 2016, participants were refining their legal-spatial consciousness as they experienced and observed variability in different jurisdictions' treatment of immigrants. Oftentimes, this awareness began emerging during childhood when their families moved to new places. For instance, Juan's family had moved to three different states since they first migrated to the United States. Their first move was to Arizona, relatively close to the border town where they were originally from in Mexico. Next, the family moved to Florida when Juan was four years old "because we had family members who lived there and my parents just didn't want to be in Arizona any more. My earliest memories are of Florida. I don't really remember Mexico or Arizona." Juan recalled that life in Florida was good initially: "My dad got a very well-paying job there, and my mom established her own home business." But then the economy declined in 2008, hitting Florida particularly hard, and his father lost his job in construction, which Juan noted "was the one of the first industries to go." The family continued to struggle economically, Juan shared, but "made it through by moving to Maryland." Beyond economic opportunity and social network connections—well-documented influences on migrant settlement decision-making[45]—Juan identified an additional factor shaping their move: "Part of the reason we moved to Maryland is because Florida stopped giving out driver's licenses. My dad's friend that was like, 'They're still giving them out here,' so we moved here. We had enough savings to make it here and get established." Juan's family, then, decided to move to Maryland in part due to the state's more integrative local policies.

Juan's family transitioned well to life in Maryland. His dad found a few different construction jobs, though eventually took a position washing dishes at a successful local restaurant chain. As Juan shared, "He started fixing stuff at the restaurant. The ceiling was falling apart and he was like, 'Oh, I can do that.' And they kind of realized they had a resource in him and hired him for maintenance management for all of their restaurants." Juan started working alongside his father for the restaurant when he was a junior in high school and created a system to track employees' hours, paychecks, and so on. "Eventually," he indicated, "it became an actual job. The owner requested for me to join the administrative team of all the restaurants as an assets manager. I go around to the restaurants and look at all of the equipment and run analytics." Juan worked for the restaurant all the way through college, and he and his father eventually formed a limited liability company to contract with the restaurant. The move to Maryland ultimately proved to be a positive economic one for Juan's family, and the driver's licenses they were able to obtain formed a critical component of their everyday security.

Despite gaining access to driver's licenses, though, Juan noted that he lost his health insurance in the process of moving to a different state: "I had Medicaid for a while when I lived in Florida. I can remember going to the doctor very frequently for different reasons, like almost every month for something or another. But that stopped once I moved to Maryland. I had Medicaid at one point, and then I just didn't the next." Juan reported that his engagement with the health care system declined considerably after he moved and lost his insurance. His experiences underscore that even states like Maryland that are known for having more integrative local policies (e.g., driver's licenses) simultaneously have other policies that are more restrictive (e.g., health insurance), with uneven impact on different immigrants.

Within Maryland, participants also encountered county-level policy differences with important implications for them and their families. Since he immigrated from Bolivia when he was five, Beto had only ever lived in Montgomery County. As noted earlier, Montgomery County is a prosperous jurisdiction known for having the most integrative policies statewide on immigration-related issues including education (for both children and adults), health care, public safety, and immigrant policing. Beto was acutely aware that his family had benefitted from settling there: "Fortunately, we moved to a county that is accountable to people living there. Montgomery County is a really great place to live if you're an immigrant. They have services and don't discriminate if you are a U.S. citizen or not. They just want to help you, and give you the care that you need." As a child, Beto benefitted from the Care for Kids program, which provides health care services for uninsured minor children living in the county regardless of immigration status. Most (but not all) of the fifteen participants who lived in Montgomery County at some point in their childhood had Care for Kids, having found out about the program through school or members of their social networks. For county residents who qualified, the program was invaluable in helping them meet their health needs—which they often came to realize with heightened clarity once they aged out of the program as adults. However, no such program was available to the other half of participants who lived outside of the county as children.

Several other participants also experienced changes to their coverage when they moved between Maryland counties. Denisse and her family had made a number of local moves since coming to Maryland from El Salvador when she was five years old: "When we lived in Montgomery County, there was a program that helped kids who were uninsured be able to go to the clinic. The program went with you anywhere you moved in the county—they'd help connect you to where you'd moved."

However, during her freshman year of high school, her family moved back to next-door Prince George's County, where they had lived initially when they arrived; as she recalled, "When we moved back to PG County at the beginning of high school, that's when we lost it. And that's how it's been for us since—we've been without health care." Denisse expressed great frustration about this situation: "Not [every county] has coverage, which sucks because some people need it, but just because of where they live, they're not able to get it." Though the distance her family moved was never very far, the change in their county of residence negatively impacted the children's access to care.

These accounts underscore that moving—between states, counties, and cities—is a common experience among DACA recipients and their families in the D.C. Metro region. However, participants' accounts also illuminate the complicated variegated policy landscape that immigrants encounter as they move between jurisdictions, even if the move happens to be a very local one, as with Lucas and Denisse. Because of this variation, DACA recipients like Lucas and Denisse and their family members of different statuses have gained and lost access to social resources like driver's licenses and health insurance. Their experiences navigating these socio-legal contexts also demonstrate that information about eligibility and access is transmitted via social networks, such as Lucas's and Juan's family friends as well as via professionals like Lucas in service settings.

As I got to know participants more, I observed that many had social networks, interests, and opportunities that led them regularly to different D.C. Metro region jurisdictions—which is common among others in the region, myself included. Participants regularly spoke about visiting family and friends and pursuing school and work opportunities in different places. As they did so, they also discerned important differences in local policing, largely drawing a contrast between Maryland and Virginia rooted in racism embedded in enforcement practices.[46] Their insights were based not only on their personal experiences but also on those in their social networks who had talked about their negative encounters, particularly in Virginia. Lucas was quite familiar with differences between D.C. and Maryland since his family had lived in both places. However, by working in clinics in different jurisdictions that served clients throughout the region, he started hearing more about others' experiences in those places, as well as in Virginia. As he noted,

"At work, we hear a lot of sketchy things from Virginia, from racist policemen to Latinos being stopped by the police for no reason. I feel like it's a different area, a different culture there. Though northern Virginia is getting better." Though he has never lived in Virginia, and personally has not spent a lot of time there, Lucas clearly identified important considerations to share in directing patients to services. His comments also underscore that even more localized contexts (like cities and towns) vary considerably and are not static in their receptivity to immigrants.

Luis echoed Lucas's perceptions of placed-based differences in policing practices in Virginia, though stemming more directly from his family's experiences. When he migrated from El Salvador with his mother and two older sisters to join his father when he was four, Luis's family settled in Virginia, where they had extended family. After his parents' divorce a few years later, Luis and his two older sisters (Angélica and Nayeli) moved to Maryland with their father, while their mother remained in Virginia. Luis generally went to see her every other weekend or so, typically taking the Metro subway to do so. In comparing life in Maryland versus Virginia, Luis noted, "There are a lot of ICE officials in the Woodbridge area where she lives. It's my impression that they're tighter in Virginia than they are here [in Maryland]. I've only every heard about two occurrences here in Maryland." Luis reported that the increased ICE presence made him anxious when he visited, but he worried even more about his mother, who did not have papers: "There were lots of ICE officials around the Woodbridge area when my mother lived there, so we were a little bit paranoid about her going out." He and his sisters were relieved when she moved: "Now she's in the Manassas area, which is really diverse so I don't think that's really going to be as much of an issue. It's good for her to be able to do a lot more of the things she likes." As Luis noted, his family is relieved that his mother is now living in a more protective location associated with decreased deportability fear.[47]

Participants also talked about how these anxieties became embodied when they were in less protective locations in Virginia. Camila had quite a bit of extended family living in the area, with her dad's side of the family concentrated in Maryland and her mom's side in Virginia. Despite being much more familiar with Maryland, she visits her Virginia-based family regularly: "Virginia is much less immigrant friendly. For my family in Virginia, everything revolves around their immigration status. My cousin didn't have any immigration status and lived in fear that she'd be pulled over by police. Those programs in different counties . . . the police could easily pull you over and ask for your immigration status. That's always in the back of my head when we go." In her comment, Camila is referencing the 287(g) program through which state and local law enforcement collaborate with the federal government to enforce immigration laws and which operates at both the county and city levels in Virginia.

As previously mentioned, Juan had lived in Arizona, Florida, and Maryland. He asserted that he felt "very much at home and protected in Maryland" but contrasted those feelings with an experience he had in Virginia in late 2017: "I went to Virginia not too long ago. I was in Richmond, and I felt not very safe. I felt very looked at, like I didn't belong. Whereas here I walk around Langley Park [Maryland] and it's like, 'Oh, my people.'" While Richmond is technically beyond the D.C. Metro region, simply being in the state of Virginia heighted Juan's sense of insecurity. Juan noted that his documents helped mitigate this fear (see chapter 2): "I try not to put myself in situations that are risky, but when I do, there's always this weird sense. In Richmond, I remember thinking that I wished I had my documents with me." Luis, Camila, and Juan's comments underscore the place-based nature of embodied immigration-related vulnerabilities and highlight Virginia as a location in which they are amplified. However, Juan's commentary also reveals the forethought and embodied alterations that DACA recipients develop to minimize risk[48]—like bringing their documents as a form of security—as they venture into less familiar or comfortable socio-legal contexts.

"The Path Has Been More Paved for Me": Forging and Deploying Navigational Capital

As they refined their legal-spatial consciousness, DACA recipients were also simultaneously cultivating navigational capital that enabled them to put their local knowledge to practical use in accessing different sectors like education, employment, and housing. Some participants—foremost among them Juan—described the "workarounds" they started developing as teenagers to navigate around restrictions related to their status, as first described in the introduction. Juan's "workarounds" enabled him to get around the D.C. Metro region when he could not yet legally drive, though he also used the term in relation to accessing higher education and health care (given that he had to figure out how to access care when he lost his insurance when he moved to Maryland). Juan's use of the term "workaround" is closely aligned with the forging and deployment of navigational capital. While there is a vast interdisciplinary literature on the practical workarounds that employees deploy within public administration and organizational settings,[49] the phenomenon Juan describes is more akin to forging and deploying navigational capital on a micro-level scale in the context of everyday life.

During phase I when many participants were in their late teens and early twenties, it was clear that they had become particularly adept at finding workarounds to navigate higher education. In many cases, they built on the experiential knowledge of their social network members,[50] most prominently siblings. In 2012, Maryland passed a state DREAM Act, the first jurisdiction to do so in the D.C. Metro region, which benefitted many participants. Initially, the law had unique requirements (in comparison with other states' DREAM Acts) dictating that undocumented students had to first attend community college for a period of two years, after which they could transfer to a university paying in-state tuition. For many, however, the transition to a university was financially challenging given that they also could not apply for federal financial aid. In 2018, after many participants had already graduated or discontinued their schooling, Maryland started enabling undocumented students to access in-state financial aid under provision 15-106.8 of the Maryland Education Article.

Given the particulars of the Maryland DREAM Act, many participants began their higher education journeys at community colleges. Several learned about a scholarship program that bridged students between the main community colleges in two counties (Montgomery and Prince George's County) and one of the state's public universities. DACA recipients were explicitly eligible for the program, which paid a major share of tuition at each school. Luis's older sister Nayeli found out about it at just the right time when she started at one of the community colleges. As she told me, "A classmate told me about the program. I remember she was like, 'You should join, they pay up to 66 percent of your tuition.' But I was like, 'I'm not eligible for scholarships, you have to be a U.S. citizen.' Then I researched it and you actually don't. You just have to qualify for the DREAM Act, so then I was like, 'This is beyond words!'" Other participants, though, unfortunately found out about the program too far into their community college or university studies and were not able to apply with enough time to take advantage of it.

Another benefit of participating in the program was that it provided Nayeli with a built-in community of fellow scholarship recipients on campus, which was especially important to her as a commuter and transfer student. The scholarship program intentionally fostered connections among each cohort of students, having them take a core course together and participate in regular programming activities. This "support system," as Nayeli called it, proved to be critical for her in 2017; as she recalled, "When the September 5th thing happened, everyone from my cohort was like, 'Are you okay? It's going to be okay. You have us. It sucks that you are in this situation, but know you're not alone.' They were just very, very supportive. They're always checking up on me." Nayeli ultimately finished her bachelor's degree in business in five years—more quickly than many undocumented and DACAmented students—while also working multiple part-time jobs. During her last semester, she attended a career fair on campus and had already lined up a human relations position at a large national retail chain store before she graduated. She was acutely aware of what a difference the scholarship made in ensuring her timely degree completion, as her older sister Angélica started community college before the Maryland DREAM Act and ultimately took ten years to finish her bachelor's degree in psychology. Nayeli reflected, "I was very fortunate—very, very fortunate—because my sister is totally different than me. There was no DREAM Act, or anything, when she started. So a three-credit course was a thousand dollars. She had to go one course at a time."

When the time came, Angélica and Nayeli ensured that Luis, who is seven and three years younger than his sisters, respectively, also applied for and was accepted to the program. Indeed, theirs was not the only family in which younger siblings were able to benefit from knowledge about the scholarship program early enough that they could tailor their applications. Luis was accepted into the program, following Nayeli's path. He ended up majoring in psychology, like Angélica, and she advised him about classes, internship opportunities, and how to position himself well for working in their field, given her years of work experi-

ence within the local labor market. Ironically, Angélica and Luis graduated right around the same time despite their seven-year age difference.
Luis recognized that as a result of his sisters' navigational capital, "I
have had it a little easier. The path has been more paved for me because
of my sisters." Nayeli and Luis also understood quite clearly that this
scholarship opportunity may not have been available to them if they had
stayed with their mother in Virginia or even lived in another county in
Maryland. Yet the siblings were not able to help their youngest sister Susana access the scholarship program since she was not able to apply for
DACA due to the 2017 DACA rescission and subsequent court decisions
that determined that USCIS would no longer accept any new DACA
applications. Susana attended community college and transferred to the
same university as her siblings, but as an undocumented student she had
even fewer opportunities and resources.

I also found that older siblings cultivated and shared navigational
capital about occupational fields that were viable options for DACA recipients as they planned their careers. When she was in high school,
Marcela applied to "all of my dream schools and got accepted to all of
them," even though she knew it would be unlikely that she would be
able to afford any of them. Instead, she started at community college in
Prince George's County and "decided to do forensic science. I pictured
working as a forensic trace analyst in the lab," she recalled. But during
her second year of associate's degree studies, "everything changed when
I did research on it to see where I could work. It said, 'To work in the
police force, you have to be a citizen.' And I asked some professors and
they said I do have to be one. So now I finished my associate's degree in
forensic science, but I can't work in it." Quite frustrated, Marcela started
thinking about "doing dental hygiene, because I actually can work in
that field. You don't need to be a citizen for that."

When she transferred to a university after completing her associate's
degree, Marcela entered as a biology major, still not entirely sure about
her postgraduation options. She completed an internship (unrelated to
her major) with a large national food and beverage corporation, building on her six years of prior experience working at a local grocery chain.
Her final semester was spring 2020, when universities went remote due
to the COVID-19 pandemic, which limited her employment prospects
postgraduation. So she decided to continue on with the corporation,

doing a six-month training program to learn how to independently manage distribution routes. Her job was based in Virginia, meaning that Marcela had to learn the geography of an entirely new place and undertake a long daily commute from Prince George's County. She contemplated moving to Virginia to minimize her commute even though she did not really want to live there, given that her social network was all in Maryland. She liked the job alright, though a few months in she started wondering if "maybe this was not the correct choice for me. Maybe I should actually pursue what I studied."

Based on the barriers and frustrations Marcela experienced over many years, her younger sister Esme approached her schooling and career planning pragmatically. For one, in high school, she found out about a dual enrollment program that would allow her to gain college credit while in high school, cutting down on tuition costs. She remembered, "I found a paper with the information in my high school. But I was worried because I thought that being DACA wouldn't count. I asked the teacher, and he said, 'It doesn't matter. They won't ask you about your citizen status.' I started the summer after junior year." Esme noted that her sister's experiences shaped her participation: "My sister's always done better than me in school. I remember she applied for a bunch of scholarships, and didn't get any. That's why I was like, 'It's free college, so I should do it.'" Esme also started college quite aware that she would need to carefully select her major and future career to account for status-related restrictions.

As she started community college, Esme planned to complete an associate of applied science in radiography. She applied to and was accepted to a nuclear medicine program. Yet because of the DACA rescission, she worried that her work authorization would expire, complicating her ability to finish the program and future employment prospects. She also heard that she might not be able to take the boards and secure a state license in Maryland because of her status, which led her to make the difficult decision to leave the program. Indeed, DACA recipients face barriers in the licensure process in many fields in health care, dentistry, and law, given that eligibility is governed by states and only fifteen states (not including Maryland until 2023) have enacted legislation to provide or improve professional licenses for targeted immigrant populations.[51] As she noted, "Because my sister went through forensic science and couldn't work in it because she's DACA, my mind was that I needed to do something that I actually can do for my career." So she dropped nuclear medicine and started taking classes in business instead. Her father helped her find a position with a friend who owned an electrical company, doing invoices and other miscellaneous tasks. However, she noted, "the business wasn't doing well, and I was not really satisfied being there."

When she was in the process of applying to work at a bank, she received a fortuitous call from a program contact who inquired about why she had stopped the nuclear medicine program the previous year. Esme explained why, and "the counselor told me, 'They're not going to ask about your citizenship as long as you have a permanent address and a social. There's no reason to. But if you have trouble in the future getting a state license, you don't need a state license in DC.'" Esme recalled, "It was such a relief, because that's really what I wanted to do from the beginning. But even in the back of my head I kept thinking, 'What if I can't take these boards, and I'm doing it all for nothing?'" She proceeded with taking—and passing—her first two board exams and got her certification in May 2021 and was just waiting on the Maryland license to come through. Postgraduation, she was pursuing job leads in both Maryland and D.C. in case she encountered difficulties gaining employment in Maryland. As she reasoned, "Based on where I live [in Prince George's County], I could get to D.C. pretty easily." Along her career pathway, Esme benefitted from her sister's experiences and knowledge, which allowed Esme to make more strategic choices but also the knowledge of a proactive counselor, who provided her with the information and assurances she needed to continue.

Like Esme, Elena also benefitted from the experiences and knowledge of her two older sisters, Pau and Sara, as she found her career path in business and information technology. When I first met her in 2016, I noted how surprisingly future minded and practical she seemed for a nineteen-year-old. Elena told me that she had started working when she was fourteen at a bridal and flower shop that her father purchased with the idea that the sisters could run and grow the business. Sara had graduated from high school the year before, and without DACA yet on the horizon in 2011, her father thought that the business would be a good economic opportunity. Elena recalled, "I was always at the shop. If

I wasn't in school or some type of after-school activity, I would be at the shop. On weekends, I was always there. It was very stressful, but also a really good learning experience." When she was seventeen, Elena started working at a local chapter of a well-known national insurance company, where her older sisters had started working after the family made the tough decision to close the shop; as she noted, "Pau got me the interview. They knew everything about DACA, so the support was already there. It was like no questions asked as far as why I'm in the situation I'm in. They were very respectful about it." Elena continued working for the agent after she started community college and once she transferred to a university. As she explained at the time, "I work full-time and I'm going to school full-time. That's how it's been since I started."

Given her long work history, it is not surprising that Elena focused on establishing herself financially early on. As she remembered, "As soon as I turned eighteen, I got my first credit card. Credit is something I've actively worked on. And I have excellent credit, which is absolutely amazing. It's helped out so much, especially my family if they need to finance anything." Elena's statements clearly indicate that she sees her solid credit as a family resource to strategically leverage. By age twenty-three, Elena had helped both her uncle, who was undocumented, and her older sister Sara, who also had DACA, purchase homes in Prince George's County. By that point, her family members were quite knowledgeable about the local housing market. Her father, who had Temporary Protected Status (TPS), had worked for the same construction company for the entire time he had been in the United States. Six years in with the company, he purchased a house in Hyattsville that the family had lived in for more than a decade when I met Elena. Over time, her parents had also purchased another home in Hyattsville that they rented out as a way to generate additional income; they also viewed this home as a bit of an insurance policy in case they experienced disruptions in employment, if her father lost status, or if either parent was deported. Thus her family members were collectively quite knowledgeable about the local real estate market. Despite her young age, Elena played a key role within her family as an economically and legally secure family member. As we will see, one of the notable trends in the third phase of research was that seven participants (29 percent of the phase III sample) had purchased homes, often describing their families as motivation for doing so.

Participants' experiences underscore the importance of forging place-based knowledge about state policies like the Maryland DREAM Act and professional licensure and even more local programs like university-based scholarships and county housing resources. Their accounts also underscore the importance of social networks for building and disseminating knowledge about these policies and facilitating access to resources like scholarship programs and counselors. Older siblings like Angélica and Marcela often had to struggle to find out about these policies and resources, while younger siblings like Nayeli, Juan, and Esme experienced a much smoother incorporation pathway and transition to adulthood and very clearly understood that this was due to the very specific navigational capital their siblings possessed and workarounds they shared. Leveraging this navigational capital became a central aspect of many participants' professional lives.

"Moving Wasn't a Big Switch for Me—I'm a Pretty Flexible Person": Moving Jurisdictions and Expanding Spatial Mobility

Though Elena embarked on homeownership deeply rooted in the jurisdiction for which she and her network possessed the most knowledge, I also found that many participants were testing out and applying their navigational skills to new jurisdictions as they embarked on moves to less familiar places. In phase III, when participants shared updates, they often began by indicating that they had moved since the last time we caught up—both within the D.C. Metro region and increasingly to places beyond. Overall, by phase III, eight participants (33 percent of phase III)[52] had made a major move to a new jurisdiction: three out of state (to Massachusetts, Michigan, and California), three from Maryland to Virginia, and four to a different Maryland county (Baltimore, Frederick, Howard, and Prince George's). Another two had moved on a more temporary basis, and another three whom I have continued to remain in touch with after phase III have subsequently moved to another state (two to California and one to Texas).

In her case, Annisa moved from Maryland to northern Virginia. She was quite comfortable within her tight-knit Indonesian community in Maryland but held a very different perception of Virginia before she moved there: "When my dad was an Uber driver, he would talk about how he would stay away from Virginia because the police are stricter . . . there were more random stops at that time." Despite her deep roots in Maryland, Annisa found herself somewhat unexpectedly moving to Virginia in 2020 after she got married to an Indonesian man whose family was based there. "When I first moved, it was really hard," she recalled. "I lived with my family all my life and suddenly they were forty-five minutes away. With work and then COVID I see them much less now." She also noted that she felt that she was not as well acquainted with Virginia as she would have liked to have been going into her move: "I worked in Maryland right up until I moved, so I didn't have time to research the policies. By the time I started working in Virginia, I was still trying to catch up and learn about everything." One of the most challenging aspects of the move for Annisa, then, was her lack of familiarity with the local socio-legal context and the fact that the workarounds that she had carefully discovered and put to use in Maryland did not extend to her new community in a different state.

Annisa found navigating different Virginia bureaucratic offices to be a challenge—especially getting a new driver's license. As she noted, "I feel like Virginia is so strict with policies and Maryland is a little more laid-back." The pandemic only exacerbated these challenges as she struggled to find a Department of Motor Vehicles appointment before her Maryland license was set to expire since the offices were open only in a very limited capacity. Over time, Annisa has settled into her new community, which has been aided by her husband's Virginia-based Indonesian social support network, demonstrating that collective ethnic capital can be essential for not only initial settlement but also relocation.[53] Annisa also found a new job as a mental health technician "doing exactly what I want to do" in northern Virginia's major health care system, which also helped ground her locally as she learned about area resources to share with her clients. Though it took her some time to cultivate legal-spatial consciousness in Virginia, Annisa eventually built her knowledge base and applied it in her own life and on behalf of her clients. In August 2020, she expressed that being a "resource person" who actively shared workarounds across socio-legal contexts was central to her identity.

Santiago also relocated to northern Virginia, in his case when he pursued a new career opportunity. Santiago had always lived and worked in Prince George's County (Maryland). Before he received DACA, he started volunteering at a youth development nonprofit organization based in D.C. and multiple Maryland counties: "There was nothing I could do about the situation with my status. So even though I couldn't work, I just kept myself busy." Once he was able to work legally, the nonprofit hired him and he steadily "worked his way up" into management "by working hard and showing people that I can do it. Even though I'm young, I have a strong work ethic and take pride in the work I do." After seven years working at the nonprofit, though, he was ready for a change and started job hunting, ultimately landing a position as a workforce development program manager in a D.C.-based organization in 2020.

Like many residents of the notoriously traffic-filled D.C. Metro region, Santiago decided that his forty-five- to sixty-minute commute from Maryland was unsustainable. He "started looking at Virginia" and decided to move there since his commute would be only fifteen minutes: "That was the main reason that I decided to move." Santiago had gained some familiarity with Virginia because his girlfriend of over two years lived there. During that time, he had been able to ascertain which areas were more immigrant friendly and gain a sense of where he would feel most comfortable living. As he shared, "I live in Arlington, right next to the Pentagon. In northern Virginia, where I live, I'm just another person. It's pretty diverse here too, like in Maryland. And I think I also got to a point that I've made peace with me being darker. It doesn't worry me like before." Santiago's residential decision making clearly reflects his attempt to minimize the perceived risk of immigration enforcement and choice of a neighborhood where he could blend in.[54] Both Annisa's and Santiago's comments underscore the importance of finding protective locations within a state that they perceive to be less immigrant friendly overall.

Other participants have moved to new places beyond the D.C. Metro region, whether on a shorter or longer term basis, in the process expanding their legal-spatial consciousness. Mae had only ever lived in Montgomery County, where she remembers "living with my mom's brother's family and then my mom's sister's family. There were a lot of people, a lot of kids, and I remember being very happy. Me and my cousins grew up really close." Like many undocumented young adults, Mae was not terribly aware of the limitations of her status until she started thinking about college. She applied to a number of different universities, though many of them were out of state, "even though I knew I couldn't go there." She ended up going to a state university in Maryland due to financial and practical reasons. Mae applied to the business school and was accepted, majoring in marketing. Though she had "always wanted to study abroad since middle school," Mae noted when she was a college sophomore, "DACA has prevented me from being able to do things like that . . . visit or volunteer in different countries."

During her final year of college, Mae landed a summer internship in San Francisco. As she noted, "It was definitely different there. But now that I have DACA, I like to travel quite a bit. I just love going on trips with my friends to national parks and things like that. So moving wasn't a huge switch for me, I am a pretty flexible person. It definitely gave me a glimpse into what life could look like, living in a different city." Mae parlayed her internship into a full-time job as a web producer as soon as she graduated in 2020. Her first year on the job was remote due to the pandemic, though she eagerly anticipated moving back to San Francisco as the office reopened. As she said, "I see myself back in San Francisco for a while. My parents aren't really that tied down to the idea of staying in Maryland. So we always joke that they'll follow me to wherever I'm living. Especially as my parents are getting older, I'd like them to be closer to me." Mae's spatial mobility has expanded considerably since I first met her in 2016, when she had never left Maryland, and may soon extend to her parents should she help them negotiate an out-of-state move.

Nancy was the participant who had moved around the most, between Maryland counties, to Virginia, and out of state. Nancy first lived in Montgomery County, where her mother's family lived, though over the next few years they moved frequently between Montgomery, Prince George's, and Anne Arundel Counties. When I inquired about their frequent moves, Nancy shared, "In the beginning, we moved to apartments because it was cheaper. Then my parents were trying to step it up a bit and moved to a house my aunt owns and rented for a year or two. Then we moved to be closer to my father's job, but then he changed jobs and wasn't in the same place anymore." When I first met her, Nancy lived in yet another jurisdiction, Baltimore City, while she attended a state university about thirty minutes away.

After graduating with a degree in electrical engineering in 2017, she and her partner took positions with a consulting firm and moved up to

Massachusetts. Though she embraced the opportunity initially when I spoke with her in 2018, she moved back to the D.C. Metro region fairly quickly: "We didn't last long in Massachusetts. I got very sick and we decided to move back. I realized my support system is here in the DMV, and I needed to be back close to home because I didn't really have any family members in Massachusetts." Once she returned, Nancy and her partner both got jobs in Virginia and lived there. She initially rented an apartment in Fairfax, which she characterized as "very immigrant friendly." However, she wanted to buy a house and found that she could not afford real estate there, so she found a place closer to her job in Manassas: "Towards D.C. there's definitely more diversity, [but] I've found Manassas to be immigrant friendly too. Though anywhere south of it is definitely not!" Nancy, then, has explored and mapped a clear line between places she feels more or less insulated against racism; however, she also acknowledges that being a light-skinned Argentinian shields her from some of the racism directed at her largely Mexican neighbors in Manassas.

Nancy also highlighted a different kind of mobility: visiting new places. Indeed, DACA has also served to increase the spatial mobility of its recipients since their bureaucratic documents enable them to securely and efficiently travel between jurisdictions.[55] Since 2016, participants have excitedly recounted the trips that they have been able to take to destinations throughout the United States and Puerto Rico, for internships, work, and leisure. As they have become more economically secure, Nancy and her current boyfriend have also started traveling more, including to places that she deems decidedly *not* immigrant friendly, like rural Pennsylvania and the Mountain West. Nancy notes, "My boyfriend and I are both Hispanic, and we've traveled a lot. There are places we traveled that we felt more normal, and other places that you can feel the tension. We went up to the mountains in the middle of nowhere Pennsylvania. We stopped at a random local diner, and when we both sat down, we're like, 'Do you feel that?'" As she traveled to Idaho, which she noted, "felt a little more iffy," she reflected, "I feel safe, even if we were to encounter problems . . . should we get pulled over, I wouldn't have to worry because he's a citizen and I have my papers with me all the time. I just feel safer with them on me."

Camila likewise found that her documents lent her security as she entered unfamiliar territory during a trip out west she took with a friend who had DACA and another who was undocumented. As Camila explained, "Yellowstone National Park's been on my bucket list so I went last summer. Being in touch with nature . . . that's my therapy. It was a fun road trip, and the landscape was breathtaking, beautiful." As she continued to talk about the trip, she revealed, "I had a sense of security in a way. My other friend who is undocumented, he did feel uncomfortable. He's like, I'm not gonna drive here. You guys can drive just to be safe." In addition to discomfort about the immigrant policing environment they might encounter, they also confronted a vastly different political and racial landscape. As she noted, "It was definitely nerve-wracking going to these states. In Montana, we stayed at this tiny, tiny, tiny town. We had breakfast at this diner and everybody there was white. There was a huge picture of Trump right at the bar. When we walked in, everybody was staring at us because we're the only three Brown kids and we felt uncomfortable. Like if we moved a certain way, people looked at us. It was an experience." Despite actual and potentially negative experiences in these new places, Nancy and Camila felt equipped to negotiate them, having gained familiarity with more pervasive racism in Virginia and armed with that experiential knowledge and their bureaucratic documents.

In addition to the moves they had made with their families as children, participants were very much on the move as they got deeper into their adult lives and professional careers. Having DACA has clearly made a major difference in enabling recipients to pursue new employment opportunities, like Santiago and Nancy, or even dream of different possibilities, like Mae. Some of these positions allow them to impart their navigational capital, as Annisa has done. The decisions they make about where to move are clearly quite intentional and informed by their sense of how receptive the new jurisdiction is to immigrants, such as with Santiago. These moves also involve mapping out local policies and becoming familiar with new workarounds, as Annisa clearly anticipated— certainly an experience that anyone moving between jurisdictions has, but with added layers of complication due to having DACA and possessing time-limited documents. Yet even as they move away from their families and into their own places, it is clear that their family relationships and D.C.-based networks still keep them connected to the region.

Conclusion

Federal-level immigration policies are not the only policies that immigrants confront—ever-shifting state and local policies also determine how immigrants are incorporated into local communities and what their lives are like on the ground. It is precisely in the context of daily life that immigrants encounter the complicated jurisdictional patchwork of policies and learn how to access place-specific social resources like driver's licenses and health care. Typically, navigating local policies would not be conceptualized as political engagement; yet DACA recipients *are* actually engaging politically as they gain specific knowledge of local policies that impact immigrants, competency in maneuvering within politicized landscapes, and skills for acquiring access to exclusionary civic institutions. DACA recipients leverage their navigational capital to pursue normal lives by taking such seemingly mundane actions as matriculating in colleges and universities, carefully planning career paths, pursuing targeted employment opportunities, figuring out the intricacies of the local housing market, and devising strategies to safely travel to new places. They harness collective knowledge and resources to overcome obstacles and successfully participate in these activities of everyday life. As I highlight in the next chapter, they also engage in specific forms of everyday activism that they perform in solidarity with other immigrants as they take more explicit political action.

4

"People Show Up in Different Ways"

Shifting Political Engagement and Emerging Forms
of Everyday Activism

In 2016, when I met Madeline, she had never participated in any kind of immigration-related activism. She got DACA when she was seventeen, though for many years she did not know anyone besides her older sister who also had it. She was not terribly comfortable sharing information about her status with most people she knew or had met on her university campus; as she noted, "It's something I keep to myself. I don't really talk to people about it in general. It's usually if it's a friend and we're alone, and they're like, 'Why are you so stressed out?' I mention my status, and they are usually really sympathetic about my situation. I had a friend who didn't even know that Black people also had DACA as well!" Madeline also did not seek out a larger community of DACA recipients, or even immigrants, on her college campus or in the suburban Maryland community in which she lived.

Despite not being involved in immigration-related activism, Madeline was deeply knowledgeable about the U.S. political process and policies that impact immigrants. "I've always paid attention to politics," she asserted. "It's interesting to me as a foreigner that I often pay more attention than people from [the United States]." In fact, Madeline had purposefully chosen to major in political science so that she could make better sense of her legal situation: "I wanted to understand what goes on in politics . . . how it works with deciding who gets to work and who doesn't, who gets to have a driver's license and who doesn't, things like that. I'm able to approach it from the perspective of a migrant, which really helps me, whether it's analyzing different conflicts or how governments process people from different cultures." As part of her major, she completed an internship at the Library of Congress, which was "the first time I got to go into places like that. It was a bit odd having a government ID. Every day when I walked by the Capitol, I remember thinking, 'Half of the people in that building probably don't even want you in this country.' That thought was always in the back of my mind."

Like many others, Madeline took the 2017 DACA rescission announcement quite hard, sharing, "I never took what [Trump] said at face value. I really didn't think he was going to do anything drastic with DACA." Two months after the rescission announcement, when I spoke with her, I inquired about how she had been doing, to which Madeline responded, "I've just been bummed out and haven't been quite right. I just kind of checked out. Before, I was always on top of the news [about DACA]. Since the decision was made . . . I don't really watch the news anymore." Instead, Madeline shifted focus to her upcoming graduation and figuring out her next steps, including contemplating the possibility of a move to Canada with her sister to reunite with their older brother, who moved to Canada after he had returned to Senegal to get paperwork in order and was unable to reenter the United States.

Yet one day in October 2017 as she entered her university library, Madeline encountered something that stopped her in her tracks: a flyer for a campus forum about "fake news," a term referencing misleading information that President Trump had parlayed into a catchphrase and propaganda tool. The event was a serious one, featuring multiple experts from across campus with different expertise on the topic. However, the flyer featured a cartoon with a graphic of an alien ship landing, with a mass of thirty or so smiling green aliens emerging from a spaceship. Toward the bottom of the flyer, there was an image of a newspaper announcing "Breaking News: 3 Million Aliens Voted in 2016," with a picture of an alien dropping a ballot into the ballot box. As Madeline shared with me, "[The flyer] was on the stand when you walk in the library. I looked at it and initially didn't really think much of it, because it was like 9:30 a.m. So then I go upstairs, I get right out of the elevator and there's another flyer. I was just like, 'No, I don't need this. Why?' Then I went to the lab to use a computer, and there it was on the library home page on the news slider. It was everywhere, and I just felt the need to say something because I thought it was insensitive to us." Madeline found the event organizer's contact information on the flyer and headed right to her office. Unable to find her, she instead sent her an email (actually copying me on the message) explaining why the flyer was offensive to

DACA recipients and immigrants on campus and tying her comments to the volatile political climate and the particularly painful timing related to the DACA rescission. Madeline received a prompt reply in return from the event organizer, who, as Madeline noted, "explained to me what the graphic designers were trying to convey. I understand it, but it was just the wrong message. They could have highlighted something else. This is people's lives. It was extremely insensitive."

I was taken aback by Madeline's actions; I had gotten to know Madeline well over the previous year as a CAB member and knew that she did not commonly disclose her status to people she knew well, let alone to strangers. Yet something had changed for Madeline. As she explained,

> I don't generally do things like that. A year ago, if I had seen that flyer, I would have thought that I didn't like it but I wouldn't have sent that email. Because I haven't been really vocal in regards to DACA and DREAMers. I don't go to the protests or things like that . . . I mostly just keep to myself. I just decided [that] I can just walk by the poster and say that I don't like it, or I can send an email to somebody and let them know why I don't like it and hopefully next time, another DACA person or immigrant won't have to feel the way I did.

Taking action in this way was quite satisfying for Madeline. "It felt good," she commented. "I was proud of myself because I thought it should have been said and I know that there are other people that aren't going to necessarily say something."

Madeline's actions are most definitely not the typical mode of activism for which DACA recipients are known.[1] Undocumented young adult activists have worked quite effectively across the country to organize political action campaigns that feature clear arguments, messages, and rhetoric that have had wide reach within public sphere.[2] These activists are typically quite outspoken, strategically sharing their immigration stories and openly disclosing their undocumented status as a means of commanding public attention and prompting political action.[3] Despite the high visibility of the youth-led social movement, though, it is quite likely that the majority of the estimated more than two million undocumented young adults do not participate in it—though no such data documenting this trend exist. Among my research participants, only eight of the original thirty (27 percent) indicated that they participated in collective political action or the organizing efforts of community-based organizations (CBOs) focused on immigrant rights. Beyond that, several who had been active in the movement as teenagers reported that their level of participation had lessened over time; by phase III in 2021, only one individual still actively participated.

Instead, many DACA recipients like Madeline prefer to keep their status quieter, sharing it only with trusted friends and supporters in very specific and limited contexts. Yet their relative quietness about their status does not mean that they are not aware of the larger policy context and immigration-related developments; indeed, as we have seen, like their activist counterparts, most possess a nuanced legal-spatial consciousness borne of their lived experiences. Madeline's backstory reveals that she has long been a serious student of the U.S. political process and immigrant experience and regularly followed developments related to DACA before it became too painful for her to continue to do so—as we have seen, a common experience. Nor does DACA recipients' relative quietness signal that they are disconnected from the struggle and immigrant rights movement overall; instead, many are politically engaged via everyday activism carried out in more mundane contexts like campuses and workplaces.[4] On a smaller scale, Madeline engages in the immigrant rights movement by educating friends about DACA and dispelling myths about its recipients when the opportunity arises. Yet Madeline also found herself taking concerted direct action in her local campus community for the first time in the aftermath of the rescission when she saw a flyer that she perceived as an injustice against her and her fellow immigrant students. Though such an explicitly political act required that she "come out of the shadows" as DACA recipient and expose herself to potential vulnerability, such small acts collectively are quite impactful in transforming social relations and potentially fostering social change.[5]

This chapter describes DACA recipients' trajectories of political engagement across time—before DACA existed, once the program was established, and after it became endangered. Although the public activism of DACA recipients has commanded significant public awareness, many undocumented young adults like Madeline have never participated in these actions or diminished in their participation over time. However, against the backdrop of the repressive state and racist political discourse about immigrants in the first Trump era, the everyday activism of DACA recipients rooted in their local communities emerged to complement more conventional forms of collective action like protests. Activism itself is conventionally linked to the public, explicit, explosive, and sometimes even glamorous elements of political life, set apart from the mundane, routine, and hidden or unnoticed aspects of the everyday.[6] Yet DACA recipients have increasingly been electing to engage politically in their normal, everyday lives as a means of contesting their precarious legal status and advocating for themselves and their loved ones.

Indeed, DACA recipients' everyday activism underscores the adaptive nature of their political engagement strategies in contributing to the larger political project of fighting for immigrant well-being and justice.[7] The phenomenon of everyday activism also raises interesting questions about the nature of activism itself, including the extent to which it must be collective, organized, and public to be regarded as activism. Mendes and Chang contend that a lack of publicness does *not* necessarily equate to a lack of activism.[8] Instead, I argue that public and everyday forms of activism can be mutually constitutive as complementary forms of resistance. As anthropologist Matthew C. Gutmann points out, overt and covert forms of resistance should be considered in conjunction, as they can "occur together, alternate, and transform themselves into each other."[9]

Undocumented Young Adults' Social Movement and Everyday Activism

Undocumented young adults have "unapologetically" staked public claims on belonging, emerging as a "politically identifiable group with a legitimate and identifiable voice."[10] As Nicholls notes, they are unconventional political actors with complex political subjectivities, defying many standard expectations about social movement participants.[11] For one, undocumented young adults make claims on the state as legitimate political subjects with rights despite not being official members.[12] Their active engagement is also notable compared to the generally lower participation and apathy of young adults.[13] The DREAMer movement is also unusual because of its emergence in a hostile immigrant context, which typically results in immigrants avoiding the public sphere.[14]

When the original federal DREAM Act was introduced in 2001, undocumented young adults did not yet exist as an organized political group on the national stage.[15] However, immigrant youth and their allies were already busily engaged in successful state-level legislative campaigns in California and Texas pushing for undocumented students to be classified as state residents for tuition purposes.[16] The DREAMer movement scaled up as part of the broader immigrant rights movement, which coalesced around the 2006 protests, which at the time were the largest mass mobilizations on any topic since the 1970s, with an estimated 3.5 to 5.1 million participants nationwide.[17] The protests served as a crystallizing moment in the political socialization of a million youth from immigrant families, many of whom had never before been politically active.[18] After the protests, comprehensive immigration reform stalled after several failed legislative attempts. In a context in which few political opportunities existed, national immigrant rights associations decided that DREAMers were a vehicle to keep pushing the struggle for immigrant rights forward as the public was more sympathetic toward undocumented youth who were brought to the United States as children by "no fault of their own," as their situation was commonly described in public discourse.[19]

After the DREAM Act once again failed to pass in December 2010, dealing a devastating blow to young activists, they retooled and started more strongly asserting autonomy and control over their place within the larger immigrant rights movement.[20] As the 2012 election loomed, United We Dream—the largest national immigrant-youth-led nonprofit organization—and its affiliates shifted efforts toward gaining "administrative relief" for "low-priority" immigrants like undocumented young adults through waves of coordinated actions designed to ratchet up pressure on Obama during his reelection campaign, capitalizing on the centrality of the Latinx vote.[21] By June 15, 2012, the Obama administration announced the new executive order, DACA, which clearly mirrored the language and arguments of these activists.[22]

Young adults' participation in the movement has frequently been mediated by CBOs that provide important resource infrastructure and impart knowledge and skills to facilitate youths' engagement in political activity.[23] Regional networks of CBOs flourished in relatively welcoming local contexts like California[24] and Illinois[25] as the movement solidified.

However, undocumented young adults operate in uneven geographies of politicization, with activism being most prominent in large central cities that have high levels of organizational density and broader ideological support for promoting immigrant rights.[26] Regional organizing efforts laid the groundwork for the establishment of national "beltway" organizations like United We Dream based in Washington, D.C.[27] Despite its centrality in the movement, the D.C. Metro region has been featured less in the undocumented youth activism literature,[28] even though D.C. is the seat of the federal government and site where youth activists from throughout the country frequently stage public actions. The large surrounding metropolitan region is also home to many long-established CBOs focused on immigrant rights that grew out of the region's large Central American community and its long-standing fight for political recognition; these CBOs afford local young adults with relatively easier access to opportunities for political engagement.

During the early 2010s, social media also emerged as a critical platform for asserting autonomy and streamlining messaging across geographic locations.[29] Youth more vociferously challenged the hegemonic frames of deservingness and worthiness that dominated policy debates and the media and rejected the criminalization of their parents by emphasizing the shared vulnerability of the undocumented community.[30] Many activists started rejecting the DREAMer label altogether given that it applies only to a select group of purportedly deserving immigrants instead of recognizing the full humanity of all undocumented immigrants.[31] The movement also become more expansive in other ways as well. Adopting the LGBTQ+ rights movement's "coming out" framing, activists organized "coming out of the shadows" campaigns to combat the social stigma of undocumented status.[32] Over time, the movement itself has taken more of an inclusive and intersectional approach, influenced by UndocuQueer and undocumented Asian American and Pacific Islander activists.[33]

Activists' claims-making strategies have evolved in alignment with new political realities,[34] underscoring that the movement is dynamic and flexible.[35] Over time, activists have shifted from targeting the policy arena through mass mobilizations, lobbying, teach-ins, and rallies to more overt acts of civil disobedience and protest like disrupting a board of regents meeting and occupying a classroom at the University of Georgia.[36] They also carry out nonstaged acts of civil disobedience at sites of enforcement like detention and processing centers.[37] Youth openly disclose their undocumented status and risk deportation as explicitly political acts.[38] Some have used social media to chronicle their experiences of self-deportation and publicized themselves destroying their Employment Authorization Card.[39]

These newer forms of high-risk activism are designed precisely to expose the violence of the state, which has become a powerful force shaping the movement, particularly during the first Trump era.[40] Indeed, scholars found that the unapologetic nativist and anti-immigrant policies of the first Trump era served to increase undocumented young adults' political engagement.[41] Activists have also critiqued CBOs' push for the "right to assimilation,"[42] shifting the gaze away from merely achieving formal legal recognition to protesting the structural forces of inequality embedded within the citizenship regime.[43] Activists instead are articulating an end goal of intersectional immigrant justice and seeking to *"live* radically"[44] by promoting self-care, #undocujoy, and freedom.[45]

Despite the increased inclusiveness and more expansive goals of the movement, many of the estimated two million undocumented young adults nationwide do not participate in public activism. Nevertheless, as Mendes and Chang point out, a lack of publicness does not necessarily equate to a lack of activism, and they therefore urge that we expand our notions of activism to include more unorthodox manifestations of agency.[46] Rather, many who do not fit the prototypical "fierce" or "daring" activist archetype may be engaged in other forms of resistance in their everyday lives.[47] James C. Scott influentially argued that everyday forms of resistance have often been overlooked with the predominant focus on organized rebellions and collective actions.[48] Everyday forms of resistance are typically more hidden or disguised, individual, and not politically articulated.[49] Yet they can be activated to resist structures of power without engaging in direct confrontation as oppressed groups are able to carve out modes of resistance in social spaces insulated from control and surveillance.[50] These "free spaces," as political scientist Chris Zepeda-Millán refers to them, are instead defined by their roots in community and rich networks of daily life.[51]

Activism itself is conventionally linked to the public, explicit, explosive, and sometimes even glamorous elements of political life, set apart from the mundane, routine, and hidden or unnoticed aspects of the everyday.[52] Mansbridge defines everyday activism as "talk and action in everyday life that is not consciously coordinated with the actions of others but is (i) to some degree caused (inspired, encouraged) by a social movement and (ii) consciously intended to change others' ideas or behavior in directions advocated by the movement."[53] Price and Rojas argue that operating within "ordinariness" of daily life can enable people to "live out the change they would like to see rather than just demand the change."[54]

Scholars examining everyday activism have frequently focused on cities and how marginalized residents contest spatial inequality in daily life—demanding their "right to the city," as phrased by influential French philosopher and sociologist Henri Lefebvre in his theorization about the nature of everyday life.[55] For instance, political scientist Jérôme Tournadre examines how Black residents of South African townships demonstrate against poor living conditions within their neighborhoods—notably far outside of the political sphere.[56] Urban studies scholar Adriana Soaita describes how a group of tenants in the United Kingdom claimed occupancy rights by calling for such practices as rent control, secure contracts with flexible cessation, and the freedom to personalize their spaces.[57] Building directly on Lefebvre's concept of counterspaces,[58] anthropologist Maurice R. Magaña demonstrates how youth activists from working-class neighborhoods in Mexico constructed their own spatial networks that combined symbolically occupied public space with physical spaces like youth-run cultural centers.[59]

Expanding the spatial boundaries of activism is particularly important for young adults, who have their own forms of political expression that may fall outside of the mainstream.[60] The everyday spaces where young adults stake belonging include schools, workplaces, and sporting events, where locally focused practices like volunteering and becoming involved in local causes can serve as vehicles for promoting civic engagement.[61] Sociologists Anita Harris and Joshua Roose underscore the importance of documenting these practices and spaces in particular for those who are alienated from formal mechanisms of political engagement, such as migrant-background Muslim youth in Australia.[62] As another such group, undocumented young adults in the United States have cultivated "safe" or "counter" everyday spaces on university campuses that have allowed them to find emotional support, share information about resources, and build social solidarity.[63] Some of these spaces have even become institutionalized through the public endorsement and financial support of university administrators and establishment of DREAMer centers.[64] However, anthropologists Mariela Nuñez-Janes and Mario Ovalle chronicle how undocumented college students in Texas forged their own "organic activism" through the practice of *acompañamiento* (accompaniment) by drawing on their shared knowledge and lived experiences to forge a collective consciousness. Creating and sustaining this youth-led group has allowed them to transform oppression into resistance by taking action in their communities.[65]

Indeed, campus groups (both formally organized and organically emergent) have been essential sites where undocumented young adults have nurtured political engagement given their limited opportunities for more conventional civic acts like voting or serving on juries.[66] Anthropologist Jennifer R. Nájera highlights how members of a campus-based California undocumented student advocacy group teach the general public about undocumented people through public *testimonio* (sharing one's story) and instructing other members of the undocumented community on how to access rights and resources. She argues that campus spaces can serve as incubators for public pedagogy as a form of everyday activism.[67] Yet college campuses are not insulated from the broader sociopolitical climate. Nuñez-Janes and Ovalle chronicle the adaptations Texas student activists have had to make to their strategies and actions over time, while Nájera documents how the election of Trump in 2016 destabilized the security that California students had cultivated in a welcoming state and campus context, corroding their safe space.[68]

Yet not all undocumented young adults come to their activism by way of organized collective action in cities or occupying campus safe spaces. Many young adults from immigrant families throughout the country manifest their activism in less obvious ways and practice "quieter" activism in their everyday lives,[69] complementing the more public and collective forms of anti-state activism in which their peers are engaged. While participating in mass mobilizations offers some degree of anonymity, DACA recipients' more personal exchanges with nonimmigrants in the intimate spaces of their daily lives potentially introduces new forms of vulnerability as they out themselves as undocumented as a component of their public pedagogy. However, as sociologists Julie Fish, Andrew King, and Kathryn Almack's analysis of LGBTQ+ people's everyday activism underscores, coming out on this interpersonal level is an explicitly political act and these smalls acts collectively transform social relations and have the potential to foster social change.[70] Everyday activists' contributions are impactful in cultivating citizen allies who support immigration reform[71] and in moving public opinion progressively in support of them, an important social movement outcome.[72] This everyday work often goes unnoticed, yet these actions play a critical role in progressive struggles for social justice.[73] Beyond that, many undocumented young adults have also had to cultivate more innovative strategies of engaging politically precisely due to repressive state actions,[74] making these everyday exchanges a more preferable mode of political engagement for some. These more overt and covert forms of activism should be viewed not in isolation or opposition but rather as coexisting in relation to each other.[75]

Trajectories of Political Engagement and Emergent Forms of Everyday Activism

During phase I in 2016, I was surprised to discover that the majority of research participants had never been involved in immigration-related activism. Several mostly Latinx participants recounted coming of age participating in CBOs' organized political action campaigns, particularly in the period before DACA came into existence. Yet as I continued conducting research, their political engagement shifted over time in response to changes in their lives as well as in the broader sociopolitical climate with the election of Trump. Thus by 2017–18, even fewer participants were involved in public collective action or CBOs' activities and campaigns. However, I started noting the alternative ways in which DACA recipients advocated for immigrants in their everyday lives, particularly in the first Trump era, though also extending beyond it.

"It Played a Positive Role in My Life for Sure": Early Involvement in CBO-Based Activism

As teenagers, eight of the thirty original participants—all Latinx, though notably from six different countries of origin—had participated in local CBOs and their political action campaigns. Most started participating in the youth programming of these CBOs as they learned about the policies that constrained their access to employment, driver's licenses, and higher education. These participants credited those organizations with affirmatively impacting their experiences coming of age without papers, such as Pau. Like many undocumented teenagers, Pau started realizing in high school that she would not be able to get a driver's license and that going to college might be more difficult than she had imagined.[76] By tenth grade, she had started actively seeking out resources to help her navigate her situation, like school guidance counselors. She eventually discovered a community-based "immigrant center that helped me become a lot more aware of what was going on." As she recalled, "We were very involved with the DREAM Act, doing marches and getting students together to go to Capitol Hill, meeting with potential donors, and stuff like that."

Pau became a youth leader in the program as one of the only participants from Prince George's County, as most of the CBOs' youth program participants were from next-door Montgomery County. In early 2012, she led an eighty-student walkout from her high school to downtown Washington, D.C., to participate in a march, noting, "My principal was not very pro-immigrant, but I asked for permission to get students together and she didn't give it to me. So we simply walked out. It was just a really badass moment." She recalled the elation she felt when the establishment of DACA was announced shortly after the walkout: "We were dancing around at [name of CBO], just celebrating. It was really, really fun." Pau reflected on the impact of the CBO on her life during that time: "It was a big help. For us to get to share our stories and for people to actually see how important of a role we play . . . was just really amazing. It played a very positive role in my life for sure."

Although Pau never formally worked as an organizer, five participants were employed by different local CBOs in 2016 when I met them. Receiving DACA had enabled several to parlay program participation, volunteer work, or unpaid internships at these CBOs into full-time paid employment with benefits. Laura received DACA when she was twenty-two, as she juggled work at a cleaning company at night while taking part-time classes at a community college during the day. She found her way to the CBO through an internship: "I started as an intern, and then I just became a volunteer. I remember my former supervisor and the committee organizer person told me to come in for a meeting, and when I sat down, they were like, 'We've seen your work ethic. We want to bring you in—not as an intern but as a full-time staff.' I was just so thrilled!" These paid positions are unique employment pathways for DACA recipients and are certainly testament to their organizing power. Laura continued working at the CBO while working on her bachelor's in social work, though the grant funding for her program was ending as she approached graduation in May 2017. As her position wound down, she started working part-time as a case manager with a local chapter of a global nonprofit organization focused on international and domestic adoption and foster care. Soon thereafter, she took a full-time position, providing postrelease services to unaccompanied minors as they transitioned out of shelters into the community.

Yet she missed the explicitly activist orientation of the first CBO where she had worked. "After the election, everything changed," she reflected. "I was working with a program that told us that we couldn't be political. Yes, we could inform clients about their rights and tell them to go to places. I was assessing twelve different things in their lives, but only one of them was immigration." Laura started "feeling like my hands were tied. I started reflecting on, as a case manager, where do I stand with this issue? I want the best for my families, but I can't tell them that they need to speak up, raise their voices. So I started feeling like 'How can I get more involved? How do I make a change?'" Laura ultimately left that case manager position to take a position as a youth organizer at yet another local CBO where she had previously volunteered before she had received DACA. Like many immigrant young adults nationwide, Laura's activism and employment are deeply intertwined, though it is also clear there are some constraints related to these positions, including their sustainability.

The majority of participants, however, were not as politically involved as Pau or Laura, either before or after receiving DACA. Several had processed their DACA applications at a CBO but were not involved in the activities of the organization beyond that. Others had no connection whatsoever to such organizations or awareness that they even existed. In fact, none of the five participants from Asian or African countries of origin was ever involved with a CBO (or even campus group) or had taken part in any organized collective action. Mae was one of the participants who was least involved in immigration-related activism. She was relatively unaware of her undocumented status during her childhood: "I didn't realize anything about what was happening. My parents didn't tell me anything. The older I got, the more I wanted to learn about it and the more I understood about why I was under [DACA] and what actually happened." A neighbor they were close to was a lawyer and helped Mae and her brother apply for DACA, though it was her brother who handled the paperwork. As I asked questions about her experiences applying, she laughed and said, "I feel like through this entire process, I've been the most unknowledgeable person about this! If you ask me, 'When did you get it?' I just don't really know." Mae's response stood in stark contrast to those of many others, like Laura, who actually identified the original date she received her approval, reasoning that it was a critical date of which to keep track.

Aside from her brother, Mae noted that she knew only one other undocumented person, but "we're not that close. I haven't asked him questions about that or anything." Mae did not seek out other DACA recipients, either in high school or in college. In fact, as we wrapped up our first interview, she noted, "I don't think I've ever talked to anyone for this long about DACA!" Being a DACA recipient was not at the core of Mae's identity. She was certainly aware of the protests immigrant young adults were leading downtown: "I think it's great for people to protest. But for me personally, I don't think protesting and thinking about DACA all the time is going to help me. I don't avoid DACA, but I just try to look past it and continually try to do well in school, go to my job, and volunteer." Mae, then, focuses on aspects of her "normal" life as a mechanism for managing anxiety related to her legal status precarity.

Other participants observed more markedly that their ethnic communities lacked organizations that focused on legal advocacy or planned mass mobilizations. As noted earlier, Annisa was deeply immersed in her local Maryland Indonesian community. As she shared, "My mom heard about [DACA] word of mouth . . . her friends let her know about it." Yet once they learned about the program, Annisa said, "My mom had to ask around with her friends for help with a lawyer and how to talk about it with a lawyer." Eventually they found their way to a recommended lawyer who specialized in DACA applications, but it was a circuitous and complicated process; her description of her experiences stood in stark contrast to those of many of the Latinx immigrants who found out more easily about CBOs that provided pro bono or low-cost application assistance. Most members of Annisa's community were not DACA recipients or even undocumented, meaning that she had to seek out resources well beyond her community, which she did once the DACA rescission happened and she looked for information about next steps. Annisa observed, "Non-Latino undocumented people are kind of like an invisible group. We're very overlooked . . . we're kind of a minority within a minority." Annisa noted that immigration status was not commonly discussed within her community, but "there are actually a lot of us [undocumented immigrants]. No one knows that. There are actually a lot of Indonesians in our community who have been caught by ICE too."

"I Was Feeling Way Too Exposed": Changing Patterns of Political Participation

By 2017–18, the smaller number of participants who had been actively involved in CBOs described changing patterns of political engagement. Elisa came from El Salvador when she was ten and recalled that when she arrived, "I was really depressed. I missed my uncle who had raised me for seven years. It was really hard for me to adapt here." Like Pau, she discovered the youth programming of a local CBO when she in early high school, which served as a positive force in her life. She shared, "Since I was fourteen, I would go and participate. I love participating because it makes me feel good about myself and I know how it helps. Even if it's just a little bit, I know that it helps. I used to do a lot of those events." Elisa recalled quite clearly how volunteering with the organization facilitated her DACA application process: "Since I worked with them, we got the chance to apply faster than everyone else. I remember I was the seventh person in the line!" By 2018, when I asked her about her ongoing involvement with the organization after the DACA rescission announcement, though, Elisa lamented, "No, I haven't really been." She continued, "It's mostly because I had a baby and I can't really go anymore because he's too little. I also had a C-section which made it hard." Despite these challenges, Elisa insisted, "I really wanted to participate—to be honest, I really did," underscoring that her commitment to the movement remained. Elisa and others noted that "adulting" infringed on their activism and made it more challenging to maintain their previous level of engagement.

Yet factors beyond adult responsibilities also profoundly shaped participants' political engagement. Pau's declining participation was particularly noteworthy. I met Pau for coffee right after the rescission announcement in September 2017 and asked her if she had gone to the student-led action on our campus or any of the protests in downtown D.C. She shrugged her shoulders and said, "I don't have time for that right now. I had class that morning and had to get to work." I was surprised at Pau's tepid response given how politically active she had always been. When I saw her next in January 2018, right after the government shutdown over DACA, I inquired more directly with her about what had changed. She lamented that she had grown frustrated with the movement: "I feel like a lot of the groups are doing very similar things, but nobody wants to just come together. Why don't you just bring the vision and work together?" Indeed, the sheer number of organizations in the D.C. Metro region and their duplicative efforts caused her frustration and made her less inclined toward participating at all. Pau also felt more broadly disheartened: "I know there is power in the people and [value in] just getting our faces out there and showing that, you know, we are real people. But, at the end of the day, they ended DACA. What are we going to do? No matter what we do, they don't care about us. So at this point, I'm like, yeah, they just don't care."

Other participants expressed their increasing discomfort with being identified publicly. In 2016 when I met Camila, she had just started working at an immigrant rights organization, her first professional job. She had grown quite accustomed to telling her own DACA story for her job, a big change from earlier in her life. As she reflected, "I used to be very quiet about it in school . . . my friends didn't even know about my status. But the people who are leaders in the movement, that's what has inspired me and that's why I am more outspoken now." Camila was devastated when DACA was rescinded but forged ahead as she had previously, participating in a series of youth-led actions in Washington, D.C., throughout the fall and winter, including the January 2018 action to pressure Congress about DACA that led to the government shutdown. She recounted that the government shutdown initially "felt like victory."

However, when the government quickly reopened without any resolution for DACA recipients, Camila recalled, "I experienced my first ever anxiety attack. I was by myself and I didn't know what to do. I remember panting and I felt like I couldn't breathe. I started thinking, 'What's going to happen to me? I don't want to go back.'" Within the next few days, she was asked to do a media interview, a common practice for her organization. She said, "I remember they asked me and usually I never refuse. That day I refused. I stayed quiet and just tried not to think about what's going to happen next." Camila's use of the word "refusal" indexes a broader practice of refusal that migration scholars have highlighted as an increasingly deployed strategy of resistance used by undocumented activists to repudiate the unpaid emotional labor involved in sharing their stories and reject the state's "game of citizenship."[77]

Angélica also began engaging in refusal after the rescission announcement. Like Camila, she worked for a youth development CBO and frequently shared her story publicly. But after the rescission, as she described, "I turned down an interview and just told her 'I'm not in the mental state to actually speak very publicly right now.' I just had to take a break because it was too much for me to handle. I honestly felt scared because I was feeling way too exposed." Instead of being an empowering act that provided validation and fostered social support,[78] sharing her story had become something that engendered vulnerability and was negatively impacting her mental health. In addition, Angélica noted that over time she had grown weary of sharing her story. As she reflected, "I shared my story at a gala once. As I was practicing for it, every time I had to repeat it, it no longer felt like my story anymore." Angélica's retreat from sharing her story can be read, in part, as an act of resistance to the commodification of it for the benefit of an unknown audience. As such, sharing one's story constitutes a form of "narrative capital" (as Gálvez refers to it) through which DACA recipients can either choose or decline participation in the moral economy in which this capital circulates.[79]

Some participants also retreated in their participation based on actual or potential experiences of being exposed and endangered. Angélica's younger sister Nayeli had not been active in the youth programming of her sister's CBO. As Nayeli explained in 2016 when I first met her, "I have a busy schedule, working three jobs and going to school full-time, which doesn't really give you free time for things like that." Angélica had often encouraged her sister to share her story too and informed her about opportunities to do so that aligned with her busy schedule. However, Nayeli also had a negative experience that changed how she felt about sharing her story:

> [My sister] asked me if I wanted to do an interview about DACA. And I was like, yeah, I want more people to know about it. After, the reporter was like, "I may need your number just to clarify a few details," and I was like, "That's fine." But she just kept harassing my phone, calling and texting me when I was in class. She went through my LinkedIn and said I was lying about my name. She was like, "Send me a picture of your license." I was like, "No, you're crazy!" It definitely made me more cautious on who I speak to.

Because of this incident, Nayeli revealed that she's choosing "to stay in my safety bubble" by protecting her story. Nayeli's brother Luis noted the implications of his sister's identity being public: "The worst-case scenario is someone sees this information and has bad intentions with it. That puts [her] at risk, but also the whole family . . . including our other family members who are not documented. It's a chain reaction really that we don't ever want to happen."

Annisa also had an experience that left her and her family feeling overly exposed. As she started connecting with others outside of her community who had DACA (including through our CAB), she had become aware of some of the Latinx-serving CBOs in the area that were convening informational sessions in the aftermath of the rescission. Annisa attended one of these events, and next thing she knew, her picture ended up on the front page of a newspaper. "It didn't have my name on it," she recalled, "but there was my face front and center. It was really annoying because when I was there, I thought it was a very safe space. I was the one that stood out, the only non-Hispanic there, so they wanted to highlight me. But I already told one of the people who asked ahead of time that I didn't want to be interviewed because my family is very careful in this area." The next day, Annisa received a call from her mother: "She was panicking, because she's the one who found out. Someone from my community recognized me . . . her friend sent it in a group chat. My mother was so scared." Annisa's picture was used without her explicit permission, putting not only her but potentially her family at risk.

This fear of exposure—or worse, being detained or deported—has made many DACA recipients understandably selective about their activism. Lucas noted that he was fairly quiet about being a DACA recipient, "except with people that I know who also need it. I don't really come out to everyone and say, 'Hey I'm a DACA recipient.' There are people who are heavily vocal against immigration reform. You don't want to hear their negative comments, and I don't want to bring that attention to myself." He discussed the conflict he felt about becoming more involved in direct action:

> You definitely think, "I should be out there fighting the fight." But when you get into the politics side of it, it gets very scary. I was at a training one time and this nurse was like, "You guys need to go out and protest more because the system is set up to leave minorities behind." And I'm just sitting there thinking, "If I was to be that radical, I would be deported." And I wanted to say something, to be like "Some of us don't have the privilege of getting arrested and then being here to tell the tale." I'm honestly scared of going there and outing myself. But at the same time I feel like I'm being a bit of a hypocrite because I always encourage us as minorities to be at the forefront.

Indeed, Lucas's sentiment was actually quite common among participants around the rescission announcement and is a phenomenon in the first Trump era others have also documented.[80] Participant after participant expressed their guilt for not being more active in the movement and expressed that they hoped that they could be more involved in the future. They described feeling a sense of duty to push for immigration reform in the public sphere as well as some obligation to participate on behalf of siblings, parents, and other more legally precarious members of their social networks who risked exposure by engaging in such public protests.

Although some participants had long histories of involvement in the movement, including as volunteers, interns, and paid organizers, different influences have altered their participation over time. For some adult responsibilities have made participation prohibitive despite their

desire to be involved, while for others disenchantment with the political process and politics, the urgent need to safeguard their mental
health, and negative experiences telling their stories have forced them
to retreat "into their safety bubbles," as Nayeli phrased it. While telling
one's story became a powerful act both before and once DACA began,
it became fraught under Trump as it likely will again in his second
term.[81] In response, some DACA recipients started engaging in more
deliberate acts of refusal, exerting control over the ways in which their
stories were being used and the terms of their political engagement.

"People Show Up in Different Ways": Emergent Forms of Everyday Activism

Although some DACA recipients are eschewing or deliberately dimin-
ishing their participation in public activism, a complementary set of
more informal and localized participatory practices were emerging,[82]
particularly during the first Trump era, though also extending beyond
it. As discussed earlier, Nayeli described her own guilt about not being
more involved in the immigrant rights movement but noted that her
boyfriend reminded her that "people show up in different ways" and that
she should recognize that she was "fighting her battle" in other ways.
Indeed, DACA recipients are "showing up" in different ways that operate
in alignment with and support of the broader movement, underscoring
the adaptive nature of undocumented young adults' political engagement strategies.[83]

Some participants felt compelled to engage in these actions for the
first time, never having spoken publicly about DACA before. Several
talked about classrooms as particularly ripe spaces for raising consciousness about DACA and strategically sharing their stories to combat ste-
reotypes and dehumanization.[84] As a South Korean, John is well aware
that most people he knows and encounters do not realize that he is a
DACA recipient. However, he also did not feel the same need to protect this personal information that others expressed: "Sometimes, if you
hang out long enough, you talk, and [your DACA status] just comes out.
[Laughs] Sometimes I go to bars or something and I take out my DACA
work visa card and people are like, 'What is that?' And I'm like, 'This is
a special card, only for special people.' [Laughs]" John noted that Presi-

dent Trump paradoxically brought more attention to DACA by threatening to eliminate it: "It's actually pretty good that Trump did what he did because before DACA was in limbo where everyone in the government was like, 'We don't want to deal with this problem.' Now there's no way they'll be able to kick us out, not just because of the money, but morality-wise. . . . people are not going to stand for that."

John has found that a lot of people have misconceptions about DACA, which he attributes in part to the media. After the rescission announcement, he noted, "I try to share [about my status] as much as possible. I feel like I did to some degree before, but it's more frequent right now because more people are aware about DACA now and they ask questions." John capitalized on increased awareness about DACA that grew precisely because of its endangerment. For John and other participants, Trump's election and targeting of the DACA program actually amplified their political consciousness and led to greater politicization. He noted that he felt a particular responsibility to interrupt his fellow students' ideas about DACA: "A lot of people just straight-up call DACA recipients Mexican. And I think letting those people know that there are other people too diminishes the racism value of saying something like that. And then I see them thinking . . . 'Wait a minute, he's a DACA recipient, and he's Asian. . . .' You can see them thinking, and that's already half the work done." Through his actions, John controlled the terms of his engagement surrounding DACA. In this classroom space, he was actually the one doing the teaching about undocumented immigrants and race,[85] demonstrating compellingly how public pedagogy serves as a form of everyday activism.

Other participants became more proactive in raising consciousness about DACA in other spaces like workplaces. As previously indicated in the introduction, Rebeca had historically been guarded about her status, experiencing it as a form of stigma during her high school years and early adulthood before DACA.[86] In addition to the professional benefits she gained with DACA that allowed her to pursue various positions in the health care field, she felt like receiving documents also allowed her to "feel like I can say something" and "defend myself" more. Like John, she started being more open about her status on Facebook, which led to her educating her coworkers about DACA, as described in the introduction. Over time, Rebeca started crafting more personal posts:

"I put pictures and everything to make it more real . . . like pictures of me graduating or certificates or awards that I have won. I want people to understand that there are so many young people going through this, and this is our life. This is where I am right now." Rebeca has been pleasantly surprised at the response she has received from her colleagues: "I actually get a lot of comments and private messages. Because people know more about it now, they can support it more too." While posting on Facebook is not inherently an act of resistance, if situated in the larger sociopolitical context, it can be read as an intentional political act.[87] In fact, online spaces can be particularly ripe sites for everyday activists to share personal stories that contribute to larger political debates while negotiating the delicate balance between being public and protecting privacy.[88]

Elena also became increasingly vocal about DACA at her workplace, a corporate information technology firm where she started immediately after graduating with majors in finance and information systems. Elena had participated in youth programming at the CBO where her older sister Pau was a youth leader as a teenager, though she noted, "not as much as [Pau]. She volunteers way more than I do. I was stuck with AP classes and involved in school, so I didn't have much time." Elena recalls being "very scared" about having to disclose her DACA status as she was onboarding with her firm: "You never really know people's political views on the matter." Right away, she recalled, "there was this big trip to India with all of the new analysts. And of course I can't travel outside of the U.S. That put me in a position . . . it sort of forced me to share my status with my managers. They pretty much had to restructure training to fit me." Despite her concerns, however, Elena ultimately felt supported:

> I specifically remember one of managers . . . I worked my first project with him right after training. He didn't know what DACA was at all . . . he didn't really know much about immigration or the immigration process at all. Or that they could get rid of DACA. He took it upon himself to learn about it. Whenever I would see him again, he'd be like, "Hey, like, I read this article," and "Hey, how are you feeling about this?" It was really good on from that point. Now I'm not scared to say hey, "I'm actually under DACA." Because if it's going to help out other people then I'm absolutely going to do it.

Elena was not the only participant who harbored these types of concerns as they launched their professional careers. Mae, for instance, was similarly concerned that she would not be able to visit with international clients, a typical duty in her position as a web producer in a corporate firm; however, like Elena she also found that her fears did not bear out in reality and that her workplace was accommodating.

During the next two years at her job, Elena became an asset to her firm beyond just her work performance, which was excellent, as she quickly received a major promotion. As she shared, "I've been involved in recruitment events and the training initiatives that we offer. If me being open about my status motivates any new analysts starting with the company in any way, then I'm going to go ahead and do it." Further, Elena noted, "From a diversity and inclusion perspective, it's been good to get involved. I want more diversity, and especially Latino representation. Because I'm probably one of the only ones in the entire D.C. office. The majority of the people in my office are white and males." Elena, then, has gone from being concerned about her employability to being an important player within her company for spreading awareness about immigration and diversifying the workforce in her firm. She sees herself staying "with the company for a very long time" in part because of the progress she has seen surrounding their support of justice issues: "They've been very vocal with the political climate. They posted something about Black Lives Matter, and even something about immigration."

Though Elena found being vocal about her status at work to be quite validating, other DACA recipients have embraced "quieter" forms of activism at work. Santiago had become involved in a youth development CBO when he was a teenager and was slated to serve as an AmeriCorps volunteer; as he recalled, "My mentor was the one who was like, 'You should apply for AmeriCorps. It would be a great opportunity, and you would get money for college.' So I applied and went through the whole process. We even called in and they were like, 'Yes, you have a Social Security, so you're good.' I got the interview and got the job. I had done the swear-in and everything and was already working. But then they were like, 'Once we put you in the system, there was a problem. We have to let you go.'" Fortunately, the CBO remained committed to Santiago and ultimately offered him a position as a case manager for a program focused on academic support, college preparation, and job readiness for local high school students, which he took on while simultaneously being a full-time student himself. A number of the program participants were undocumented youth, for whom he could serve as a role model and source of information. Knowing their specific constraints, he directed them to resources beyond the CBO. As he explained, "I'm part of a committee that gives scholarship to low-income youth. Since I received it, I became part of the alumni committee. This is one of the scholarships I try to refer a lot of my students to when I know they're undocumented since they accept students regardless of legal status. I'm putting my energies into that."

Angélica, who worked at a different branch of the same CBO when I first met her, also performed tasks that went above and beyond her specific work responsibilities as a case manager running after-school programming and interfacing with local school systems. Specifically, she became involved in helping youth fill out their initial DACA applications when they were still being accepted, which was not technically part of her job. As she said, "I have my application on my computer, just in case if I need to go back and see how I did it. And, it's very good, because I am able to help these kids." She prided herself on being able to "pick up on little clues" that her students might be undocumented (like making up excuses about why they delayed getting a driver's license) and might be able to benefit from DACA. As Angélica noted, she would frame it as, "'Are you by any chance struggling like I am?' Then I share my experience, and then that would get them to be like, '[Gasp]. Me too. I thought I was alone.'" Though she was deeply committed to providing this form of assistance, she did so outside of the scope of her day-to-day work responsibilities.

In fact, Angélica noted the dearth of legal services available through her organization: "We don't have a lot of immigration assistance even though we see a lot of clients and families that need it. One of the things I was able to push forward was getting accredited to be able to provide some legal assistance. I did the class and passed the test, and now I'm able to provide legal advice. I've been advocating more in that sense." Angélica's advocacy work is with mixed-status families like her own and is focused on improving the lives of all members regardless of their status. As she noted, "I was able to hold two different clinics for unaccompanied minors and another that was safety planning for families in case of deportation. That was completely new to [the organization]. That's been my method of activism." As I first noted in the introduction, she reflected that this "hands-on work" was ultimately more directly impactful than being one more person in a big rally.

Although most participants did not participate in conventional "methods" of activism throughout the first Trump era, it is clear that they were very much politically engaged through everyday activism as they went about their daily lives. College campuses and increasingly workplaces were particularly ripe spaces for this mode of activism, though participants also talked about places of worship and other spaces too. Although taking such action could potentially introduce new forms of vulnerability as DACA recipients come out to fellow students, coworkers, and parishioners, participants actually found the opposite to be true: their acts of public pedagogy made an impact in pushing these people and places to be more inclusive. For those who worked in service-oriented positions serving youth, sharing their status was an effective mechanism for providing support and mentorship to similarly positioned youth in ways that extended beyond their work roles. These smaller-scale actions also meshed well with the constraints ushered in by the pandemic, particularly given the health risks associated with attending large-scale public gatherings. Everyday activism also flourished in virtual space as people limited their face-to-face interactions with others to mitigate risk.

Conclusion

The undocumented youth movement is well-known for its overt acts of political resistance and highly coordinated mass mobilizations, including those staged at prominent locations of the federal government in Washington, D.C. Much less attention has been paid to how DACA recipients who are not activists and do not participate in these mass mobilization events engage politically, especially as they grapple with the fallout of their indeterminate legal situation. Previously, I demonstrated how DACA recipients negotiated exclusionary local immigration-focused policies by deploying navigational capital to gain access to targeted resources in the D.C. Metro region. In this chapter, I described additional mechanisms through which DACA recipients engage more directly in contesting immigrants' exclusion—through their public pedagogy and other actions they take in their daily lives to support immigrants. They have seized on opportunities to educate others about immigration and make a difference on a local scale, drawing from a different knowledge base and skill set. Indeed, DACA recipients are politically engaged on multiple fronts as they build confidence and exert control in their daily lives. Their actions demonstrate how political belonging is staked effectively in the realm of the everyday in ways that also serve to bolster the immigrant justice movement overall. The movement also benefits from DACA recipients' leveraging of their navigational capital and political commitments to help family and community members access local resources—including critical ones during the pandemic, which we turn to in the next chapter.

5

"I'm in a Good Position to Advocate Now"

Brokering Care in Service of Immigrant Well-Being and Justice

By the time she hit her mid-twenties, Camila was well established in her career and had begun thinking about buying a house. She received DACA soon after graduating high school and had been steadily employed since, building credit and saving money. When I first met her in 2016, Camila had just started a position as an education organizer with an immigrant rights nonprofit on a grant-funded program focused on promoting parental involvement in the Prince George's County public school system. Camila believed deeply in the program: "It helps parents be more active with their kids in school. We help them by giving them tools for reading report cards, interacting with teachers, things like that." She then took another position within the nonprofit as a youth organizer running a program with immigrant youth in Montgomery County, where they focused on campaigns like the extension of the Maryland DREAM Act. Camila reflected, "I feel proud of the work that I've been doing with them. It helps that I'm a DACA recipient. They see how I am when I'm action." Camila's positions built on both her nuanced place-based knowledge of local resources as well as her ability to effectively share this information with local immigrant families.

Camila continued to live with her family, playing a critical role in household maintenance as the oldest child with the most stable employment. Eventually, she noted, "We were living five people in a three-bedroom apartment and we pretty much outgrew it. It was very dense and very confined. I really wanted to give my family a bigger place to live." No one in her family had yet purchased a house, so Camila turned to her friends: "I had a few friends who were DACA recipients who had already bought their first homes. And I was like, 'If they can do it, I'm pretty sure I can do it. I have a good credit score. I have nothing to lose by trying.'" Camila's friend gave her the contact information of a real estate agent who knew how to work with clients with DACA. "I found [a house] that made me say, 'This is my house!' I feel it," Camila said. "I didn't hesitate, and we were able to get it." Camila's whole family moved to the house, which ended up being fortuitous when the pandemic hit. Camila got COVID early on and could actually isolate from her family members. "Imagine if we were all cramped in our small three-bedroom apartment with only one bathroom!" she exclaimed. Camila was pleased with her decision to buy in Montgomery County: "Now that I'm a homeowner, I know that a big chunk of the budget comes from their property taxes. So I'm pretty happy that if I'm paying this much money, it's going to people that really need it. I'm satisfied with the services and resources that Montgomery County offers even to residents who are undocumented."

Around when she bought her home, Camila started a new job at a nonprofit organization focused on preserving and expanding access to affordable housing and implementing neighborhood revitalization programs. Camila was becoming quite an expert on housing in the county. She explained that in addition to her normal work role, during the pandemic "I've turned into kind of like a social worker over the last year. We help our residents apply for rental assistance programs—state and local programs. We also created an organization that was intended to help those residents who have been struggling or impacted by COVID. Most of the residents I help belong to immigrant communities. I identify with them." Camila is able to help community residents quite effectively in her relatively well-resourced county. In her de facto social worker role, she also benefits from exchanging resources that fall outside of the scope of housing with her sister, Lucy, who works at a community health clinic (CHC) in the county serving a similar demographic. Camila's nonprofit also expanded its services, including hosting pop-up vaccine clinics at different properties. As she said, "The clinics are definitely serving the people that need it the most. Being at these clinics makes me feel a sense of fulfillment, that I'm doing what I'm supposed to be doing." Yet Camila's work also became quite heavy during the pandemic; as she recalled, "I did have a moment where I broke down. The calls I was receiving . . . just to hear their stories . . . how they're struggling and the lack of access they have to certain resources. It was heartbreaking. I just didn't have the ways to help them."

Camila's professional trajectory clearly demonstrates the benefit of work authorization for DACA recipients.[1] She received DACA with ideal timing as she graduated high school and entered the professional workforce, quickly establishing herself in the nonprofit sector in different service-oriented positions focused on immigrant advocacy. Camila has achieved professional success and, just as importantly, fulfillment, as she has settled into her career as an advocate and flexed her skill sets with new opportunities. She has also built solid credit, saved money, and embarked on homeownership, all important benefits of DACA in bolstering recipients' incorporation pathways. Her family has also become more established, underscoring that protected legal status can benefit not only DACA recipients but also members of their mixed-status families.[2]

Over the past decade, Camila has also cultivated and deployed navigational capital in facilitating fellow immigrants' access to education, youth development, and housing resources by sharing the workarounds she has honed. As we have seen, this nuanced place-based navigational capital is rooted in specific socio-legal contexts—Prince George's and Montgomery Counties, in Camila's case. Indeed, leveraging navigational capital is central to her work as a nonprofit advocate. Navigational capital has typically centered on educational settings with college-aged populations.[3] Yet less clear is how young adults deploy navigational capital in their adult lives as they embark upon professional careers and facilitate immigrants' access to other sectors like housing. Many DACA recipients have entered service-oriented careers and been lauded for filling labor shortages in fields like education, social services, and health care that have been particularly impacted by the pandemic.[4] DACA recipients in these positions serve as professional brokers who address structural inequalities and facilitate immigrants' access to social institutions.[5] However, Camila's commentary also reveals the challenges inherent in this work as they regularly confront limitations in how much they can actually do if immigrants are prohibited from accessing social resources or if such resources simply do not exist.

Camila's experiences in purchasing a home also illuminate how, into adulthood, navigational capital emanates from social networks outside of institutional spaces. Even DACA recipients who do not serve as professional brokers in service-oriented careers also harness navigational capital to benefit their families and communities by taking advantage of their economic stability and relatively more secure statuses. Anthropologists have examined such acts through the lens of care, encapsulating a dynamic process of circulation mobilizing different social actors, relations, and community resources.[6] Indeed, care is often undergirded by moral sentiments and deep commitments to others,[7] as Camila's commentary reveals. Care practices like Camila's are frequently performed in the context of mundane life.[8]

This chapter describes various configurations of care within which DACA recipients are embedded. It argues that DACA recipients deploy their nuanced placed-based navigational capital to broker care for more economically, socially, and legally precarious family and community members as they seek to promote immigrants' access to resources, security and stability, and overall well-being. These practices bridge conventional distinctions between public and private caregiving, care paid and given, and intimate and institutional care work.[9] Their reflections on their care practices also underscore that DACA recipients envision them as political acts meant to promote immigrant well-being and social justice. This frame is shared and deployed by those like Camila who are well versed in immigrant rights discourse stemming from their involvement in immigrant rights advocacy, but also notably by others who are not engaged in public activism but nonetheless view their everyday care practices as contributing to the larger immigrant justice project.

Performing Brokerage, Leveraging Navigational Capital, and Engaging in Care Practices

This chapter builds on and complexifies the concept of brokerage, a mechanism through which intermediaries facilitate immigrants' access to social institutions,[10] by linking it synergistically to navigational capital and care. Human development and education scholars have demonstrated how minor children in immigrant families frequently play crucial brokerage roles in facilitating their families' incorporation into U.S. society.[11] Children often start brokering by translating and interpreting for family members,[12] though they also convey information about U.S. social and cultural norms that they gain by attending school.[13] For many, performing this work is a normal, everyday activity that they may not consciously realize they are even doing.[14] As intermediaries between their families and local institutions, children's brokering work facilities families' access to education, employment, housing/residential spaces, financial services, and health care.[15] Teachers, social workers, doctors, and others in underresourced institutional settings also depend heavily on these children's contributions, often out of sheer necessity.[16] Indeed, children's brokering work is of critical political importance for bridging major structural exclusions experienced by marginalized immigrant communities.[17]

Through brokering, children in immigrant families cultivate and assert their burgeoning navigational capital.[18] While the concept of navigational capital originated in educational settings to examine how students of color persist and achieve,[19] Yosso observed in her original formulation of the concept that these navigational skills extend into other realms such as the labor market, judicial system, and health care system.[20] Scholars have started describing health-related navigational capital as immigrants negotiate constrained access to health care and forge alternative health care spaces like community clinics and flea markets[21] and organize to advocate for their health and well-being.[22] Exclusionary immigration policies also necessitate legal brokerage since young adults with more protected legal statuses are better able to access and share legal resources with more legally precarious family members.[23] In these roles, they explain details of new policies, assist in navigating the immigration bureaucracy, assess risk in applying for services, and help buffer the effects of immigration enforcement.[24] Young adults' contributions to their family stem not merely from their greater familiarity with U.S. society but from their enhanced legal security, which enables them to more safely navigate spaces that represent greater risk, underscoring the place-specific nature of navigational capital.

Much of the aforementioned brokering work would be classified as *informal*—which is to say, performed by nonprofessionals as unremunerated labor. Another distinct literature on brokering captures the more *formal* professional roles that immigrant, children of immigrant, and coethnic employees play in addressing social inequalities in school-based[25] and health and social service settings.[26] Such positions are particularly prevalent in CHCs in the health care safety net and are known by a range of labels including *promotoras de salud* / health promoters, lay health educators, patient navigators, and community health workers (CHWs). CHWs are prized for their linguistic and interpersonal skills, knowledge base (including about the community), trust with and respect for patients, education and capacity-building proficiencies, and outreach and advocacy skills.[27] Brokers in CHCs often "buffer" their clients from the impact of the complexities of system changes stemming from health care reform and exclusionary policies.[28] These providers creatively bend rules and go above and beyond for their patients in underresourced settings.[29] Brokers flex to meet community needs and often perform work that extends far beyond their envisioned roles and scope of care.[30] Despite their demonstrated value, scholars also note the challenges inherent in professional brokering, stemming from the fragility of their employment and the lack of appropriate remuneration for the services they provide and emotional labor they invest.[31]

Sociologist Laura López-Sanders cautions against seeing only how brokers enable access in an affirmative light, noting that the dual nature of brokerage is such that their actions may also serve to hinder immigrants' access.[32] She describes the ways in which brokers bridge access gaps for undocumented immigrants by connecting them to services, coaching them, and dispelling rumors or incomplete information; however, she also highlights how their actions can simultaneously hinder access as they scrutinize cases and perform bureaucratic filtering resulting in patient dissatisfaction and distrust.[33] Brokerage has also been destabilized and diminished through increased formalization and scrutiny with health care reform,[34] underscoring that brokers are ultimately quite constrained as they negotiate deeply entrenched structural inequalities in the health care system. Scholars have also found that brokers experience a tension in serving as an extension of the state and its formal institutions when they perceive themselves instead as agents of change in empowering local communities.[35]

Despite the phenomenon of brokerage being well articulated in both literatures, less attention has been paid to the ethic of care that undergirds brokers' work, whether they are formally embedded in service bureaucracies or not.[36] Care emerged as a vast field of inquiry in the social sciences in the 1980s as a critical frame for making sense of neoliberalization and emergent global and gendered inequalities and the precarity they produce.[37] Care is seen as a mechanism for addressing persistent forms of exclusion and domination produced by dominant liberal forms of care like welfare and humanitarianism, which are particularly pronounced for noncitizens.[38] Care is often envisioned as a positive activity that compensates for the limits of other ideologies like freedom, choice, rights, and citizenship.[39] As anthropologist Tatjana Thelen points out, care is often deployed "to argue for a seemingly more inclusive or impartial ethic of care."[40] Scholars recognize that caregiving is fundamentally a moral endeavor or imperative,[41] often situated within a larger moral economy.[42]

A feminist approach to care underscores that it is a dynamic process of circulation that mobilizes different social actors, relations, and community resources[43] and often operates outside of the direct purview and funding of the state and its institutions within families and communities that vary considerably in the way they distribute care.[44] Care is understood to be fundamentally relational[45] and rooted in communal ties and intersubjective experience.[46] Scholars have pointed out that care work is frequently shouldered by females and devalued given that they often receive little to no fiscal compensation or recognition for it.[47] Care roles also shift across gendered life course phases including childhood, young adulthood, adulthood, and elderhood.[48] Indeed, care also connects people within and across generations.[49] Many immigrants are embedded within global care chains in which women migrate to participate in wage labor, with ripple effects within families and multigenerational households back in their countries of origin.[50] In the United States, children in immigrant families perform care work for older generations as "active participants in the circulation of care processes within community networks."[51]

Thelen cautions that a more critical anthropology of care "needs to denaturalize it and pay attention to its transformative potential as well as its downsides,"[52] underscoring that care can produce differential access to care and thereby marginalization. Care work is often embedded in power asymmetries and is ripe for exploitation and co-optation.[53] Care can be directly entangled with state violence, emergent inequalities, and exclusion and dispossession[54] and be used to compensate for institutional neglect and to coerce people into new forms of surveillance and unpaid labor.[55] Thus it is worth noting, as Indigenous studies scholar Hiʻilei Julia Kawehipuaakahaopulani Hobart and gender studies scholar Tamara Kneese urge, "who is uncared for, who receives care and who does not, and who is expected to perform care work, with or without pay."[56] Scholars speak of the "tensions and frictions"[57] as well as the "ambivalence and contradictions"[58] inherent in care work. Care work can also unwittingly and perniciously reproduce social conceptions of legitimacy and deservingness, positioning some groups against others in determining who is worthy of care.[59]

Yet Black, Latinx/Chicanx, and Indigenous feminists have long contended that care is often fundamental to the pursuit of social justice and collective social movements.[60] Care often serves as the basis for solidarity and advocacy,[61] as an alternative to moral sentiments like charity, sympathy, or pity.[62] Instead, as gender studies scholar Aisha Finch notes, care amplifies the value and worth of those who are deemed to be marginalized or less valuable.[63] Hobart and Kneese argue that care "is a vital but underexamined praxis of radical politics that provides spaces of hope in dark times."[64] Anthropologist Miriam Ticktin articulates the power of care as having "revolutionary, transformative potential."[65]

While care is frequently embedded within collective social action in more exceptional moments, it is also a part of the fabric of everyday and mundane life.[66] Anthropologist Cati Coe, for instance, argues that political belonging can be forged through care work and "claimed and denied in multiple contexts that do not, at first glance, appear political." She describes how African immigrant home care workers stake belonging in the United States through their care of the U.S.-born elder population.[67] Care work can be a particularly impactful mechanism for those who lack formal citizenship rights,[68] serving to generate membership in multiple social formations, including the nation but also humanity at large.[69]

Care is also necessarily responsive to political exigencies; as Ticktin points out, "There are new forms of need resulting from austerity and anti-immigration policies, ultra-right-wing forms of abandonment, and, most recently the world-changing COVID-19 pandemic and the deep racial stratification and violence it has revealed."[70] Anthropologist Carolina Nvé Díaz San Francisco likewise acknowledges that the pandemic increased the burden of care multidimensionally, amplified by "COVID-19 stressors of racism, social determinants of health, language limitations, migration status, isolation, poverty, and underlying conditions."[71]

Yet amid these profound challenges and constraints, people have culti-vated creative and novel care arrangements in their daily lives.[72] DACA recipients have been at the center of these care configurations as particu-larly apt advocates for immigrant well-being and justice.

DACA Recipients' Brokering Work and Everyday Care Practices

Indeed, the benefit of my longitudinal design is that I have been able to observe participants' evolving care practices, including during the pan-demic, when the need for such acts was amplified. I have found that DACA recipients have become quite adept at identifying local resources and deploying nuanced place-based navigational capital to broker care for more precarious family and community members. Three sets of care practices are presented below—facilitating access to services, leveraging economic security, and advocating for community well-being—grounded in a deeper examination of participants' experiences over the past decade since many first received DACA and entered the job market as work-authorized young adults.

"I Love Looking for . . . and Sharing Resources": Care as Facilitating Access to Services

Into their twenties, my research participants' lives changed as they planned their future careers and came to specialize in different posi-tions and fields. For many participants, their career paths ended up being quite circuitous as they discovered a range of fields (for example, forensics, international development, and cybersecurity) in which they were unfortunately unable to work even with their DACA work authori-zation, as lawful permanent residency or citizenship was often required. Nearly half of the participants (fourteen; 47 percent), though, ended up working in health care (nine; 30 percent) and social services (five; 17 percent) in line with their career aspirations, but also in positions that were also ultimately beneficial to family and community members.

One such participant was Angélica, whose first job in the formal economy was as a social worker in a youth development nonprofit. Since DACA did not exist until she was twenty-one, Angélica spent three years after high school taking community college classes one at a time in Montgomery County while working under the table at an automotive glass company and in a medical office. After she transferred to a four-year university and declared her major as psychology, Angélica completed an unpaid internship at the nonprofit that eventually led to her being offered a full-time position. She immediately quit her other jobs, recounting, "I was like, 'Okay, I have a social [security number] now, I can do something better.' I was so relieved." Over the next few years, Angélica's career at the nonprofit flourished and she gained more and more knowledge about the resources available to immigrant youth and their families in Prince George's and Montgomery Counties and in D.C., as the nonprofit, which had multiple offices in the region, served all of those catchment areas.

Simultaneously, Angélica took on more and more responsibility at home as the oldest sibling. Her parents separated when she was in high school, and the oldest three siblings lived with their dad in Maryland. As she noted, "From the moment I finished high school, I started contributing at home. I needed to buy food and help my dad, especially because there were two other kids at home that needed to be taken care of. I just didn't have the luxury to spend more money on school." Indeed, oldest siblings like Angélica often take on increased responsibilities at home from an early age, particularly if they possess more secure legal statuses.[73] During the next few years, Angélica's position at the nonprofit was also the most stable in the household, as her father, who was undocumented, moved from job to job.

None of Angélica's family had health insurance when she was growing up, and they sought care only irregularly, largely at nearby CHCs. Angélica's younger brother, Luis, had several chronic conditions that needed regular attention, though they ended up going to different clinics depending on where they were living. Over time, Angélica accumulated knowledge about multiple CHCs in the region. Angélica had a health situation that resulted in a major bill that interfered with her ability to pay tuition, and her father had an accident that caused them to wrestle with how medically necessary it was that he seek care given the potential cost, ultimately deciding that he needed medical attention. Through these experiences, Angélica learned about how to best access different health-related resources. She noted that even when her work positions were focused on youth development or educational access, she provided a range of different services to her clients, including health referrals. She generously shared this place-based navigational capital with her family and friends as well as members of our CAB who did not have insurance or established access to care. For instance, during a CAB meeting in January 2019, she provided another CAB member with personal contact information for someone she knew could help her friend in getting an appointment sooner at a CHC that was notorious for its long waits.

Angélica continued to get promoted, moving into management, first at the same youth development nonprofit and then in a large public school system in Prince George's County as a resource advocate. In addition to her caseload at work, she observed that she also "case-managed" her dad: "I always joke around, with one of my coworkers who I talk to a lot, that it feels like I'm case-managing my dad. I'm doing finances with him and am like, 'No, this is how you save money,' or 'Look, this is why this job is not good for you. You need to leave that other job and switch to something more stable.'" She continued, "I got him an appointment at the doctor's so he could start getting annual checkups because I tell him, 'You're not getting any younger.'" Along with her younger sister, Nayeli, Angélica also "case managed" their younger brother Luis's mental health crisis in 2017 by directing their collective financial resources to purchase health insurance for him, helping him figure out where to seek care, and paying for the significant expenses incurred for his treatment over time.

Angélica's brokering skills were beneficial for her clients, but also clearly for her friends and family members. Yet by the time she was twenty-eight in 2018, Angélica exclaimed, "I'm tired. I tell my sister, 'I shouldn't be this tired at the age that I am. I'm exhausted!'" After Nayeli graduated with a degree in business and immediately landed a corporate job in human resources management, Angélica sat her down and told her, "'I need you to step up and take a little at home too.' She was able to pick up a lot . . . now the load is shared between the two of us. I've honestly been taking a little step back . . . for my own mental health." The weight of performing so much care work over time clearly took its toll on Angélica. During the initial period of the pandemic, much of Angélica's work was remote, though she also did "hands-on" work making educational supply kits for children in their program and doing weekly food distributions. She was, however, able to spend more time at home: "I'm actually enjoying being at home. I was moving so much for so long that I kind of enjoyed staying put. I've been drawing more, which is something that has been nice to get back. I've been reading more. I feel like I'm reverting back to who I used to be, if that makes sense." It is clear from Angélica's commentary that the weight of performing such intensive brokering can take a cumulative toll, serving to undermine her own well-being even as she works toward improving the well-being of others.

Like Angélica, Annisa's care practices as a self-proclaimed "resource person" also blur boundaries between personal and professional, as well as self, family, and community. As previously noted, Annisa grew up in a tight-knit Indonesian community in Montgomery County (through which she found out about DACA) and received DACA during her junior year of high school. Even after she received DACA, though, Annisa reported that she had struggled with "the mental toll" of uncertainty about her temporary status and "deportation anxiety" given that her parents had no form of legal protection. Luckily, Annisa had regular access to care through Montgomery County's Care for Kids Program when she was a child. However, when these mental health challenges resurfaced after her coverage ended at age nineteen, it was harder for her to access care. Once again through their social network, her family discovered a Muslim-run CHC where, as she noted, "you don't need papers. You just have to be from the area, from the state of Maryland." This resource was critical for her family, as Annisa's mother "had lots of medical problems and was hospitalized a lot. That was when we were deep in debt because of all we had to pay." These medical problems and associated expenses weighed heavily on Annisa as she started at community college and her mother got diagnosed with a rare form of cancer. Her family once again leaned on the Indonesian community for information about resources; as she noted, "We found financial assistance through nongovernmental programs. So we found out about it word of mouth. There's a lot of people in our community that help each other out." By Annisa's second year of community college, her mother's health improved and she was able to focus more on her studies.

Annisa declared psychology as a major when she transferred to a four-year university, realizing that her career prospects were likely better in that field than in her other passion, art. Around that time, Annisa recalled, "I went to this Islamic convention and a lot of the speakers were psychologists. They knew how to speak to people, and were really in touch with their feelings and knowing about people. I admired that. And I also kind of liked staying in touch with my faith, too." At the university, Annisa took a counseling psychology class that also shaped her path. "At first I'd get so nervous because I wouldn't know what to say," she noted. "But we learned the different techniques and applied them. I loved doing that . . . and just love having contact with people and hearing their stories." During college, Annisa obtained an extremely limited health insurance plan for the express purpose of fulfilling the school's health insurance requirement; she knew that actually finding a provider through the plan would be challenging and cost prohibitive. In the absence of formal care, Annisa found her support system on campus through the Muslim student group and chaplain. She also benefitted from interfacing with other DACA recipients on campus, which she had not done as much previously. As she explained, "It's just nicer when you're around people who are in your same status. They understand what you've been through and they can help you too with the resources and how to work around them. Knowing the workarounds has really helped."

Annisa graduated in 2017, but found herself in "a dazed and confused state. I was like, 'What do I do now?' It was really intense." In addition to normal postgraduation stressors, Annisa was contending with the DACA recission announcement and its implications for her future. She lamented that even though she had graduated, "my resources are [on campus]. Campus is my go-to place just to talk about or find other people in this situation." Annisa continued to go to campus regularly to see the Muslim chaplain and hang out with friends who had not yet graduated, which she was able to do since one of her part-time jobs was on campus as a research assistant for a project on reading comprehension among English language learners. She even started participating in the campus programming for undocumented students. Her other position during that time was off campus as an early intervention therapist for children with autism, which required that she travel throughout the region.

When I caught up with Annisa in 2020, her life had changed considerably. She had met her eventual husband at an Indonesian Muslim convention and relocated to Virginia, where her husband's family lived, once she had gotten married—despite the negative perception of the state that she previously held. Though it was initially "really hard" being forty-five minutes away from her family and community, Annisa found a wonderful job opportunity that served to ground her locally: as a mental health technician in the area's major health care system. She shared, "I was excited to start because I'm working in more of what I want to do. Sometimes I work in the hospital and sometimes I work in the outpatient building. I've learned so much about the county and its resources." Indeed, Annisa's job was structured around her ability to find and share the workarounds, a skill that she had been honing as a young person navigating constrained access to resources in both university and community settings. By phase III, it was clear that she took particular pride in sharing her knowledge: "I'm definitely a resource person. I love looking for resources and I love sharing resources. Essentially, if I had a good experience with that resource, I give it back to whoever needs it." In this reflection, Annisa is referring not only to her clients but also to anyone within her social network who might benefit, demonstrating the expansiveness of her brokering and the lack of boundary between the professional and personal. As she began her position in early 2020, Annisa also benefitted from having comprehensive health care coverage—which was critical when she got COVID very early on in the pandemic in March 2020 and required emergency care. As she noted, "I feel so privileged to be where I am with insurance and a job that pays well." When she became a long COVID patient, her coworkers shared their banked paid time off with her, allowing her to recover for longer, and her insurance enabled her to access a behavioral coach who helped her manage her COVID-related anxiety.

While she was in a good position, Annisa simultaneously felt "heartbroken" about the challenges the rest of her family continued to face during the pandemic. Despite living further away in Virginia, Annisa contributed to her family materially "with the money I have saved up in case of emergencies." She also exerted the navigational capital she had accumulated over the years (in personal and professional capacities) as a resource finder, focusing a lot of her energies on her younger sister, who is also a DACA recipient: "She and I went through the same things, so I'm there so she doesn't feel so alone." Annisa connected her sister to her previous contacts on campus (where her sister had subsequently enrolled) and then set to the task of trying to find a therapist who would see her sister despite being uninsured. As another complicating layer,

Annisa noted that their mother really wanted her sister to have a Muslim therapist. So Annisa made a list of all the Muslim therapists in the region she was able to find and "told her to email each one of them to ask, 'Do you do a sliding scale for no insurance?' She sent a bunch of emails and finally found one that was able to take her." The therapist was reasonably affordable, and her sister's mental health improved from her therapy sessions.

For more than a decade, Angélica and Annisa have been building local knowledge about resources throughout the D.C. Metro region. This knowledge initially stemmed from their and family members' challenges in trying to access resources without status, and then with their temporary DACA status (which notably did not improve either woman's access to care initially). They understood the implications of these exclusions intimately, having dealt with expensive bills stemming from accidents and health crises that impacted their families' economic stability. Angélica and Annisa's experiences underscore how place-based navigational capital is often collective knowledge that permeates social networks. Since their arrival, Annisa's family leaned into their social network as a resource to find legal, health, and other resources—a network that Annisa now contributes to as well. As they have gotten deeper into their careers, both women spend considerable time in their daily lives deploying navigational capital not only as skilled professionals but as care practices that permeate their social networks. Angélica joked about "case managing" her clients and her father simultaneously, while Annisa discovered resources not only for clients but also for family and community members. Both women are thriving in their careers as professional brokers; they have gotten promotions and switched to more rewarding positions (in both material and social terms) that value their knowledge and expertise. Yet is also clear from Annisa's concerns about her family's continued vulnerability and Angélica's commentary on the cumulative weight of performing such intensive care work that it is challenging to sustain over time and necessitates prioritizing self-care as well.

"The House Is in My Name, but We All Live Here": Care as Leveraging Economic Security

While Angélica and Annisa honed their navigational capital as professional brokers, many of those who did not work in service-oriented fields were also deeply engaged in care work. In fact, those who worked in more financially lucrative positions in corporate settings often leveraged their economic security for the benefit of their families as acts of care. One of most notable trends during phase III was how many participants had purchased homes as they became more deeply immersed in their adult lives; seven participants (29 percent) had successfully purchased homes, and additional participants also aspired to but had encountered barriers in accessing loans or just were not quite ready yet. Participants indicated that homeownership was a particularly "proud moment" (as Beto phrased it) and tied homeownership to their broader sense of belonging, asserting sentiments along the lines of Laura, who said, "Buying a house is what I think about when I think about being American. That's how I've envisioned my American dream." Most notable in their discussion of homeownership, however, was the fact that participants often described pursuing it for the benefit of their family and as a means of ensuring household security—which proved to be critical for some families during the pandemic.

Jenny was one such participant, who took on increasing responsibility within her extended family members' care configuration as she moved deeper into her career. Jenny migrated to Maryland from El Salvador when she was seven and immediately became part of an extended household consisting of her parents and brother, and two different aunts and their spouses and children. As Jenny noted, "We all lived together. That's how they were able to sustain us financially. Because sometimes, at some point, someone lost their job, and then the other family would take over and help pay for rent." When they were young, Jenny's mother took care of Jenny, her brother, and her cousins while her father, uncle, and aunt worked to support the family.

Like for Camila, DACA arrived with perfect timing for Jenny—she had just graduated from high school and was about to begin community college. Jenny worked on her associate's degree in biotechnology for four years while also working to pay for school. Her interest in biology was not all that surprising, given that her father had worked in El Salvador as a biologist and her mother as a dentist, though they had migrated because they did not make enough money to live there. While she was pursuing her associate's degree, Jenny saw a flyer for a research internship: "Luckily, it was only for community college students, so I was able to get it. I started out as an intern for that program, which was for one whole year, and then afterwards, I asked my mentor if I could stay and he said yeah. So I've been working and going to school part-time."

Eventually, the balancing act became difficult given the distance between the lab and her college. Jenny had also started a job at a drug store and eventually became a pharmacy technician, reasoning, "I was considering going to pharmacy school in the future. So I was like, 'I'm going to explore pharmacy to see if I like it.'" Jenny transferred to a state university, which she chose because of its statewide reputation as a research-oriented school and the potential to work in a research lab. As she approached her last semester as a biology major, Jenny very begrudgingly had to take a semester off to save money, as we learned during our second interview. She lamented, "It's pretty stressful because I didn't want to stop going to school because I was so close. I'm almost done." Jenny ultimately decided not to pursue pharmacy school in part because of the uncertain future of DACA; as she shared, "I needed a career that had a shorter [training period]. After I graduate, I need stability." After she graduated in December 2018, Jenny started at a nonprofit laboratory, where she stayed for a year before taking a position in the biotechnology industry so that she could "push herself more" and earn a higher salary. With this greater economic security, she bought a house even farther away from the Montgomery County community where she had lived since she arrived in the United States in Frederick County, and in early 2020 she moved the whole extended family there. As she noted, "In my family situation, we all go together. The house is in my name, but we all live here. It's everybody's house."

Unfortunately, Jenny's mother was diagnosed with breast cancer in 2020; as Jenny recalled, "It was really hard to deal with at the beginning, with her diagnosis and then COVID all going on at once." Luckily, Jenny's mom, whom she had previously characterized as a "super resource" in her first interview, discovered a program that paid for her treatment at a hospital some forty-five minutes away from their house without traffic, since their family had moved to the outer suburbs. Jenny's family strategized about how they could ensure household economic stability while also caring for her mother. The arrangement they developed was that "my aunt stopped working to become my mom's care worker. My aunt used to work like twelve-hour shifts every day. My responsibility was to keep the income coming in to pay for the mortgage and [expenses]." Jenny's contribution was particularly important given that her father lost many hours of work as a mechanic and the whole household got COVID early on, compromising their ability to work. Her younger brother and cousins—who worked in the financially lucrative electrical engineering and computer science fields—also started "helping with the bills. It's a community of everybody around here. Emotionally, too, we all have to take care of each other . . . we help each other out."

Though she was not a direct caregiver, either at work or at home, Jenny played a critical role in her extended household's care configuration as she settled into her professional career. Ever since she had arrived in the United States, Jenny's family collectively strategized about the distribution of productive and reproductive labor in the household. While her mother was the primary caregiver and the other adults worked when she was younger, as the younger family members matured, pursued schooling and then careers, they assumed responsibility for the economic security and well-being of the family, underscoring that care relationships shift across the life course and in response to evolving family needs.[74] As with Angélica and Annisa, Jenny was the eldest sibling/cousin and modeled an ethic of care and familial investment for her younger siblings and cousins, who began sharing in care responsibilities.

Elena similarly leveraged her professional success and economic stability to promote her extended family's well-being. As previously discussed, Elena's path to her bachelor's degree was also well paved thanks to her middle sister, Pau, who had discovered and received a scholarship to help pay for college. Elena went to one of the participating community colleges first and purposefully selected business as a major, as she knew that would situate her favorably for being admitted to the program. In fact, she noted that she had shifted in her career aspirations a few times as she realized certain fields, like criminology and forensics, would not be an option for her without lawful permanent residency. She worked at a local office of a major insurance company for a few years while she attended community college and university and was poised to participate in a training program that would have enabled her to open her own agency down the line. However, as she recalled, "We didn't find out until after starting the process that you have to be a [lawful permanent] resident to do it, which was a real downer. That ended my plan of advancing within the company." She ultimately redirected to finance and information systems as her majors, hoping that she would not encounter the same obstacles in those fields.

As we saw earlier, Elena began focusing on building economic security as soon as she received DACA. She worked full-time for the insurance company throughout her community college and university years. By the time she graduated in May 2019, she immediately found a job in a corporate information technology firm, having completed internships and done extensive research about postgraduation employment options. She already had considerable savings and had built solid credit, which she was conscious about doing for her own sake but also with an eye toward her family. As she became established in her position as a financial specialist for an information technology firm, Elena helped both her uncle, who was undocumented, and older sister, also a DACA recipient, purchase homes in Prince George's County. Her family members had quite a bit of collective experience with real estate, though she played a key role in their planning as one of the most economically and legally secure members of the extended family. Although Elena was quite eager to purchase her own home, she prioritized helping her family members first. As she noted, "When my dad asked, 'Hey, you can you do this for your uncle?' my reactions was like 'Sure, I'll do it for my family.' If my work and my success can help other people, then I'm always down to help." Yet as she noted, it was "a lot of pressure" and she did not completely think through the implications for subsequently purchasing her own house. Yet by September 2022 Elena had saved up money by living in the house she cosigned for with her sister and was able to purchase her own home too.

Pau also became more deeply immersed in the local real estate market after she graduated with a bachelor's degree in economics. Like Elena, Pau had worked in the insurance industry for many years as a full-time employee as she worked her way through college. Pau had also participated actively in immigrant rights organizing when she was in high school (see chapter 4) and carried forward this activist orientation during her college years when (at age nineteen) she started a 501(c)(3) nonprofit organization, "applying what I learned in school" to provide scholarships to undocumented students. Pau was also able to fundraise through her church, where a lot of community-oriented professionals attended, and also "built partnerships with small businesses that are pro-immigrant." She also completed an internship with a community development corporation in Prince George's County. After graduating in December 2018, Pau held a few different positions before deciding to be a real estate agent based in Prince George's County, where she had lived since she came to the United States. Although not a homeowner at that point, Pau was well acquainted with homeownership by proxy as she learned from her dad, sisters, and extended family members. She prides herself on facilitating homeownership in the Latinx community and being able to offer bilingual services to clients.

Yet Pau's interest is not merely on homeownership but on advancing household security broadly. As the pandemic introduced new forms of household precarity for the local Latinx community, Pau was appalled that immigrants were excluded from the Coronavirus Aid, Relief, and Economic Security (CARES) Act in 2020. Though several local nonprofits mobilized and started distributing resources, Pau grew concerned that the most vulnerable immigrants were still being left out of these organizational efforts given the high demand for services and limited resources. So she and three of her friends created a crowdfunding campaign for emergency funds for immigrants. When the first coronavirus economic impact payments went out, their campaign—which they blasted on social media—urged people to donate some of their payment if their employment had not been disrupted. Just as with the local organizations, they quickly realized that demand far outpaced what they had been able to raise.

With the benefit of work authorization, Jenny and Elena were able to start establishing credit and saving money early on. Both women hit a few roadblocks as they contemplated their future careers as DACA recipients, though they ultimately figured out viable and satisfying careers and established themselves professionally fairly quickly. Even as they achieved professional success, both Jenny and Elena remained focused on their extended families and engaged in care practices oriented toward promoting their collective economic security. Jenny purchased a home for her extended household and looped in her brother and cousins in the care configuration to contribute so that her aunt could stop working to focus on taking care of her ill mother. Elena was able to leverage her economic security and place-based navigational capital to help her sister and uncle purchase homes. Meanwhile, Elena's sister Pau applied herself to promoting immigrant families' household stability as she specialized in working with the Latinx community and providing bilingual real estate services; yet Pau's care work also extended beyond her clients as she focused on the household security of immigrant community members impacted by the pandemic, organizing a crowdfunding campaign to ensure that the money raised went directly to the most needy. During the pandemic, DACA recipients like Pau have proven to be particularly apt "creative problem solvers of new possibilities"[75] as they strategize novel ways to ensure that community members' urgent needs are being met. Pau's care work in both of these realms was in service of immigrant justice: a frame that she learned in her teenage years when she became acquainted with immigrant rights activism and I saw being evoked more and more as participants discussed how their care practices articulated with the broader immigrant justice movement.

"I've Become Much More Vocal": Care as Advocating for Community Well-Being

Like Pau, Beto was engaged in multiple types of care work that he saw as being interconnected and performed in service of the community. Beto became interested in biology in high school and originally wanted to go to medical school. "I wanted to help people and I thought that was the way to do it," he recalled, "but now I'm like, 'There's a different way you can help people.'" One outlet for helping people he pursued was volunteering at a fire station in Montgomery County, which he started doing in high school: "If it wasn't for DACA I would never have been able to volunteer there. They required a Social Security number." Beto subsequently took classes to become an emergency medical technician (EMT) so he could expand his role at the fire station. Around the same time, Beto also registered as a "healthy volunteer" at the National Institutes of Health, participating in around six clinical research studies.

Beto graduated with a bachelor's degree in biology in 2018 and began working at a research lab sequencing proteins within cells as an intern while also working part-time at a homeless men's shelter as a supervisor. Though these were very different work roles, Beto saw them as informing each other: "What I'm doing now is very community-driven. When I come to work at the lab, I think about my research going into helping find some sort of biomarker, or cure. Then I go to the shelter and see clients coming in where they're basically at the lowest point in their life. Then we turn it around and just help them out to get on their feet again." In addition, Beto continued to volunteer as an EMT once a week, growing his skills by taking additional firefighter courses and becoming certified in rescue tech so that he could participate in search and rescue missions and vehicle extrications. Beto also spent considerable time engaged in care practices within his family: "My mom's health has been really bad in the last few years. She was in the hospital for a while like a year and a half ago . . . it's a blessing she's back with us. But she's not really mobile, so it's hard to take care of my little brother. So I drive her around and help."

In 2021 when I caught up with him, Beto had worked in several research laboratory positions throughout the D.C. Metro region since, as he shared, "the pandemic made biotech boom. There's lots of money being thrown into science. It was the middle of the pandemic and I had recruiters telling me, 'Go for this job,' or 'You have great experience, go to that job.'" Like Camila and Jenny, he leveraged his economic security to buy a house: "My family encouraged me to get my foot in the door. I was very fortunate. I wanted something where I'll be able to continue providing for my family." During the early pandemic, Beto cut back on his volunteer hours at the fire station as he tried to minimize his potential for exposure given his mother's health problems. His father was an essential worker in water, sewage, and construction, "so there were no breaks for him. They just told him to wear a mask and try your best not to catch anything." Luckily, his mother managed to avoid getting COVID and being hospitalized.

Around this time, Beto also had to renew his DACA status. During a previous renewal, he had actually lost his position as a medical scribe when he went out of status due to processing delays, though he acknowledged that this was when he redirected to completing his fire training, which he was glad to have done. In March 2021, however, he noted that his DACA renewal experience was probably "the complete opposite of all the other stories you heard," referencing widespread social media commentary on COVID-related delays in the renewal process that left many others' employment endangered. While he submitted his application only a month in advance, Beto's approval moved quickly:

> I can't give you anything concrete, but I think the reason that it went faster was the sheet you fill out—I think it's worksheet 765—where they ask what your reason is for pursuing a work permit. So I let them know my story: that it's critical for me to have the opportunity to keep working doing research on COVID in the middle of the pandemic, I need to continue volunteering at the fire station because there's so many patients with troubles. So I let them know that when you give me a renewal, you're extending these actions that are very important. I think that's what gives them the push to be like, "Okay, we need to process this faster." I think that might have done it.

Beto provided care as a family member and volunteer fire worker during the pandemic, but his vision of what "actions" he performed in service of the community went beyond more conventional notions of care. Specifically, he envisioned his lab-based research as a form of care work and investment in improving the well-being of his fellow Latinx community members. In fact, he felt that this work, when coupled with his direct care provision, actually facilitated his rapid DACA renewal process. Thus, Beto argued that his care work (in multiple simultaneous realms) constitutes a basis for making claims on the state and ultimately signaled his political inclusion. Anthropologists Whitney L. Duncan and Lupita Nabor Vazquez also found that Latinx immigrants asserted new political subjectivities in the throes of the pandemic on the basis of their self-perceptions as engaged members of U.S. society.[76]

Lucas likewise places care at the center of his work as he also fights for immigrant well-being in his position as a CHW. As we saw earlier, Lucas initially settled in Washington, D.C., before moving to Maryland when he was a teenager. In high school, when he was unable to legally work, Lucas started volunteering as a health advocate at a children's hospital in D.C. As he recalled, "I couldn't get a driver's license or really a job, so I did a lot of volunteer work when I was in high school, just for experience." Receiving DACA at eighteen right after he graduated, Lucas recalled that he "had to work. I was helping my dad with construction-related jobs, but then got a really good opportunity to do [information technology; IT] work for a company in D.C. I was able to do that because I had done something similar in high school. The guy who was in charge of IT would always teach me how to do basic stuff and also talked to me about the network certificates that you have to take if you want to do IT jobs in the area." Even though he could not legally work as a teenager, Lucas found ways of gaining experience in the health care system and IT field that situated him well for employment once he became work authorized with DACA. Despite the economic potential of working in the IT field, Lucas felt drawn to public health: "Computer science can be very isolating at times, whereas with public health, it's super fun to interact and talk to different people and provide services." His first paying job in public health was with a CHC and focused on the interface between public health and technology management—a perfect combination of his interests. Over time, he continued to work in CHCs and started specializing in HIV/AIDS prevention services. As we saw earlier, he found that he was most effectively able to leverage his place-based navigational capital in Washington, D.C., a socio-legal context with better access to care for undocumented immigrants.

Lucas held several positions in public health before becoming a CHW. As he amassed more experience in health care, he became a strong proponent of the peer advocacy model, tailoring his work toward LGBTQ+ people of color by sharing facets of his own experiences as a Latinx queer man. As he noted, "In public health in D.C., they're focusing more on peer advocacy . . . realizing that information is much more easily given that way, and that people are more receptive to it when they see that it's someone that looks like themselves." In recognition of his specialized knowledge as a peer advocate, the state of Maryland invited Lucas to serve on a statewide advisory committee. Lucas was honored to serve on this committee for an initial two-year term and continued on for an additional term. One of the primary tasks of the committee is to advise the Department of Health on the certification and training of CHWs. As the work of the group continued, they moved from advising about "general CHW certification to what the training requirements for

CHW specialty certifications might look like." In addition to CHW advocacy, Lucas reflected, "It's been a really great learning opportunity. I've learned so much about legislation and how things work in Maryland's government. It motivates me to try and be more active on that front when it comes to advocating for other causes like Medicaid expansion."

Even as he became an advocate on a larger scale, Lucas remained focused on providing direct care to clients as the pandemic hit. Lucas had a brief period of telework, but "came back on site" fairly quickly: "As CHWs, we're at the front of things, letting patients in, screening them, asking questions about symptoms. We had the full PPE gear and everything." He acknowledged, "It was really scary at first, because we didn't know much about the pandemic . . . but people still needed to get care, so we didn't stop." In fact, Lucas's clinic "was one of the few places around the DMV that was still doing HIV and STI testing. Those sexual health services were very much needed." In addition to the clinic, Lucas also worked on a mobile health unit that traveled around the region on the weekends and evenings. Lucas and his colleagues were easily able to roll COVID-19 into their workflow: "The core of the work that we do is still HIV and STI testing. But we can do COVID vaccination at the same time when we are able to have the nurse with us. It works really well."

While the mobile clinic was quite effective, Lucas started realizing that they needed to devise even more innovative strategies to reach the most vulnerable: "There's lots of hesitancy and medical mistrust among immigrant populations and Latinx folks. So we started a web series through Instagram and Facebook Live talking about our experiences getting the COVID vaccine, in English and Spanish." As he shared, "People were asking questions, like, 'What's going to happen with my information? Will it go to the government?' And I came forward and was like, 'I'm on DACA—technically undocumented—and I'm doing this because it's the right thing to do to protect myself and others. You're not going to a government agency to get tested or get the vaccine, you're coming to a community clinic like ours.' We talked about patient rights and confidentiality." Lucas reflected, "I've been very hesitant in general to say that I'm undocumented. But I realized it's better for me to be vocal about it, so other people can see and relate. I share my experience with anyone that is willing to listen and bring awareness about this issue and immigration at large. I've become much more vocal recently."

Indeed, Lucas attributed some of his speaking up more to the stalemate over DACA, which was a shift from his previous lack of public activism: "I've been kept in the same situation since 2012 and not much has changed. I just want to push more now." In addition to being fed up, Lucas noted, "I'm in a good position to advocate now. I'm much more financially stable, have a good social network—people that support me—and feel like I can take bigger risks now." Lucas also noted the particular value of intersectional mobilization: "When it comes to immigration and to police brutality, it's just systematic racism, anti-Blackness, xenophobia, homophobia, and misogyny. But now, it's like, we have lots of common goals. I'm of the mindset that the better off other people are, the better off I am as a person too. If the person next to me is thriving, I have much more chance of thriving and being success as well. It's not a zero-sum game. But there's still a lot of work to do."

Examining their experiences, it is clear that Beto and Lucas are motivated by service and a deep commitment to improving the well-being of immigrant communities. Indeed, this orientation is a central facet of their identities and, for Beto, the basis of his claim for political inclusion. Both Beto and Lucas perform care practices in the form of direct service, in both volunteer and employment capacities. Yet both see their care practices articulating on a larger scale—for Beto, as a researcher seeking to make novel discoveries related to COVID-19 that will improve health outcomes for the Latinx community and for Lucas as an invited member of a state task force trying to improve the health care infrastructure statewide. Interestingly, neither Beto nor Lucas came to their advocacy through participation in CBOs or the immigrant rights movement, unlike Camila and Pau. Yet the way they narrate their care practices is very much in alignment with the frames deployed by immigrant justice CBOs and activists, suggesting that these frames are also resonant ones for those who perform their advocacy in the context of everyday life.

Conclusion

DACA recipients effectively leverage their navigational capital and multifaceted skill sets to broker care for more precarious family and community members, as another node of everyday activism. As central figures within complex care configurations, they have demonstrated resourcefulness in facilitating immigrants' access to services, security and stability, and well-being. The everyday care practices they perform in service of others are another mechanism through which DACA recipients contest immigrants' marginalization and exclusion in local communities in their daily lives. DACA recipients' care practices are essential for sustaining collective well-being in more normal times but were particularly critical during the height of the pandemic when the deeply entrenched inequalities faced by structurally marginalized communities were particularly pronounced. In response, many DACA recipients started framing their care practices as political acts carried out in support of the broader immigrant justice movement and some even fashioned new political subjectivities. Their actions can be viewed as prefigurative politics, in which people embody and enact the socialities and practices they envision for broader society and the future.[77]

Writing in 2021, in the throes of the pandemic and national reckoning over racial justice, Ticktin describes a politics of *structural* care, which she formulates in conversation with her colleague, political scientist Deva Woodly and their colleagues,[78] as part of their timely special issue on the politics of care. Ticktin argues that structural care is "about healing social ills through social action based on a vision of everyone as interdependent," which ultimately enables "new political formations come into being."[79] The descriptor "structural" firmly centers the deep structural inequalities that create the need for such care in the first place, emphasizing the critical importance of structural policy solutions, in this case to address immigrants' ongoing legal precarity. However, as a more liberatory and expansive concept, structural care also foregrounds the importance of people "showing up" for each other as relational acts carried out in the everyday in pursuit of broader well-being and justice, which the conclusion takes up.

Conclusion

Beyond DACA—Showing Up for Immigrants and Immigrant Justice

The DACA anniversary made me sad, to be honest. [Pause] I don't want to cry. [Starts crying] But it's been almost a decade since this program was in place and they haven't done anything. There's no willingness to fix it.
—Camila, June 21, 2021

Today is the nine-year DACA anniversary. But I don't follow it like I used to anymore. I get texts about what's going on—like I recently got a bunch that they were going to protest today. But I am not as active as when I was younger. I have a lot more going on. Being a grown-up, I'm like, "Am I going to miss work to go protest?" I just can't, I'm busy helping my patients.
—Esme, June 15, 2021

DACA is definitely still in the news. There's a protest today there in D.C. . . . it's nice to see that activism out there. But the way I've been able to weather [DACA uncertainty] is because of my support system and helping my community at home.
—Beto, June 15, 2021

As of late 2024, DACA recipients were *still* navigating prolonged policy limbo, with their status more endangered than ever, and without a more permanent resolution to their legal status precarity on the horizon. Yet another DACA anniversary (or "DACA-versary" as some DACA recipients refer to it) passed on June 15, marking the twelfth year since the program was created. Despite the positive connotation with the word "anniversary," my participants did not regard this date as a celebratory occasion each year as it passed, as Camila's comments (and tears) underscored. Around the time of the ninth DACA-versary in June 2021, I was in the middle of conducting phase III interviews and happened to conduct two interviews (with Esme and Rod) on June 15 itself. I conducted nine interviews total that month, and the passage of the anniversary—and the notable lack of action surrounding DACA or broader immigration reform—was very much on participants' minds.

Though they recognized that DACA was "definitely still in the news" and even reported receiving targeted communications from CBOs about "what's going on," no one I met with that month participated in the mass mobilizations taking place in D.C. Esme noted that she had "a lot going on" as a grown-up, a sentiment echoed by many participants as they juggled work and other adult responsibilities. Indeed, Esme noted that she was "busy helping [her] patients." Yet beyond logistics, for Camila and others, it was frankly too painful to participate in these actions, as it served as a potent reminder of congressional inaction over the past decade and their and their family members' ongoing vulnerabilities. Instead, Rod reported "weathering" this fraught milestone—and his uncertain situation more broadly—by leaning in to his support system and channeling his energies into helping members of his community behind the scenes instead of participating in public protests.

Esme, Rod, and Camila's comments underscore several key dimensions of DACA recipients' experiences that have been highlighted throughout this book: the harmful impact of legal status precarity on DACA recipients' well-being over the course of the DACA program, the critical importance of their social networks in providing mutual support, the eschewing of more conventional modes of activism like participation in mass mobilizations, the busy lives of DACA recipients deeper into adulthood, and the everyday actions they take to promote immigrants' well-being, like providing care to patients and volunteering in their communities. As this book has argued, DACA recipients' response to prolonged legal status precarity has been to forge political inclusion in the everyday by deploying navigational capital and engaging in everyday activism in solidarity with other immigrants. Indeed, one of the enduring legacies of the DACA program—regardless of its ultimate fate—is how recipients responded to deeply unsettling uncertainty by pursuing surprisingly normal lives and channeling their energies into advocating for and ensuring the well-being of others.

Fighting for Policy Reform at Multiple Levels

Despite their remarkable resiliency and resourceful advocacy, DACA recipients are still regularly subjected to multiple forms of violence enacted by the state and remain structurally vulnerable by policies that intentionally produce legal status precarity,[1] which deeply impacts their incorporation trajectories, as well as overall health and well-being. Unquestionably, the most impactful way of alleviating DACA recipients' legal status precarity and ending the ongoing legal challenges to DACA would be Congress finally passing immigration reform to provide DACA recipients—and other immigrants with precarious legal status—a mechanism for accessing a more stable and permanently renewable status with a pathway to citizenship. Such structural reform would substantively address the precarious circumstances of millions of immigrants in the United States as well as positively impact the broader well-being of mixed-status families and communities nationwide.[2] One major takeaway from the DACA experiment is that temporary solutions (such as those taken through executive action) are insufficient and that more permanent structural fixes are necessary to address gaps in the immigration system.

As scholars have strongly contended for decades now, opportunities for permanently legalizing status are particularly impactful for young adults early in their transition to adulthood.[3] However, gaining a more permanent status would obviously still be quite beneficial for undocumented immigrants who came as young children but are now more deeply into adulthood in their twenties and thirties—like most of my research participants. Moreover, while gaining status would be individually impactful for all DACA recipients, it would also be immensely beneficial for their family and community members and greatly facilitate the brokering and care work they perform. If these family and community members who have been in the United States for decades without formal legal status were also eligible to benefit from a broader and more inclusive version of reform, (former) DACA recipients could more effectively promote their well-being without running up against the exclusions and intractable barriers that stymie their best intentions and efforts.

During the 118th U.S. Congress, new bipartisan reform bills were introduced to address the legal situation of DACA recipients, including a more expansive House bill that would have provided a permanently renewable status for millions of undocumented immigrants. Immigration reform that includes more than just DACA recipients would unquestionably be the fruition of decades of advocacy and a hard-fought victory for the broader immigrant rights movement. However, it is highly unlikely that the 119th Congress will prioritize such reform. Many undocumented activists, though, have pushed for an end goal that extends beyond just legalization and maintains a critique of entrenched regimes of power, instead emphasizing broader intersectional justice and alternative liberation projects beyond the purview of the state.[4] Even with a large-scale legalization program, many immigrants would still be left out of reform and subject to multiple forms of state violence; thus, organizing to contest border and interior enforcement, oppose mass deportation, put an end to the expansive immigrant detention infrastructure, and revamp the asylum system all remain critical to the broader immigrant justice project, especially into the second Trump era.

This book has made clear that, in the absence of federal immigration reform, state- and local-level policies play a consequential role in shaping immigrants' everyday lives in local communities nationwide. Such policies have proliferated in the absence of federal reform over the past few decades and in some cases (depending on the jurisdiction) have gone much further in expanding immigrants' rights and opportunities to flourish and forge belonging in local communities. Thus, states and localities remain critical levels to harness advocacy efforts and push for reform.

In some jurisdictions like Washington, D.C.—the most immigrant-friendly jurisdiction featured in this book—purposefully inclusive policies have facilitated immigrant incorporation and fostered immigrants' active participation in community life. Immigrants with precarious legal status have been able to access driver's licenses, health care coverage, tuition equity, local financial aid, and excluded worker funds and live their lives in a sanctuary jurisdiction without concern about district employees inquiring about residency or citizenship status or cooperating with federal immigration agencies. Though Maryland trends more integrative, it maintains restrictions related to immigrants' health coverage and several jurisdictions still participate in 287(g) agreements. Yet the recently passed Healthy Babies Equity Act (2022), Professional Licensure Act (2023), and Access to Care Act (2024) on the state level portend potentially more inclusive policies to come that merit concerted focus and continued advocacy. At the county and even city levels, there is also great potential for the passage of integrative policies like those in Maryland extending health care coverage to undocumented minors (as in Montgomery County) and allowing for noncitizen voting in communities like Hyattsville, right down the street from my university. Regional CBOs with a deep history of successful advocacy (like Casa de Maryland, La Clínica del Pueblo, and CARECEN in the D.C. Metro region) offer ample opportunities to become involved in political action campaigns focused on these state and local issues as well as periodic mass mobilizations in support of reform at the federal level.

Though this book has briefly described these different policy levels, issues, and arenas of potential engagement, I have purposefully limited the discussion of them and do not call on readers to get involved in immigration advocacy only in these ways. Many immigration-focused books and articles over the past twenty years have concluded by enumerating areas in which policy reform is urgently needed and the advocacy channels through which readers might become more involved in fighting for reform. In *We Are Not Dreamers*, Abrego and Negrón-Gonzales call out many researchers' "failure to reciprocate with undocumented immigrant communities, rarely using their skills to support the advocacy work that they document." As part of this critique, they present a brief guide on research ethics for scholars conducting research on/with undocumented youth created in the aftermath of the first election of Trump by anthropologist Gabrielle Cabrera (an author featured in the volume) as well as Ines Garcia and an anonymous student. A key component of their guide is the pointed and poignant assertion that "'Policy Recommendations' at the end of articles are not enough." Instead, they advocate that scholars conduct ethical research that engages the community throughout the process.[5] Though I began my research for this book before that volume came out, I have endeavored to take such an ethical and collaborative approach to conducting this research, as described in greater detail in appendix A.

However, I also heed the editors' and authors' call to think more about how academics and nonacademics alike can harness our commitment to social justice, knowledge (of various forms), and skill sets (whatever they may be) in support of immigrants as they seek to flourish in their everyday lives even amid structural marginalization and exclusion.[6] Following the lead of the DACA recipients featured in this book, I ask how the different forms of capital we possess can be leveraged through forms of everyday activism carried out on a smaller, yet potentially quite impactful, scale. As social movement scholars have noted, such small-scale actions are also essential for movement building.[7] Anthropologist Savannah Shange notes that even with abolition as a larger social movement goal, scholars should "bring abolition home" by taking action and contributing to ongoing campaigns in our everyday lives.[8] While this book has been dedicated to capturing how DACA recipients leverage alternative forms of capital and perform everyday activism, I also urge readers to think about how all of us (as committed "citizens" regardless of our immigration statuses) can and should show up for immigrants and immigrant justice in our everyday lives.

Beyond "Policy Recommendations": Showing Up for Immigrants in the Everyday

In the aftermath of the DACA rescission announcement in September 2017, support for DACA recipients was at an all-time high as more people became aware of DACA recipients' tenuous legal situation. Countless universities, nonprofit organizations, and foundations issued and posted formal statements on their websites strongly and unequivocally asserting, "We stand with DREAMers." Indeed, some 143 business associations and companies—many of them top *Fortune* 500 companies—filed a friend of the court document conveying their support of the program and its recipients.[9] Ordinary people also tweeted and posted about DACA recipients and DREAMers on social media using hashtags like #SaveDACA, #DefendDACA, and #StandWithDreamers. Online merchants sold Stand With DREAMers–inspired merchandise like T-shirts, posters, and stickers. Indeed, on my campus more colleagues than ever asked me about DACA and felt compelled to signal their support by placing signs on their office doors.

During phase II, conducted in 2017–18 in the aftermath of the rescission announcement, many participants shared that they were pleasantly surprised by the unexpected support and solidarity offered to them by people they encountered at school, workplaces, houses of worship, and other places they frequented in their everyday lives. These supportive actions were well received by DACA recipients as they contended with the actions of an aggressively anti-immigrant president and ongoing assaults on their health and well-being. Yet as time continued on and DACA began a winding and confusing journey through the judicial branch (eventually amid an emerging global pandemic), many of these pronouncements of solidarity faded. I talked about shifting public support quite a bit with my research participants during the middle and later parts of the project. By phase III, in 2020–21, they reported feeling like their cause had been "forgotten"—though they acknowledged that DACA had gotten terribly confusing over time and that even they had taken a step back from following ongoing DACA developments.

As I contextualize their experiences, I see quite clearly that "standing with" DACA recipients and/or DREAMers is an easier though much more limited political engagement strategy that does not necessitate a deeper and longer-term commitment to promoting immigrant justice. As I think critically about the limits of just "standing with" immigrants, I realize how substantively different it is to "show up" instead, drawing from my participants' use of the term. A key distinction between standing with and showing up is that the latter requires substantially more intention, investment, and action sustained over a much longer period of time. Showing up can also be more revelatory of deeper interpersonal relationships and reciprocal exchanges that unfold over time as a cornerstone of scholarly praxis, as described in appendix A.[10] In line with key themes from the book, showing up requires you to think about what skills and forms of capital you have and can leverage to benefit the immigrants you know and those you do not, and what creative avenues and channels you can find for leveraging them. As sociologist Robert C. Smith notes, showing up entails saying yes when asked for help, offering to help when you can, and acting when opportunities arise based on the relationships you have already forged.[11]

Over the years in which I have been engaged in this research, I have endeavored to show up for participants in ways that have not yet made it onto these pages; indeed, these actions are not central to participants' experiences, stories, and perspectives, and I realize that I often think of them as off-stage modes of reciprocity that are revelatory of moral and ethical engagement and deeper political commitments. Viewing them through a different lens, however, these types of actions are a useful vehicle for thinking through the potential of everyday activism for all of us, regardless of what social positions we occupy. In that vein, I urge readers to think about how they might take such actions and offer some examples, ideas, and resources about how academics and nonacademics alike can show up for immigrants in their everyday lives which will be ever-more important during Trump's second term. As the introduction described, my participants talk about "showing up" for immigrants in two different respects: showing up as a relational act as a way of offering support during challenging times and showing up in support of the movement for immigrant justice; each mode of engagement is described below.

Showing Up for Immigrants

In the realm of the relational, showing up for immigrants involves listening deeply and carefully, bearing witness to immigrants' experiences, remaining present and engaged over time, and being responsive to their needs as you become aware of them regardless of the social positions and professional roles you occupy. I offer a few brief examples from my research of ways that I and my student collaborators have found to show up for undocumented young adults, which has entailed different actions depending on our positionalities and realms of knowledge. Showing up has also evolved as participants' needs have shifted and as we have gotten to know them better over the years. Showing up for participants has most often entailed more individualized and tailored actions since we were not collaborating with a CBO or working within a cohesive, preexisting community of DACA recipients.

During phase I, we examined barriers to accessing resources as a topic of research inquiry, though also with a practical eye toward inventorying and sharing information. After we officially wrapped up each interview, we shifted gears out of research mode to check in with participants about their awareness of local resources. Initially, we focused on and shared quite a bit on campus-based resources given that the majority (though not all participants) were students. While I had known about these resources and could sometimes facilitate contact, my student collaborators had more direct experience with actually navigating them as fellow students, commuters, and members of immigrant families. They knew, for instance, that it was incredibly challenging for students to get a timely appointment at the university counseling center based on their own and other friends' experiences. By the beginning of phase II, though, we learned that a practitioner who specialized in working with immigrant students conserved appointments specifically for them, so we could give participants more specific advice about accessing this limited resource. For the subset of (eight) participants enrolled at the University of Maryland, College Park (UMD) during phase I, we ensured that they were aware of this counseling resource as well as the student health center, undocumented student center, and student groups focused on immigration issues. For participants who were not students on our campus, we searched for comparable resources on other local campuses.

Another subset of participants were transferring from community college to much larger (and, for some, quite intimidating) university campuses. As transfer students, they sometimes lacked resources and built-in community as they made their way to and around unfamiliar campuses. One participant found this transition to be quite disorienting as she navigated the massive UMD campus, particularly given that she was a commuter who lived and worked full-time off campus.[12] I checked in with her regularly during her first semester at UMD (even though I was on parental leave), helping her to find programming for commuters, food security resources, activities that aligned with her interests (e.g., club soccer), and immigration-focused student groups and services. She eventually found her footing on campus, through a newly formed student group focused on immigration and programming run by the undocumented student office.

Realizing that the transition between community college and universities was particularly challenging, I strategized with some of the students while they were still in community college about their next steps. One participant had just started taking community college classes when we met her in 2016. She shared that she was aspiring to transfer to UMD in a few years and eventually wanted to go to medical school but was not sure what she needed to do to prepare. I reviewed online information with her about the university's pre-health office and found the relevant contact information, following up with her a few weeks later about it. Another participant enrolled in community college in 2016 was interested in moving to Southern California, where her boyfriend at the time was relocating, after she finished her associate's degree to continue her schooling. I put her in touch with a colleague at the California state university where she was hoping to transfer who was well connected to their DREAMer Center and would ensure that she received the information she needed. These campus referrals and connections can be critical resources for young adults in exploring options, even if they do not end up ultimately pursuing them.

Beyond campus-specific resources, our research team also shared relevant community-based resources. For instance, we learned that one participant lived in Montgomery County and had younger siblings who were undocumented minors. Having learned what a valuable resource the Care for Kids Program had been for many of our Montgomery County–based participants, we shared information about the program (which he had not heard about) so that his family could look into enrolling his younger siblings. My student collaborator Alaska was particularly well positioned to share information about Montgomery County resources, as she had worked in several different positions in the county in emergency care and occupational therapy. As they became more deeply immersed in their professional careers, student collaborators Delmis and Ana became quite knowledgeable about specific resources in Prince George's County and D.C., respectively. During phase II, one participant was pregnant and about to lose health insurance through her father's insurance since she had turned twenty-six. The timing of her loss of coverage was particularly stressful given her pregnancy. Based on where she lived (in Prince George's County), I provided her with information about a clinic that specialized in pregnancy care and served predominantly immigrant women that I knew about from previous students who had interned and done research there. After significant effort spent exploring her options, she was ultimately able to effectively navigate her way to giving birth at her preferred hospital.

During phase I, we discovered that many participants were interested in connecting with other DACA recipients and deepening their networks. As noted in the introduction as well as in appendix A, we formed a CAB composed of four members of the original research team and eight DACA recipients who met twice a year over a period of years. During our first two CAB meetings, we mapped out local (campus- and community-based) resources that had been mentioned in phase I, that CAB members then added to so we could share them with participants as we continued into phase II. Over time, the CAB itself also transformed into a space for emerging young professionals to share navigational capital related to legal, health, education, and legal resources. Over the life of the CAB, members graduated and transitioned into professional roles that built their knowledge base and facilitated access to new resources. For instance, Delmis's postgraduate position at an immigrant rights CBO made her a go-to resource for regular updates on DACA as well as obtaining referrals for legal services; one CAB member sought additional guidance on the implications of her move across state lines on the processing of her DACA renewal. Five members worked within health care and social services and freely shared resources about clinics and programs, while three members worked as advocates within school systems or educational nonprofits and shared employment resources with each other during our meetings, also interfacing with each other regularly in their professional capacities. These exchanges underscored the horizontal solidarity incubated through the CAB and noninstitutional pathways through which navigational capital also moves. While the CAB is a somewhat unique space, other institutional spaces (like research labs and student engagement centers) and spaces created by undocumented students themselves (like student groups) can also serve as effective vehicles for horizontally transmitting navigational capital.[13]

As a multigenerational college graduate and university professor, I am also well positioned to provide targeted support to immigrant young adults in anticipation of, and during, their transitions into the workforce and graduate school. Indeed, over my decades of collaborating with young adults in immigrant families—many of whom are first-generation college students—I have found that sharing academic capital is one the best forms of reciprocity I have to offer. As with previous research projects, I regularly read and provide input on application materials. In August 2017 as the DACA rescission loomed with increasing likelihood, one participant was quite anxious about entering the job market and preparing her application materials. We got together to strategize about how to approach her search (as a DACA recipient with potentially endangered work authorization) and I provided feedback on her cover letters and resume. Based on her experience and accomplishments, she soon found a satisfying job in her field. As another participant who attended my university graduated and solidified his plans to apply to graduate school, we got together to discuss crafting a personal statement; I shared insights from my own experience as a regular reviewer of graduate program applications (albeit in a different field). Once he drafted his statement, I provided feedback and encouraged him to speak more directly to how his status had shaped his path and desire to continue on to graduate school. After he was admitted to the program and began teaching his own class sections as a graduate assistant, we got together to talk about pedagogical strategies and classroom management.

Showing up for participants has also meant being available to their family members and friends. Several participants had younger siblings who were either aspiring to or beginning their studies at my university, and I encouraged them to share my contact information with their siblings so that they knew they had a resource to rely on once they arrived on campus. One participant talked with me and Alaska fairly extensively about the field of anthropology after our initial interview. Subsequently, she asked me if I would meet with a friend of hers, who was undocumented, about majoring in anthropology and postgraduation employment options. I answered her friend's questions about anthropology, which she ended up majoring in, but also discovered that she was interested in pursuing occupational health. Though I did not have expertise in this realm, I put her in touch with Alaska, who worked in the field, as well as another graduate student (also coincidentally from an immigrant background) who was enrolled alongside Alaska in a class I was teaching at the time and was an occupational therapist. Years later, I wrote her a recommendation to a clinical nursing program where she is currently training—and offering me periodic updates. This experience also illuminated the professional licensure challenges faced by undocumented immigrants.

I offer these as examples of small but impactful actions that academics can take in support of immigrant students that can easily be folded into everyday academic life. While many professors regularly take similar actions in support of their students, doing so with particular sensitivity to immigration-related considerations and constraints is critical. Campuses remain important potential spaces of inclusion and belonging for immigrant students as well as those from mixed-status families. Many campuses—whether they are community colleges or four-year universities, publicly or privately funded, large, medium, or small in size—have DREAMer centers or offices that provide critical resources for students related to financial aid, career advancement, legal services, health services, and counseling services. Institutional support for these centers varies widely depending on the campus types and the administration's support of and investment in them, and they also operate in alignment with the state's education policies. California's immigrant-friendly policies and state universities' institutional investment in undocumented students have enabled them to thrive on these campuses.[14] These centers have become all the more important since the government stopped accepting new DACA applications, leaving thousands of undocumented college students and aspiring college students without the opportunity to gain even a temporary form of status and in need of substantial support as they attempt to follow the lead of older DACA recipients.

I have realized from my conversations with colleagues that many faculty and staff members are not aware that such centers or offices exist. I encourage readers working in academia, if they have not already, to become more involved in the activities of these centers and offices on their campuses and/or explore the resources they offer not only for their students but also for themselves. Many also have resources for administrators, faculty, and staff, including regular "UndocAlly" trainings for those interested in learning about how to serve as allies for immigrant students, which present a good opportunity for doing more than just "standing with" immigrants. Many also have more immediately available tips on how to create a more welcoming environment for immigrant students. Most are easily identifiable through a basic internet search, though some are embedded within other student service offices or units. It is also worth noting, however, that there are also campus safe spaces that exist apart from these centers that have been forged by marginalized youth themselves and emerged more organically as they seek to create networks of support and solidarity.[15] As my participants' experiences underscore, both formal and informal campus spaces can serve as important incubators of everyday activism and sites for the horizontal transmission of navigational capital rooted in shared experience and collective knowledge.

Beyond these physical centers on campuses, numerous national or-ganizations (including United We Dream, Informed Immigrant, and the President's Alliance on Higher Education and Immigration) offer on-line toolkits and webinars oriented toward supporting undocumented students' educational pursuits as well as their mental health and over-all well-being. In my field, the Anthropologist Action Network for Im-migrants and Refugees (AANIR; for which I am a Steering Committee member) curates a range of resources including webinars and lectures, resources for educators, and syllabi and teaching materials. Those who work in primary and secondary schools will also find that a plethora of resources exist and are easily searchable. Government entities like the Department of Education and nonprofit organizations like the Ameri-can Federation of Teachers offer national-level resources, while many state- and local-level school systems, organizations, and groups offer more tailored local resources oriented toward serving immigrant stu-dents and promoting college access.

For those who work in health care and other service-oriented profes-sions, both national and local resources and toolkits oriented toward promoting immigrants' access to care and mental health resources are plentiful—particularly for youth, who are often eligible for a wider range of services. United We Dream, Informed Immigrant, and UndocuBlack offer mental-health-focused resources for practitioners and providers. In response to the DACA rescission announcement, many professional organizations, including the Association of American Medical Colleges, American Nurses Association, American Psychological Association, and National Association of Social Workers, strongly renounced the re-scission and held trainings for their membership about how to support DACA recipients. Some of these trainings are available as continuing education courses (i.e., continuing education units and continuing med-ical education) required to maintain professional certification. Given the urgency of immigrants' circumstances in the second Trump administra-tion, I imagine new trainings and resources will be developed and made widely available by these and other organizations. If your professional role is not included in the above, I urge you to seek out personal and professional opportunities to show up for immigrants in your everyday work life.

Showing Up for Immigrant Justice

Beyond showing up for the immigrant young adults I am privileged to know and learn from through my research and being a university professor, I also think regularly about how to show up for the immigrant justice movement, in support of access, inclusion, well-being, and justice for all immigrants. Previously, I have done so by participating in CBO activism and immigrant rights organizing with and alongside immigrants. Such fierce organizing will continue to be critical during Trump's second term and beyond. Beyond that, as a professor whose research focuses on immigrant justice, I have taken part in such activities on my campus as planning and tabling at events oriented toward promoting a more inclusive campus culture, developing content for and participating in "train the trainers" sessions for our campus UndocTerp program, sponsoring student clubs focused on immigration-related issues, serving on committees awarding scholarships for undocumented students, presenting on mixed-status families and mental health vulnerabilities at the counseling center and medical school, and participating in different campus-based public events on immigration. Beyond these activities, though, showing up for immigrant rights has entailed responding to opportunities as they arise and finding new footholds.

As an educator, I have a clear platform for showing up for immigrant justice: teaching about and challenging students to think critically about DACA, immigration, and the forces constraining immigrants' incorporation into U.S. society. One of the primary courses that I have taught since my first semester at UMD is a general education class on immigration taken by 60 to 120 undergraduate students at a time from all different majors and backgrounds, the majority of whom will likely never set foot in an immigration-focused class again. The course fills multiple requirements (ensuring that it is always full), though many students are drawn to it because they or their family members are immigrants and/ or they are curious to move beyond political rhetoric about immigration to actually learn more about immigrants' everyday lives. At the flagship campus of a more integrative state in the hyperdiverse D.C. Metro region, I am fortunate to teach diverse students along many axes of identity. I also teach upper-level electives that focus on global migration and health as well as health inequities in the United States that attract a range of different students, including anthropology, public health, and public policy majors as well as those aspiring to pursue health-related careers or go to law school.

On Tuesday, September 5, 2017—the day of the DACA rescission announcement—I remember clearly wishing that I could go to D.C. to join in the #DefendDACA protest. However, it was the second week of the semester and I was more in instructor than researcher mode, with multiple classes to teach that day, making my participation an outright impossibility. Yet I started realizing that I had a different platform for showing up for immigrant justice that day: teaching about and fostering student engagement on the topic. So instead we talked extensively about DACA, as I explained the confusing set of twists and turns that had led to that point and what it showcased about trends in immigration policymaking. I fielded numerous questions and set the stage for this being an evolving story that we would continue to follow. Each time I teach the course, there's a different unfolding story related to immigration that I have the students track and complexify—for example, the European refugee "crisis" of 2015, the impact of the COVID-19 pandemic on immigrants in 2020, and the U.S. pullout of Afghanistan and subsequent mass displacement of Afghan refugees in 2021. Indeed, DACA was the major story we followed for the fall 2017 semester.

I came to see quite clearly that I was actually where I should have been that day; my way of showing up for the movement was not downtown protesting but rather in the classroom on my campus helping my students make sense of DACA. That day, a junior economics major came up to me after class to introduce himself and let me know that he had taken this class precisely because a DACA recipient friend of his from Honduras (whom I knew) had recommended it to him as a way of making better sense of her situation and showing up for her. Shining a light on DACA was also beneficial for my students who were DACA recipients. A few class sessions later, a freshman finance major who had not yet said anything in class let me know that he was a DACA recipient who came from South Korea when he was three years old. In a written assignment, in which the students analyzed mainstream news stories on immigration, he shared further about his experiences and how they shaped his interpretations of these news stories. This student was not interested in speaking about DACA in class or even sharing with other students that he held this status. Yet his comments on assignments throughout the semester signaled that he appreciated it being so openly and supportively discussed in a classroom setting.

By centering DACA and immigrant justice in my teaching, students also feel comfortable sharing information about immigration-focused events taking place both on and off campus. I generally make in-class announcements when these events enter my radar, though students also have a pulse on a wider range of activities and events. I purposefully create the space for students to share this information and find that they frequently take the opportunity to do so, especially in smaller classes. Over the years, students have shared information about student group meetings, initiatives led by these groups (e.g., a student-organized petition calling on the administration to increase services available to immigrant students in the aftermath of the 2016 election), and fundraisers for scholarships, among other topics. During the spring 2022 semester, a student with DACA in my Global Migration and Health course was quite involved in the campaign to enable DACA recipients to access state licenses for professional practice. Early in the semester, she made an announcement about the campaign and shared ways of getting involved, evoking great interest and enthusiasm. After sharing the information (in the process disclosing her status), she spoke regularly in class about the range of policies impacting her and her family members' health and well-being. Her presence, willingness to share, and dynamism greatly enhanced the learning environment and served as the impetus for her classmates to become more involved.

Over the course of this project, I underwent professional transitions as I got tenure and took on administrative roles. With accumulated experience in navigating my campus and greater professional security, I also see new outlets for everyday activism beyond the classroom where I can take advantage of my increased access to different spaces. On college campuses, people often speak of the importance of cultivating allies who support humane immigration reform.[16] Indeed, many DREAMer centers nationwide explicitly invoke allyship in the branding of their trainings and certifications oriented toward making campuses more inclusive and supportive environments for immigrants with precarious legal status. Yet anthropologists Ruth Gomberg-Muñoz and Mark Schuller make impassioned calls for engaged scholars to go beyond mere allyship.[17] Taking the alternate position of accomplice, Gomberg-Muñoz argues, instead involves relinquishing the "deceptive comfort" of allyship and squarely recognizing that we are, indeed, complicit when we allow the system to persist. Instead, she implores that "we take an unambiguous stance in a struggle that already envelopes us, and that we leverage and sacrifice relative protection, access, and prestige in service to the subversion of oppressive systems."[18]

As I seek to more directly confront undocumented students' and scholars' institutional marginalization and exclusion, I have discovered different institutional footholds for pushing back. On the threshold of tenure, I began serving as graduate director in my department, which means that I have a direct hand in trying to make our graduate programs more inclusive in general and specifically for immigrant-origin and international students, which I have very much focused my administrative energies on—particularly in the aftermath of the U.S. Supreme Court's 2023 decision preventing universities from considering applicants' race in the admissions process and subsequent efforts at more systematically implementing holistic review principles. My administrative role also gives me access to conversations, connections, and awareness of processes beyond what I was privy to as an individual faculty member. Three years into my term, the university debuted a new fellowship program aimed at increasing doctoral program diversity. When I opened up the fellowship guidelines, I was indignant to discover that only U.S. citizens and permanent residents were eligible for it. Because of my role, I knew whom to contact about it and proceeded to do so. I received a fairly tepid response about the administrative reasons why this was so (namely, that DACA recipients fell in between conventional categories of domestic and international students, who were explicitly excluded from this fellowship) and that they would not have a mechanism for discerning if an applicant had DACA. Because of my knowledge of the graduate admissions process and the new software system, I knew that DACA recipients were actually quite identifiable within the system, as I had been surprised to see it as a unique category on a report we had previously generated for our department's admissions process. I pointed this fact out in a series of follow-up exchanges about the topic. Ultimately, this administrator "considered" adjusting the language of the call to include DACA recipients, though did not do so in that cycle. However, I have continued to raise the issue, in tandem with the university's undocumented student coordinator, and his successor subsequently took it up for further consideration, ultimately deciding to open up eligibility to DACA recipients and other categories of immigrants with work authorization. Of course the state university system in which my university is embedded must also be held accountable to immigrant students who are not work authorized and pushed to follow the lead of the University of California system, which is taking steps toward opening a pathway for hiring undocumented students.

Another DACA-related exclusion became clear to me when I was trying to bring on a DACA recipient colleague as a postdoctoral fellow to work on this research project. My colleague and I quickly confronted a major impediment: the university's fellowship program—which explicitly identifies diversifying faculty as a program goal—extends eligibility only to those with U.S. citizenship or permanent residency. I had learned from my research that DACA recipients are often excluded somewhat unwittingly from such opportunities. If a salary, stipend, or other type of payment is involved, it is often more important that applicants are work authorized (rather than being a citizen or resident per se) so that they can be properly entered into administrative systems; indeed, DACA recipients are and can be. I took my indignation about this exclusion to a dean, fully expecting that they would politely hear me out and offer no remedy. I was taken aback when they actually put hours of their own administrative time and concrete resources into devising a plan involving a financial commitment from different units that would enable her to come on board.[19] Ultimately, the dean's solution was a workaround, meaning that other DACA recipients were likely encountering the same barrier that still needs to be more comprehensively addressed at an institutional level. However, the experience underscored to me that it is always worthwhile to confront these exclusions with campus administrators to push for more systematic change.

Both of these examples accentuate quite clearly that there is still much work to be done to make university campuses more immigrant inclusive and specifically call out exclusions built into many "diversity" initiatives; my campus is definitely not unique in this respect. Nor do I mean to suggest that these actions are exceptional; in fact, my colleagues also actively call out and seek to remedy exclusionary policies and practices on their campuses—especially as we all get more securely into our academic careers and are in better positions to do so. Indeed, my colleagues and I have forged the AANIR collective as a space for sharing strategies and unique forms of capital for advocating for immigrant students. These examples also highlight the importance of everyday activist work on our university campuses—and the particular importance of ratcheting up the actions you take as you move up the academic hierarchy and have access to new people and spaces for contesting exclusion and inequality—including, though certainly not limited exclusively to, immigrants.

While these examples are very specific to academic life, they also speak to larger processes in operation in other institutional contexts. I urge readers to think about what everyday actions they can take to change their workplaces by taking advantage of privileged access to particular spaces and pushing back directly against exclusionary policies and procedures that disadvantage immigrants. There are also explicit resources to support such efforts. With decades of experience in higher education settings, groups like the Intercultural Development Research Association (IDRA) and National Association of Student Personnel Administrators (NASPA) are focused on supporting student affairs professionals committed to educational equity. In the realm of health care, the Association of American Medical Colleges and National Association of Social Workers have become increasingly vocal in advocating for DACA recipients' access to medical training—as well as broader reform. Undocumented youth have also been leaders in the fight for more inclusive training and professionalization opportunities, including the long-established Pre-Health Dreamers group. DACA recipients themselves are certainly leaders whose lead we should all follow, regardless of one's professional workplace and roles. In this spirit, I remind the reader once again of the everyday activism of participants featured in this book as they have pushed their workplaces to be more accommodating of immigrants' circumstances and inclusive overall.

Everyday Activism Beyond DACA and Beyond Immigration

As DACA recipients have made abundantly clear through their remarkable and sustained activism in the twenty-first century (in both public and everyday forms), their fight for immigrant well-being and justice has never *only* been about them. Indeed, DACA recipients are deeply embedded in family, community, educational, professional, and national networks that have led them to vociferously resist the DREAMer narrative that exceptionalizes them as being somehow more deserving than other immigrants.[20] Engaging in everyday activism and sharing alternative forms of capital can and should extend well beyond just DACA recipients and immigrant young adults (despite them being the focus of this book) to a wider range of immigrants, in tailored ways that attend to their particular circumstances. In recognition of this broader purview, activists have increasingly been pushing beyond rights and political inclusion as the target, pushing instead for broader justice, freedom, and liberation.[21]

Regardless of whatever potential immigration reform may come to pass and whenever it may come into being, millions of immigrants will likely be left out of such reform *in the best case scenario*, underscoring that there is much work yet to be done. The quest for immigrant well-being and justice will certainly forge on through more conventional organizing and coordinated political action campaigns waged on federal, state, and local levels; however, it will also necessarily involve concerted actions carried out in the realm of everyday life. These everyday actions typically tend to go unnoticed, yet they ultimately play a critical role in moving forward progressive struggles for social justice.[22]

Undocumented activists have also forged a movement known for its increasingly intersectional character as they link their cause to other social justice movements to collectively contest pernicious and persistent forms of inequality in the United States. Everyday activism also has salience well beyond immigrants to others marginalized by the state, neoliberalism, and the global capitalist system. Indeed, critical migration scholars like anthropologists Heath Cabot and Georgina Ramsay have urged scholars to "deexceptionalize" displacement as being a particular condition of migrants, instead recognizing that experiences of dispossession and alienation are the more normative experiences as people live in a world of seemingly perpetual crisis.[23] This broader purview also aligns with the ways in which people use the phrase "showing up" as a rallying call around a wider set of social movements organized around combating inequality. This phrase has widespread use in other social movements including racial justice, criminal justice reform, economic and worker justice, LGBTQ+ justice, and climate and environmental justice. In fact, a national organization—Showing Up for Racial Justice, formed in 2009 in the wake of the election of President Obama and the racist backlash that ensued—is explicitly built on this concept in encouraging white people to "show up" and join their campaigns to work toward actualizing racial and economic justice.[24] Through his history of transformative social movements across different time periods, American studies scholar Daniel Martinez HoSang highlights new visions borne of collective experience that have emerged that center human difference, vulnerability, and interdependence in pushing for "a wider type of freedom."[25]

Scholars have also increasingly endeavored to reveal the interconnections between economic insecurity, political instability and war, white supremacy and xenophobia, climate change and environmental disasters, and the global pandemic as unifying dimensions of humanity that produce widespread experiences of precarity.[26] As anthropologist Anna L. Tsing intriguingly ponders, "Most of the time we imagine such precarity to be an exception to how the world works. . . . What if, as I'm suggesting, precarity *is* the condition of our time?"[27] Yet even amid "capitalist ruins,"[28] as Tsing aptly characterizes the contemporary era, scholars urge that we illuminate how people "imagine and carve out spaces of collective and individual flourishing"[29] as they tap into deep resourcefulness, creativity, and imagination to do so.[30] Indeed, in this book I have described how DACA recipients have marshalled their resourcefulness and creativity in pursuit of normal, flourishing lives even amid structural marginalization and as their communities are aggressively targeted by state violence.

Schuller makes an impassioned call for widespread *radical empathy*, arguing that "we each need to be willing to stand up for others caught in the system, being denied health care, or clean water, or the right to worship, or freedom from sexual harassment or assault, or the right to safety when going to the bathroom, or the right to exist because they too are human, and because we need everyone's perspective to survive."[31] Accordingly, he urges readers to join "in solidarity with marginalized groups engaging in local struggles for liberation."[32] Education scholar Roseann Liu and Savannah Shange critique the call for empathy as the foundation for multiracial alliances built on notions of shared suffering that gloss over differential experiences of state violence; they instead put forward the concept of *thick solidarity* to argue for a form of empathy "that layers interpersonal empathy *with* historical analysis, political acumen, and a willingness to be led by those most directly impacted."[33] Indeed, my participants have taught me that joining in these local struggles and forging thick solidarity through more traditional activist modalities are not the only ways to become involved in these interconnected and ongoing struggles for liberation. With a broader goal of collective liberation, anthropologist Andrea M. López has also urged scholars to think concertedly about how to actualize justice "in the meantime."[34] In addition to higher-profile coordinated political actions, everyday life is and should be a critical site for locating creative forms of political engagement "in the meantime" that operate in conjunction with more conventional forms of activism as overlapping pathways for forging social change.[35] Indeed, my participants' experiences underscore that we can and should think creatively about how different types of actions— including those that we take with great intention and care in the context of everyday life—articulate with each other and ultimately contribute meaningfully to advancing intersectional justice.

EPILOGUE

As I was putting the finishing touches on this book, the 2024 U.S. election happened, with devastating impact for immigrant and many other structurally marginalized communities. Trump's second term is ushering in a new chapter of brazen state violence and racist political discourse targeting immigrants and stoking immense fear in immigrant families nationwide. The reelection of Trump and Republican majorities in the U.S. House and Senate in the 119th Congress render DACA more endangered than ever and foreclose the likelihood of Congress passing inclusive immigration reform in the near future.

Immigrant activists, allies, and accomplices have long been bracing and planning for this reality and are already organizing fiercely throughout the country in support of local immigrant communities. Undocumented activists will continue to adapt their strategies to meet the moment, and lead by devising new ways of confronting and critiquing repressive state violence. They will be joined by well-established organizations showing up for immigrant justice, activists from other social justice movements forging strategic alliances, and new supporters showing up in sometimes-unexpected ways precisely because of immigrants' pronounced precarity in the second Trump era. I encourage the reader not merely to "stand with" but also "show up" for immigrant justice in the years to come.

Yet as before in the first Trump administration, many undocumented immigrants may be too cautious or anxious to participate in public campaigns and mass mobilizations, despite feeling a sense of deep responsibility to advocate on behalf of their families and communities. In the aftermath of the election, United We Dream and other organizations have also reminded undocumented young adults that engaging in radical care—whether it is self-care or caring for others—is also essential in fighting against oppression and can even provide hope during dark times. These forms of care and everyday actions are also creative, adaptable, and generative, serving as a powerful complement to public activism. Thus, everyday activism will continue to be a critical component of undocumented young adults' resilience strategies in their continued quest for justice and well-being. Though speaking during the previous Trump administration, Juan's optimistic insights about immigrant young adults' fortitude and transformative potential ring true again now: "I don't know a single person that has DACA that isn't extra resilient, extra resourceful. That's the resilience that you have to develop to survive, but also to thrive. I've learned to appreciate the resilience and the motivation that I've developed. It makes me more confident to tackle bigger challenges than I thought that I could."

ACKNOWLEDGMENTS

First and foremost, I am profoundly grateful to the immigrant young adults (now just *adults*) who generously shared their experiences with me during a particularly unsettling period of their lives. While our initial conversations in 2016 centered around the positive developments that DACA helped usher in, over time DACA transformed into a source of great stress and uncertainty. Yet they continued to share their updates and led me to see how they were flourishing despite the challenges they faced. I also appreciate the subset who participated in the DACAmented Dream Team—which took on a life of its own and became a critical source of sociality, support, and solidarity for all of us. I have tremendous gratitude for the manifold contributions of my research team, Alaska Burdette, Ana Ortez-Rivera, Delmis Umanzor, Kaelin Rapport, and Umai Habibah, who inspire me with their dedication, drive, compassion, and kindness (of which I have been the recipient numerous times). The team's contributions were essential at every stage and made the project better in every possibly respect. Convening this research team and forming the CAB have been among the most fulfilling experiences of my academic career.

I thank Cirila Estela Vásquez Guzmán for her friendship and our many conversations about DACA, including related to my burgeoning ideas for this book, as well as Ewaoluwa Ogundana Obatuase for her input and for priming my interest in professional licensure. Both Estela and Ewa are passionate scholars and advocates whom I am privileged to know and learn from. I am also grateful to Elizabeth Hanna Rubio, Lupi-Quintero Grady, and Cecilia Dos Santos for sharing their local CBO and community knowledge and facilitating contacts with potential participants as the project launched. I wish to thank the University of Maryland (UMD)'s Yvette Lerma Jones and Laura Bohórquez Garcia for distributing information about the project and acknowledge them and Rocio Fregoso-Mota, Perla Guerrero, and Janelle Wong for their tireless advocacy on behalf of immigrant students and students from mixed-status families on our campus. The Center for Global Migration Studies is an important immigration hub on the UMD campus; I thank founding Director Julie Greene and Executive Director Kate Keane for their efforts in creating my position through the immigration cluster hire and bringing me on as Associate Director of the center. I also thank the subsequent Directors, Colleen Woods and Madeline Hsu, for their leadership and collegiality.

UMD has been the ideal place in which to carry out this project and write this book. I received generous institutional support through several UMD mechanisms. The initial phase was funded through my startup funds from the Department of Anthropology as well as through a Research and Scholarship Award from the Graduate School. Subsequently, I received two generous rounds of funding through the Dean's Research Initiative of the College of Behavioral and Social Sciences. I greatly appreciate (former) Associate Dean for Research Jeff Lucas's guidance in crafting these applications, and his and (former) Chair of Sociology Patricio Korzeniewicz's willingness to brainstorm alternative options for funding DACA recipient consultants and scholars. Most recently, I benefitted tremendously from a UMD Division of Research Independent Scholarship, Research and Creativity Award that enabled me to complete this manuscript in conjunction with my sabbatical. I am immensely grateful to Sybil Paige for adeptly managing all of these submissions and awards.

Next, I would like to thank my other colleagues and students in the Anthropology Department for their ongoing support. I thank chairs and cherished mentors Paul Shackel and Barnet Pavão-Zuckerman for their wisdom and belief in me and my work, as well as Judith Freidenberg and Janet Chernela for their mentorship in the earlier phases of the project. As I initially conceptualized this project, Judith Freidenberg brought me into the local fold, graciously sharing her knowledge, contacts, and ideas. I am also grateful to Jen Shaffer for stepping up as Director of Graduate Studies while I was on sabbatical completing this book, as well as to Nadine Dangerfield for being a wonderful partner in running our graduate program and for always providing moral support in just the right way. I also thank my UMD colleagues and co-conspirators Andrea López and Matt Thomann for always having my back and (re)building together a thriving and supportive Medical Anthropology community. I am also grateful to UMD students (several now doctors or soon-to-be doctors) Emiliano Campos, Nic Galloway, Emilia Guevara, Magda Mankel, Silvana Montañola, Sammy Primiano, Cinthya Salazar, John Salerno, and Rachel Smith for our productive conversations that have pushed my thinking in new directions. I also thank Julieta Ferrera for her meticulous editorial assistance. I also benefited from stimulating discussions with my insightful students in my courses on Immigration Policies, Global Migration and Health, Health Disparities, and Qualitative Methods. Indeed, everyday activism is a concept that resonates with them deeply, which led me to think about it more and eventually as the book's organizing framework.

Earlier drafts of ideas that informed this book were presented in numerous sessions of the American Anthropological Association and Society for Applied Anthropology Annual Meetings as well as the inaugural Im/migrant Well-Being Conference (organized by Elizabeth Aranda and Elizabeth Vaquera). Participation in these sessions and engagement with colleagues sharpened my focus and strengthened my arguments. I also thank Thomas Rachko from the Im/migrant Well-Being Scholar Collaborative for arranging meetings with congressional offices as I sought to more broadly disseminate these research findings and advocate in the policy sphere. Throughout this project, I have benefitted tremendously from the support and inspiration of my AANIR colleagues, particularly fellow steering committee members Whitney Duncan, Lauren Heidbrink, Sarah Horton, Mariela Nuñez-Janes, Kristin Yarris, Nolan Kline, Bill Lopez, and Tobin Hansen. During the interminable COVID-19 years in which Zoom was one of our few professional engagement outlets, our AANIR meetings, conversations, conference presentations, book plannings, and informal check-ins were a professional lifeline and always serve as inspirational reminders of resourceful ways of showing up for immigrant communities. I always look up to and look forward to catching up with Debbie Boehm and Sarah Horton and treasure their encouragement, advice, and feedback. This project definitely benefitted from extensive collaborations and many years of discussions with my mentors and colleagues in the UNM School of Medicine, among them Catie Willging, Miria Kano, Andrew Sussman, Julia Meredith Hess, Angélica Solares, and Jacque García Sánchez.

Though I completed my doctorate long ago, my dissertation chair Louise Lamphere continues to show up to every single conference presentation I give and offer her constructive critique, unwavering support, and invaluable career advice. I am also incredibly fortunate to have cherished grad school and lifelong friends Nicole Coffey Kellett, Lisa Jane Hardy, Gwen Saul, and Lara Gunderson as faithful members of my support network and valued advice givers. I also appreciate the support of my nonacademic friends—particularly Ami Retamoza, Joy Ferrante, and Andy and Jen Fitch—who (indirectly) challenged me to describe this project in more intelligible ways.

I am also grateful to New York University Press for their sustained interest in my work. Since I first met her in 2016, my interactions with senior editor Jennifer Hammer have been engaging and productive. I am very appreciative that she kept checking in with me regularly about the status of this project during the long pandemic years until I finally had something to share. I have valued her clear communication and steady guidance throughout the publication process. The recommendations made by the two anonymous external reviewers also strengthened the manuscript in important ways. I also appreciate editing, design, and production director Valerie Zaborski, copy editor Joseph Dahm, and editorial assistant Brianna Jean for their assistance and flexibility in transforming the manuscript into its final book form. I also thank Arc Indexing, Inc. for creating the index for the book.

Finally, I am and will always be grateful for the support and love of my family throughout this project and every phase of my academic career. My parents Rich and Judy—editor and teacher extraordinaire—lovingly imparted the skills and sensitivities that have served me so well in work and life. I am beyond pleased that my father now uses his red pen quite sparingly when he reads what I write. My sister Diana and I have gone through so much together—especially the extreme ups and downs of the period in which this project unfolded—and she is always one of my best sounding boards and supporters. My partner Matt always shows up for me and our family every day in so many ways. I am immensely grateful for his love and encouragement, especially as I attempted to keep this project moving forward. Finally, I thank our daughter Marisa for bringing our family so much joy with her bright smile, passionate personality, and endless enthusiasm. Though I sincerely hope that the world will be a more just place as she comes of age politically, I know that she will put that light, passion, and enthusiasm to good use in advocating for social justice issues that inspire her.

APPENDIX A

Research Design and Methodological Reflections

The research design of the project upon which this book is based can be easily described in more conventional scholarly terms as commonly featured in peer-reviewed academic journals and books. Yet the evolving story of the project reads quite differently and is revelatory of deeper connections and collaborative relationships forged over a period of years.[1] I first present the nuts and bolts of the research design and then describe the evolution of the project in a more nuanced manner that attends to larger discussions about critically engaged scholarship.

RESEARCH DESIGN

Everyday Activists is based on a longitudinal, mixed-methods research project focused on DACA recipients living in the Washington, D.C., Metro region. The research protocol was approved by the Institutional Review Board of the University of Maryland, College Park. The research was conducted over a five-year period (2016–21) during three distinct phases: (I) when DACA was fully intact (in 2016 before the election), (II) after the 2017 announcement endangering DACA (2017–18), and (III) during the protracted legal battle over DACA after the 2020 Supreme Court decision (2020–21). I conceptualized the project and am the principal investigator, though I conducted it collaboratively with a research team of five student researchers and a Community Advisory Board (CAB) of eight DACA recipients.

DACA recipients are not a preexisting or cohesive "community" but rather individuals who fall under an externally created state classification based on common bases of experiences: being born outside of the United States, immigrating before age sixteen, spending at least part of childhood without authorized immigration status, and being young adults (specifically, thirty-one or younger on June 15, 2012). Conducting research with a group characterized by its loose organization, vulnerable status, and youth required special recruitment strategies.[2] Initial recruitment strategies consisted of tapping into research team members' personal networks, distributing a recruitment flyer through youth-focused CBOs, and posting a recruitment flyer to a social media group organized around DREAMer activism, which yielded an initial thirteen participants (seven, three, and three, respectively). We then used a snowball sample, which was particularly appropriate for this "hidden population."[3] Many participants did not regularly share their status with others—even close friends—meaning that recruiting participants via trusted contacts was essential. These referrals ultimately yielded another seventeen participants, bringing us to thirty total for phase I. Despite our best efforts at recontacting participants, we could not reach five individuals in phase II and lost an additional participant to attrition in phase III, bringing the number who participated in all three phases to twenty-four. In total, we conducted seventy-nine interviews.

Phase I and phase II data collection took place in person at participants' choice of location, which included offices, workplaces, restaurants and coffee shops, and public spaces and parks throughout the D.C. Metro region. After being consented, participants filled out a four-page questionnaire and then participated in a semistructured interview lasting between forty-five and ninety minutes. We were prepared to conduct data collection activities in Spanish (as I know advanced Spanish and two team members had native fluency) but ultimately conducted all research activities in English, with some participants interspersing Spanish words or phrases. Phase III consisted of semistructured interviews conducted online over Zoom due to COVID-19-related research restrictions. During phase I, I conducted each data collection activity along with one student researcher so that they could practice research skills and take on a more active role over time. After phase I, the students started graduating and transitioning to jobs and graduate school; nonetheless, three continued to participate as time and other constraints permitted. Into phase II, researcher pairs conducted nineteen interviews and I conducted six solo. For phase III, researcher pairs conducted fifteen and I conducted eight solo.

The research team designed the data collection instruments together in early 2016, stemming from our research questions and drawing from established and validated instruments. The questionnaire collected basic demographic data, including age, gender, ethnoracial background, country of origin, household composition, income, and educational attainment. It also included measures adapted from the Health Information National Trends Survey (HINTS),[4] which gauged access to health care, health coverage, type of coverage, frequency of visits to a health professional, self-report rating of health status, diagnosed conditions, and social network communication, as well as the validated Patient Health Questionnaire (PHQ-4),[5] which assessed psychological distress. The semistructured interview explored participants' lives pre- and post-DACA, including their immigration story, experiences learning about and applying for DACA, the impacts of DACA, DACA's influence on their health, and their changing health status and state of mind, overall well-being, identity, and belonging. Additional items were added in phases II and III to capture life changes (e.g., job transitions and moves), the shifting sociopolitical climate (e.g., the DACA rescission and Supreme Court ruling), experiences navigating the immigration bureaucracy, and strategies for maintaining well-being.

We used SPSS statistics to analyze questionnaire data and QSR NVivo to analyze interviews and field notes. We created a codebook and entered the questionnaire data into SPSS for analysis. Given the small sample size, the questionnaire data have largely been used for descriptive purposes. All interviews were recorded (with permission) and transcribed verbatim for subsequent analysis, which followed principles of grounded theory.[6] During phase I, we first selected an initial set of three transcripts to open code individually.[7] We then met as a team to review the set of transcripts line by line, identifying and refining codes and establishing a preliminary coding scheme. Next, we chose another two transcripts to test and refine the coding scheme, continuing that process until we constituted the full set of codes and reached consensus about their application. Three team members then coded a set of transcripts to ensure interrater reliability. Once the coding scheme was finalized, we coded all transcripts in NVivo and then generated reports and created analytic memos to review together during weekly team meetings.

Between phase I and phase II, we added a participatory component by forming a CAB—the DACAmented DREAM Team—which met twice a year over the next four years, initially in person, though online starting in 2020 due to the pandemic. CABs serve as infrastructure for building academic-community partnerships that are collaborative, seek to co-construct knowledge production, and aim to combine knowledge and action for social change. CAB members are selected based on their lived experiences, local knowledge, and specialized skill sets.[8] They provide valuable insight about the research topic and input on research activities at any or every stage (depending on how deeply collaborative the project is), including designing the study and study instruments, strategizing about and facilitating recruitment, participating in data collection, analyzing data and validating interpretations, and disseminating findings.[9] Among other activities, members of the DACAmented DREAM Team helped shape research directions, provided input on study instruments, served as a member check on interpretations, and collaboratively coauthored a publication. We presented CAB members with analytic memos and elicited feedback on emerging findings, starting with phase I data. After phase II data collection wrapped up, we repeated the same analytic process, including developing a coding scheme, coding systematically within NVivo, and eliciting feedback on analytic memos from the CAB. Moving into phase III, I developed the coding scheme and coded the data within NVivo. During this phase, though, I also took a qualitative longitudinal case study approach,[10] reviewing transcripts from the same twenty-four individuals across the three time points to develop case profiles.

We disseminated our findings through different modalities. The first dissemination activity was a community meeting we convened in March 2017 to present emerging findings to participants and supporters. We presented results at numerous national professional anthropology conferences as well as on campus (at an event oriented toward fostering local community connections, at two student-organized conferences, to a medical school student group, at a counseling center workshop, and at university-wide events). We have also published manuscripts, in both peer-reviewed journals and an editor-reviewed journal focused on applied anthropological practice, in which three students and the CAB published articles (the latter of which was also translated into Spanish). We have also contributed to more public-facing blogs, statements, and op-eds on DACA and immigration. This book, which I conceptualized building from the project I led over a five-year period, is the culmination of these activities. While I have coauthored extensively with my collaborators, I

Figure A.1. The DACAmented DREAM
Team at work, June 2018. Source: Christina
M. Getrich.

am the sole author of this book due to book publication norms and the potential burden of time involved in coproducing a manuscript of this length, and out of respect for my collaborators' busy schedules and focus on other endeavors in their adult lives. Despite being the sole author, I sought (and secured) team members' permission to be acknowledged for their substantial contributions. I also presented the book's findings to team and CAB members for their input, and they ultimately enthusiastically endorsed this final product of our collective labor.

SCHOLARLY PRAXIS AND AN EMERGING METHODOLOGY
OF EVERYDAY ACTIVISM

Though the above iteration of the research design highlights all of the relevant methodological details, it does not fully capture important contextual dimensions of the project, including its beginnings, how it evolved over time, and how relationships shaped it, as well as how it is informed by larger debates about critically engaged scholarship. I did not initially design this project as a three-phase longitudinal project carried out with student and community collaborators; rather, the project evolved iteratively over time as unforeseeable developments related to DACA and the pandemic transpired and relationships with participants took it in new directions.[11] I also made methodological adaptations to the project in response to intensifying appeals in the late 2010s to decolonize anthropology and the research enterprise itself amid the first election of Donald Trump, national reckoning over racial injustice led by the Movement for Black Lives, and recognition of the social inequalities laid bare by the COVID-19 pandemic, as I described in the introduction.

Several influential works emerging during this time shaped not only my theoretical approach but also my thinking about methodology and scholarly praxis.[12] These decolonized, coproduced volumes are formidable exemplars of engaged scholarship, advancing longer-standing critiques of applied anthropology conducted in the colonial mold. Applied anthropology has a long and fraught history, criticized for its lack of theoretical rigor as well as its ties to colonialism and applied anthropologists' complicity in perpetuating hegemonic power structures. Yet scholars have noted the wide complexity and diversity of work that falls under the broad rubric of applied anthropology, including approaches that presage more contemporary concerns like collaboration.[13] At the beginning of the twenty-first century, a repositioning toward pragmatic engagement and convergence around shared goals and interests stemming from distinct applied, practicing, and public interest traditions ushered in more collaborative partnership arrangements, expanded public dissemination of findings, and resulted in targeted efforts to influence policy.[14] Some of these interests in pragmatic engagement are also key features of participatory approaches like participatory action research (PAR), community-based participatory research (CBPR), and community-engaged research (CEnR) found in anthropology but also commonly in fields like education and public health, underscoring that other disciplines are also deeply engaged in reshaping research practices.[15]

Although more engaged and participatory approaches have become more commonplace, there is still a lack of clear consensus about what exactly "engagement" means; as anthropologist Angela Stuesse, points out, "The term 'engagement' . . . has as many meanings as it does users."[16] Engaged scholars range from more limited forms of social critique in academic and public forums to direct advocacy, collaboration, and activism.[17] Anthropologist Setha M. Low acknowledges that engagement is "practiced in different geopolitical contexts, under diverse social conditions, and during distinct historical moments"; she offers a unifying definition of engaged anthropology as "those activities that grow out of a commitment to the informants and communities with whom anthropologists work and a values-based stance that anthropological research respect the dignity and rights of all people and have a beneficent effect on the promotion of social justice."[18] Anthropologist Ashanté M. Reese points out that in the Black feminist anthropological tradition, being an engaged anthropologist in this manner is not "separate or optional" from "regular" anthropology but rather is central to actualizing the potential of the discipline.[19]

Anthropologist and Indigenous scholar Shannon Speed makes the case for a critically engaged *activist* approach that includes both sharp critical cultural analysis and engagement with research participants directed toward a shared political goal, arguing that such an approach is ethically and practically warranted.[20] Driven by a politics of liberation, activist-scholars regard research as a tool that marginalized groups can use to effect social transformation toward greater equality and justice. Activist-scholars tend to take a longer-term and more horizontal approach to collaboration as they forge explicit political alignment with those organizing for social change.[21] Some medical anthropologists like Adrienne Pine, Dvera Saxton, and Nancy Scheper-Hughes have called for an even more radically engaged mode of embodied ethnographic praxis involving *compañerísmo*, or being a companion in the struggle,[22] extending beyond activism in its level of political commitment, moral engagement, and embodied investment in organizing for social change.[23]

Many immigration scholars have taken critically engaged activist approaches, making interventions into disciplinary debates about decolonized theory and praxis while working alongside and in collaboration with immigrant communities in pursuit of rights, justice, and liberation. Below, I situate this project within these theoretical and methodological currents, by examining its background and beginnings, how we collaboratively forged the next phase, and how the project transformed during the pandemic. In doing so, I also consider the potential of everyday activism—not merely as an academic phenomenon to be observed in others but also as a mode of scholarly engagement.

BACKGROUND AND PROJECT BEGINNINGS

My motivation for beginning this research was multifaceted and shaped by my background and social identities as well as my training in applied anthropology and interdisciplinary, mixed-method research. I share information about my positionality to provide readers with a sense of "how, why, and in what ways" this research project was conducted as well as to offer a reflexive account of the power relations imbued in the research.[24] I was motivated to conduct research where I grew up in the D.C. Metro region once I returned as a UMD faculty member. I was born in D.C. and spent my first few years in Silver Spring (in Montgomery County), before moving to Gaithersburg, where I spent the majority of my childhood in middle-class townhouse neighborhoods. At that point, Gaithersburg was at the edge of the D.C. Metro region (as people thought and talked about it), though the boundary subsequently expanded further (see chapter 1). The D.C. Metro region was undergoing its transformation into a hyperdiverse immigrant gateway, which was reflected in my childhood schools, neighborhoods, and friendships. I am white and a few generations removed from my family's migration experiences; on my father's side, my immigrant great-grandparents migrated from Poland and Lithuania in the late 1800s and labored in the anthracite coal mines of central Pennsylvania, where my father grew up in a community that was (and still is) quite stratified by national origin and ethnicity. Though I did not know the sociological terms at the time, as I grew up I was particularly intrigued by the experiences of my first-, 1.5-, and second-generation Latinx friends (in particular, from Mexico, Argentina, Colombia, and Ecuador), which only intensified as I studied Spanish in middle and high school and eventually college (including studying abroad in Ecuador).

Though my roots are in the D.C. Metro region, I completed graduate school in the Southwest, first at Northern Arizona University (NAU) for my master's and then at the University of New Mexico (UNM) for my doctorate and postdoctoral fellowship in the UNM School of Medicine (SOM). Over the next fifteen years, I conducted research in California (San Diego) and New Mexico (Albuquerque and rural communities statewide), with my immigration-focused research centering mostly on the experiences of Mexican immigrants and their children. I was trained as an applied anthropologist at NAU and focused on border enforcement policies and immigrant rights activism for my master's project. My dissertation project focused on mixed-status families in the U.S.-Mexico borderlands, which became a longitudinal project that formed the basis of my first book. This project demonstrated to me that chronicling the experiences of a smaller set of participants as they transitioned to adulthood was an ideal approach for understanding the incorporation trajectories of young adults from immigrant families—especially against the backdrop of a changing immigration policy landscape.[25] During my doctoral training and subsequently during my postdoctoral fellowship at UNM, I collaborated with colleagues in sociology, economics, psychology, psychiatry, public health, and medicine on mixed-method projects focused on health disparities and primary care health service delivery to Latinx, American Indian, and other marginalized populations in constrained service environments in one of the economically poorest—though culturally richest—U.S. states.

In 2014, I came back to the D.C. Metro region when I took a faculty position at UMD (in Prince George's County) and moved back to Silver Spring, not far from where I lived as a child. As I reacclimated, I wanted to start a locally based project exploring immigrant young adults' experiences in the D.C. Metro region—a much different sociolegal context than the communities in the U.S. Southwest where I had conducted most of my previous research. As an area resident and professor at a public university with a sizeable first-, 1.5-, and second-generation immigrant student body, I knew that local immigrant young adults were likely to be of incredibly diverse national origins, mirroring the broader regional pattern (see chapter 1). DACA had also just recently been created, which also presented a unique temporal opportunity to understand more about the impact of status gains, a welcome shift from my previous focus on immigration-related policy exclusions and the health-related implications of racialized enforcement.

For many critical immigration scholars, taking an engaged approach involves partnering with CBOs or coalitions and networks focused on immigrant rights, health care access, environmental justice, worker rights, and legal advocacy.[26] I had also previously taken this approach, collaborating with an immigrant rights CBO for my master's research, youth development CBO for my dissertation, and network of CHCs during my postdoc and as a research scientist in the UNM SOM. As an initial step for this project, I began as I had previously done: by volunteering at a local CBO's DACA clinic starting in fall 2014. The CBO ran a monthly clinic to provide application support to individuals submitting an initial application or renewal. Volunteers attended a brief training and then assisted with filling out the application, reviewing supporting documents to ensure that it was complete and ready for the legal team's final review. Volunteering provided me a sense of the bureaucratic processes to which DACA recipients were subjected and provided a window into their lives in the D.C. Metro region as we talked through their migration and settlement experiences.

I also participated in collective mobilizations organized by this CBO and student groups on my campus, which I had likewise done previously in California and New Mexico. My student collaborators and I participated in a range of different actions throughout the D.C. Metro region including regular May Day protests in support of immigrant and workers' rights and protests at the Supreme Court in support of the ill-fated Deferred Action for Parents of Americans (DAPA) executive action and during the opening arguments in the DACA rescission case. As I continued volunteering at the CBO, though, I started noting that many people who came to the DACA clinic did not participate in the CBO's regular programming or public actions, which made me start wondering more about the experiences of DACA recipients who were not active in organizing spaces. I also knew that I did not want to limit the focus to college campuses and students. I started envisioning a more decentralized project that delved into the experiences of nonactivists and nonstudents throughout the DMV region.

As scholars have worked in immigrant advocacy spaces, they have often wrestled with balancing their different roles and commitments as well as the complex relationships they forge with collaborators that defy easy categorization.[27] A critical step in thinking through the nuances of these relationships is reckoning with power imbalances that often exist for scholars with more secure statuses (like lawful permanent residency or citizenship) that insulate them from the violence of the state.[28] Stuesse, for instance, squarely acknowledges that her status "as a citizen proffered a myriad of daily privileges that granted me access to research subjects, spaces, and security" not available to her fellow poultry justice advocates in Mississippi.[29] Public health scholar William D. Lopez likewise describes intersecting forms of privilege—like citizenship, skin color, and professional status—that facilitated his research on the impact of immigration enforcement in Michigan, which he carried out in collaboration with an immigrant rights coalition. He urges engaged scholars to leverage this privilege: "Those with citizen status can and should advocate in places where our undocumented neighbors cannot."[30] Other power imbalances that are particularly salient in research with undocumented young adults are professional status, age, and generation.

For me, these power imbalances existed in relation to both student and DACA recipient collaborators. Recently, scholars have started detailing more about their collaborative relationships with students. In *We Are Not Dreamers*, Abrego and Negrón-Gonzales describe the genesis of the volume as their shared experiences mentoring undocumented students researching different aspects of undocumented life in the United States.[31] Anthropologist Rebecca Berke Galemba describes how her project focused on wage theft and undocumented workers was initially constructed as a classroom-community partnership with a CBO; subsequently, multiple waves of students continued to participate as the scope of the project expanded and are featured in the resulting ethnography.[32] As this project solidified in 2015, a few of my standout students expressed their eagerness to gain more hands-on experience in applied immigration solidarity work, and I decided to form a research team. Our team consisted of undergraduate students Alaska Burdette, Ana Ortez-Rivera, and Delmis Umanzor, who joined the project first and remained on the project for its duration (years after they graduated), and graduate students Kaelin Rapport and Umai Habibah, who participated for a shorter period during and immediately after earning master's degrees. Although I occupied a position of power relative to the students, as a professor and someone who was in charge of their training and assigned them grades, the hierarchical nature of this relationship transformed over time, as I describe below. Into phases II and III, Alaska, Ana, and Delmis became my "former students" and turned into invaluable long-term collaborators who continued to participate out of their own multifaceted commitments to participants and immigrant justice.

The students' contributions were invaluable and majorly facilitated the research. As a nonimmigrant and relatively new (re)transplant to the region, I was still forging connections with local immigrant communities of which I was not a member, whereas several of my students were from and/or already deeply embedded in them. Four came from immigrant families; one was born outside of the United States (in Pakistan), and four were U.S.-born but had parents from El Salvador, Honduras, and the United Kingdom. Some of their families were quite similar to our eventual participants' families in multiple respects, including their country of origin, neighborhoods of residence, and socioeconomic status. Despite team members' immigrant roots and sensitivity to immigration-related issues, the team was ultimately composed of U.S. citizens and residents with more secure status than our research participants. As white citizens, Alaska and I also did not directly experience the impact of the racialized anti-immigrant and anti-Muslim attacks that proliferated once Trump took office and deeply affected other team members, their families, and research participants. Team members occupied positions of relative privilege (each in our own way) and reflected on this regularly during our team meetings as we sought to adopt a collective posture of humility and solidarity.[33]

My student researchers' contributions were readily apparent and greatly appreciated in every phase. As we designed study instruments initially, they thought about how family members and friends might respond to questions and made helpful wording recommendations. For instance, Delmis pointed out that instead of asking what year participants had migrated, we should ask their age when they came, since that is more commonly how youth she knew talked about their arrival and would be easier to answer. They were also the same age and generation as DACA recipients, while there was a much larger age gap between me and participants, as I had just turned forty. Indeed, my student collaborators mentored me about designing study instruments and tailored recruitment approaches that resonated with their generation and life circumstances, highlighting quite clearly that students are not the only beneficiaries of academic mentorship relationships.

As we began recruitment, we brainstormed a list of people in our personal networks who we knew had DACA, with the students contributing the majority. Their contacts were childhood friends, friends of friends, extended family members, family friends, and coworkers. The student researchers greatly facilitated trust building between me and our initial participants as they essentially vouched for me, signaling that I was trustworthy and that the project was being conducted in an ethical and respectful manner. These endorsements also carried major weight as participants referred us to their DACA recipient family members and friends, conveying to them that we could be trusted with their stories and that participating was worthwhile. There was also a status differential between me and the DACA recipient participants given that I was a professor and many DACA recipients were students (though not my students). The presence and participation of student researchers helped to bridge some of that differential. Over time, I found that most participants appreciated having a professor with whom they had no official academic relationship as a resource, and I was more than happy to share advice and academic capital.

Each team member also had different place-based connections that facilitated the research in unexpected ways. Alaska, Delmis, and I all lived in and mostly grew up in Montgomery County, so our connections ran deeper there, while Ana had lived in and had ties to both Prince George's County and D.C. As we began data collection, each of us was able to build specialized rapport with participants who lived in the local communities most familiar to us. For instance, as Ana and I interviewed a participant in Gaithersburg not far from my childhood neighborhood, the participant and I realized fairly quickly that we knew someone in common: my beloved middle school Spanish teacher who had subsequently become a county resource advocate for Latinx families and mentored him in accessing college. Recognition of our shared connection greatly facilitated rapport and defused some of the awkwardness of the interview encounter. As Ana and I got situated for an interview with another participant, who had been referred to us by a friend, they recognized each other from attending the same high school in the same graduating class and quickly determined that they knew people in common. This surprise connection put both Ana, who was new to conducting interviews, and the participant, who was new to participating in research, at ease. This individual ended up being one of our richest initial interviews and someone with whom we forged the deepest relationships over time.

BUILDING THE NEXT PHASE: FORGING ACCOMPANIMENT
IN THE FIRST TRUMP ERA

Even after we had wrapped up data collection and were deep in analysis, we remained focused on maintaining relationships we forged with participants, especially after President Trump was elected and inaugurated and started escalating his attacks on immigrants and DACA recipients. We also felt a new urgency in sharing findings via community channels and decided to hold a community meeting in March 2017 to

present preliminary findings and plan next steps, and invited participants, their friends and family members, and community and university
supporters. In addition to providing useful feedback, participants who
attended urged us to continue with the research, given the increased
vulnerability of DACA recipients, and indicated that they would like to
become more involved. We brainstormed about what form that involvement might take, ultimately deciding to create our own space and way
of holding space in the form of the CAB. CABs are particularly productive structures for collaborating with immigrant communities due
to their focus on trust, respect for community norms, and consideration of immigration-related vulnerabilities.[34] They can be particularly
advantageous in addressing mental health trauma and distress related to
migration, settlement-related stressors, and ongoing legal status precarity.[35] CABs are also beneficial with undocumented youth specifically in
reckoning with their marginalized status, addressing their limited access
to care, and promoting overall well-being.[36] I already had experience
with CABs from my six years at the UNM SOM working with research
groups that had advisory boards of primary care clinicians and community members.

We were intentional in ensuring that the CAB had individuals from
different countries of origin; who represented different ages, life course
phases, gender identities, sexualities, and religious backgrounds; lived
in different jurisdictions within the D.C. Metro region; and ranged from
being full-time college students to nonstudent / full-time employees. It
was important to us to represent the diversity of our sample (since we
were not working within a single "community" of DACA recipients) and
forge connections, as some DACA recipients had expressed that they felt
isolated and were looking to connect more with other DACA recipients
since they did not know many others with the same status. CAB members were valued as consultants and remunerated accordingly for each
meeting in which they participated (including out of pocket when my
grant funding for the meetings dried up).

The first meeting took place on August 22, 2017—unbeknownst to us,
exactly two weeks before the DACA rescission announcement. Some
members knew that Trump intended to take action to end DACA, although for others this news came as an unsettling shock that we then
processed together. From our first meeting, then, the DACAmented

DREAM Team (as we named it that day) served as more than just a research entity—it was a vehicle for disseminating information and a safe space for providing social support in response to political instability.[37] We spent a good amount of time initially establishing relationships and building community, which was especially important given the weight of the DACA rescission news and the chaos that it ushered in during subsequent months. We also charted out the next phase of the project, which focused on DACA recipients' mental health and access to resources—topics that members identified as being critically important.

After the rescission announcement on September 5, I paused the beginning of the intended phase II interviews out of respect for participants' mental health. Instead, I reached out to participants individually to check in and got together with them to provide support in whatever way I could. When CAB members signaled that they were ready a few months later, we began phase II. We had completed one-third of the interviews by the second CAB meeting in January 2018, which enabled us to present some initial themes and iteratively add new topics to inquire about for the remaining interviews. The second meeting took place immediately after the three-day government shutdown over DACA, which occupied our attention. The timing of the CAB meetings often coincidentally corresponded to major developments related to DACA, including another government shutdown (the longest in U.S. history), federal court decisions about lawsuits related to DACA, and the Supreme Court decision blocking the Trump administration from ending DACA, which kept the research in sync with the changing DACA landscape. The CAB provided a critical space to learn about and process these updates and lend support as members contended with ongoing uncertainty. Over time, and as more members settled into their careers, the CAB also became a space for emerging professionals to share navigational capital related to health, education, and legal resources, underscoring the horizontal dimension of solidarity.

As the CAB shifted in form and purpose over time, we started thinking about it as a mode of *acompañamiento* (accompaniment)[38] in conversation with colleagues from the Anthropologist Action Network for Immigrants and Refugees (AANIR). AANIR is an informal collective of engaged anthropologists working with immigrant communities founded in November 2016 in the wake of the election of Trump to strategize about how to best support immigrant collaborators, students, and friends experiencing attacks on their safety, health, and well-being.[39] Many engaged scholars recognize the centrality of accompaniment, rooted in the tradition of Latin American liberation theology, to their research methodology. In their collaborative volume, scholar-activists Pedro Santiago Martinez, Claudia Muñoz, Mariela Nuñez-Janes, Stephen Pavey, Fidel Castro Rodríguez, and Marco Saavedra define accompaniment as "walking alongside undocumented immigrant experts and others marginalized by the U.S. state and capitalist economic system . . . as a way of life involving a relationship of mutuality and reciprocity towards our collective liberation."[40] In their edited volume stemming from AANIR discussions, anthropologists Kristin E. Yarris and Whitney L. Duncan note that accompaniment represents a decolonial form of ethnographic engagement with immigrants but also a relational and care-based form of solidarity grounded in universal humanity and explicit acknowledgments of power.[41]

As the CAB continued forward in 2018, these relational and care-based dimensions became more central as we became more invested in each other's lives. As our relationships complexified, the boundaries of our roles also shifted and blurred.[42] We celebrated milestones like one member finally getting a driver's license (after a multiyear quest), graduations, new jobs, new relationships, and trips taken; members also provided support to each other as they dealt with DACA-related frustrations (like not being able to pursue a job because of status-related exclusions) and the challenges of adulting as a DACA recipient. In phase II, I was also pregnant. I kept conducting research until two weeks before my daughter was born, deciding to finally stop when I was having trouble walking up stairs and sitting comfortably (and attentively) for the duration of an interview. Our CAB stuck to our regular meeting schedule, holding a meeting weeks before my daughter was born, and at their insistence my daughter joined us for her first meeting when she was five months old. Since then, I have not had an encounter with either a team or CAB member in which they have not inquired about my daughter, asked to see pictures, and marveled at how much she has grown. Years later, I continue to get thoughtful Mother's Day messages from them too. Indeed, they unquestionably showed up for me during a major transition in my life, underscoring how care can flow bidirectionally in relationships carefully forged over time and through the research process. Motherhood has also shifted how I conduct research, as I have different constraints on my schedule and it has been harder to attend CBO activities and mass mobilizations, especially during the pandemic; thus, I have come to rely all the more on everyday activism as a mode of practice (as I describe more in the conclusion). The pandemic also ushered in methodological innovation by necessity in ways that strangely aligned well with being the mother of a toddler.

TRANSITIONING TO PANDEMIC-BASED RESEARCH, SOCIALITY, AND SOLIDARITY

The onset of the COVID-19 pandemic in early 2020 necessitated a major shift in how *everyone* conducted research, shifting to what anthropologist Nicholas Long refers to as "lockdown anthropology" of newly emerging social worlds.[43] The CAB easily transplanted into this new realm. In fact, during our January 2020 meeting, we had already decided to meet more frequently, despite the increasing logistical challenges of doing so, and to experiment with holding virtual meetings. Ana, who had always been our most tech-savvy member, ushered us into the digital space. As the pandemic intensified, we held monthly meetings that became more social and supportive in nature. One of our early exercises in reconfiguring how we engaged with each other was to generate a monthly prompt and have each member populate a shared slides document with a meme or GIF that captured our response. Our responses reflected our intense need for connection, as we talked about missing giving people hugs, being able to see crazy/funny coworkers in person, and going to concerts and bars with friends.

We also started using the space to forge new forms of sociality and configurations of care that did not require physical copresence.[44] Some CAB members confronted COVID-19 every day in their jobs as a paramedic, mental health provider, and information specialist in a public transportation system; they updated us about how things really were out in the world. We, in turn, provided them support in confronting illness, death, and the heavy weight of their work. Those of us who worked remotely were grappling with a different set of challenges: disruption to our normal workday routines and social isolation, which was impacting our relationships and challenging our capacity to provide more normative forms of care. The CAB meetings offered a brief but regular respite from work and caregiving responsibilities and dose of therapeutic connection. As an already-established network, members also shared information about supporting more vulnerable immigrant community members through a food drive put on by the CBO where one worked as well as a crowdfunding campaign for emergency funds for immigrants left out of pandemic relief. The CAB served as an innovative mode of "corona sociality" through which we cultivated evolving forms of care and support for each other.[45]

These changes also underscored that research itself can take on the form of care and investment in human relationships.[46] In the initial months of the pandemic, the CAB provided a space to forge a different kind of intimacy rooted in our common humanity and need to accompany each other through great uncertainty and abrupt changes to our everyday lives. As Saxton notes, this type of relationship building—forged on a foundation of trust and shared commitments to effecting social change—can itself constitute a form of activism.[47] I would argue that such relationship building can also form the basis of *everyday* activism. We remained focused on DACA and our shared commitments to promoting immigrant well-being and justice. As we all adapted to our new circumstances, another major development related to DACA transpired: the July 18, 2020, Supreme Court ruling blocking the Trump administration's termination of DACA on the grounds of it being done "in an arbitrary and capricious manner." From the vantage point of a few years later, it is clear that while the ruling did not spell the end to DACA, it perpetuated continued uncertainty.

With the CAB's endorsement, I decided to begin a third phase of research to continue to track the impact of this prolonged uncertainty on DACA recipients' lives. Given the severe restrictions on human subjects research due to the pandemic, phase III had to be conducted on Zoom. Despite the inherent challenges of Zoom-based research, the platform actually worked well because I had already cultivated relationships with participants and we could laugh about the awkwardness of the Zoom encounter and the propensity for family members (including my lively toddler) and pets to interrupt at inopportune times. As we resumed more normal work responsibilities, doing Zoom interviews actually fit more easily into their schedules. The virtual platform also worked well for me as a mother of a toddler at home who was juggling online teaching and professional responsibilities, as I was able to do many of the interviews at night. I managed to do an initial push of interviews during summer 2020 and wrapped them up in 2021. Alaska, Ana, and Delmis joined me whenever they could, despite increased demands at work as well as Ana and Delmis beginning graduate school.

While the logistics of conducting "home-bound pandemic ethnography" were manageable for me, as anthropologist Sarah B. Horton reflects, doing this style of research also underscored the very different pandemic realities and exposures to risk borne by my participants and their families.[48] My position as a remote worker diminished my COVID risk substantially; however, as described earlier, several participants got COVID early on in the pandemic, very likely from workplace exposures. Several others who worked in remote work configurations were still quite concerned about family members who worked outside of the home in food service, health care, emergency services, and waste management. Some ended up having family members who had lost jobs or had hours cut substantially move in with them.

Hearing these stories and talking about the challenges participants were negotiating, however, also shed light on DACA recipients' overall incorporation trajectories. Many had solid professional careers that allowed them some privilege in moderating their exposures by working from home or hybrid schedules. Some participants who I knew did not have health insurance in previous phases now did and were able to obtain care when they got COVID. Those who were taking care of more vulnerable family members were doing so from positions of relative economic security. Despite the despair of the pandemic, participants focused on how surprisingly well they were doing as they told me about all of the changes in their lives. This instead became the focal point of this phase—and the project overall—as I sought to avoid producing an account of suffering, instead highlighting participants' navigational strategies and creative forms of resistance beyond political protest.[49]

CONCLUDING METHODOLOGICAL REFLECTIONS

This book represents my efforts at thinking through and actualizing different ways of critically engaging with DACA recipients in their everyday quest for well-being and justice. Though my analysis is substantially informed by both (former) students' and community collaborators' insights, I am ultimately responsible for the arguments presented in this book, including their shortcomings. As I demonstrated, my methodological approach shifted considerably as the project unfolded. Initially, I set out to conduct immigration research in the manner I was accustomed to—by collaborating with CBOs and their members in support of their existing initiatives and actions in advancing immigrant justice. However, I started becoming interested in DACA recipients who were not active in organizing spaces and did not know many other DACA recipients. As I went about building this alternative project, I embraced the opportunity to work with a different set of collaborators, and together we composed a sample of diverse DACA recipients with unique experiences unlike those conventionally captured in the literature.

After the initial phase of research, we added a participatory component in the form of the CAB in response to community input and the collective desire to continue the research. Though the project ultimately was not as fully participatory or collaborative as I might have liked, the CAB participated at critical steps in the research process (refining study instruments, facilitating recruitment, analyzing data and validating interpretations, disseminating findings, planning subsequent research) and ensured that we remained focused on what mattered to them most. They have unquestionably been vital collaborators, enhancing the research immensely. Yet the CAB also took on a life of its own and transformed into something unexpected: a space (eventually one that did not require physical copresence) through which we accompanied each other by offering deeply politicized forms of care before and during the pandemic, even as we maintained our focus on advocating for well-being and justice for DACA recipients. As the project continued on, I also actively maintained relationships with non-CAB members and sought to support them (and members of their social networks) through a variety of different mechanisms described in the conclusion.

As I started thinking through everyday activism as a theoretical construct to make sense of the alternative ways in which participants were "showing up" for DACA recipients and immigrant rights in the first Trump era, it also started resonating with me as a methodological approach. While this project was not "activist" in the sense in which I and most scholars conventionally use the term (given that I was not collaborating with CBOs or activists themselves), I started recognizing the ways in which I was engaging in everyday activism. Some of my everyday activism was, indeed, rooted in deep investments in relationships and forms of care circulating within the CAB especially. Though I also started realizing that it entailed sharing academic capital as a multigenerational college graduate and university professor—which I elaborate further in the conclusion. I have come to see that the relational aspects of this project and the ways that I reciprocate and advocate for immigrants in the everyday are indeed activism too, albeit a less conventional form. This realization has been particularly profound for me during a period in which I was constrained (as were so many others) from doing research and engaging in activism "as usual" due to the pandemic. Indeed, everyday activism can and should be a critical element of the newly emergent patchwork ethnography that relies on innovative ethnographic strategies that maintain the commitments of long-term fieldwork while "fully attending to how changing living and working conditions are profoundly and irrevocably changing knowledge production."[50]

APPENDIX B

Participant Demographics

Pseudonym	Birthplace	Age at arrival	Age in 2016
Angélica	El Salvador	11	25
Annisa	Indonesia	4	20
Antônia	Brazil	8	22
Beto	Bolivia	5	21
Camila	El Salvador	14	23
Denisse	El Salvador	5	18
Diego	Colombia	11	21
Elena	Honduras	8	19
Elisa	El Salvador	10	20
Emine	Liberia	4	20
Esme	Honduras	5	19
Isaac	El Salvador	8	19
Jenny	El Salvador	7	22
John	South Korea	10	22
Juan	Mexico	2	20
Laura	Mexico	14	26
Lucas	Mexico	10	22
Luis	El Salvador	4	18
Madeline	Senegal	5	21
Mae	South Korea	6	19
Marcela	Honduras	8	21
Miguel	Peru	13	25
Nancy	Argentina	11	21
Nayeli	El Salvador	7	21
Pau	Honduras	10	21
Rebeca	Peru	15	28
Santiago	Nicaragua	9	21
Sara	Honduras	13	24
Veronica	El Salvador	8	20
Yvette	Peru	15	28

Gender	Highest schooling completed	Most recent job position
F	Bachelor's	Programs manager for public school system
F	Bachelor's	Mental health technician in major health care system
F	Professional certification	Ultrasound technician in major health care system
M	Bachelor's	Research associate at biotechnology firm
F	Some college	Community engagement specialist at nonprofit
F	Some college	Retail associate
M	Some college	Human resources program assistant
F	Bachelor's	Financial specialist for information technology firm
F	High school	Medical receptionist
F	Bachelor's	Registration clerk in major health care system
F	Bachelor's	Distribution manager for food and beverage corporation
M	Some college	Interpreter for public school system
F	Bachelor's	Lab technician at biotechnology firm
M	Some college	Unemployed
M	Master's	Business systems manager at engineering firm
F	Bachelor's	Social worker at mental health service nonprofit
M	Some college	Community health worker in community health clinic
M	Bachelor's	Program assistant in science and technology nonprofit
F	Bachelor's	Information specialist for public transportation system
F	Bachelor's	Web producer for software development company
F	Professional certification	Nuclear medicine technologist
M	Bachelor's	Construction worker
F	Bachelor's	Electrical engineer
F	Bachelor's	Human resources manager at construction company
F	Bachelor's	Real estate agent
F	Master's	Social worker for public school system
M	Bachelor's	Workforce development program manager
F	Master's	Accountant at large professional firm
F	Some college	Retail associate
F	Bachelor's	Information technology specialist

NOTES

INTRODUCTION

1 All names used in the book are pseudonyms.

2 The label "DREAMer" originally described undocumented youth activists organizing for the passage of the Development, Relief, and Education for Alien Minors (DREAM) Act first introduced in Congress in 2001. The DREAM Act has subsequently been introduced with strong bipartisan support at least eleven times in the subsequent twenty years but has never passed. It is important to note that not all DREAMers are DACA recipients, as many youth were ineligible for DACA or did not apply for it because of the cost, the inability to furnish necessary documents, or concerns about the government possessing their personal information. It is also the case that not all undocumented young adults identify with the DREAMer label; in fact, many who initially embraced the term have subsequently rejected it, as it upholds them as model neoliberal subjects within the U.S. meritocracy who are deemed to be more deserving of belonging than other undocumented immigrants (see Abrego and Negrón-Gonzales, *We Are Not Dreamers*, 8–11, for more on the rejection of the DREAMer narrative). I follow my participants' lead by largely eschewing the DREAMer label, instead referring to them principally as DACA recipients.

3 Scholars have coined a range of different terms to capture immigrants' in-between statuses, including semi-legality (as described by sociologist Agnieszka Kubal in "Conceptualizing Semi-legality in Migration Research"), transitory legality (as sociologist Marie Mallet and political scientist Lisa García Bedolla present in "Transitory Legality"), and legal status precarity (as used by sociologists Elizabeth Aranda and Elizabeth Vaquera and anthropologist Heide Castañeda in "Shifting Roles in Families of Deferred Action for Childhood Arrivals," and geographers Marie Price and Giancarla Rojas in "Ordinary Lives and Uneven Precarity of the DACAmented"). Aranda, Vaquera, and Castañeda define legal status precarity as "the politically induced condition in indeterminacy," or "life without the promise of stability," drawing from anthropologist Anna L. Tsing, *Mushroom at the End of the World*, 20. Philosopher and gender studies scholar Judith Butler has popularized the term "precarity" more broadly as a "politically induced condition in which certain populations suffer from failing social and economic networks of support and become differentially exposed to injury, violence, and death. Such populations are at heightened risk of disease, poverty, starvation, displacement,

and of exposure to violence without protection. Precarity also characterizes that politically induced condition of maximized vulnerability and exposure for populations exposed to arbitrary state violence and to other forms of aggression that are not enacted by states and against which states do not offer adequate protection" (Butler, "Performativity, Precarity and Sexual Politics," ii; see also Coutin et al., "Deferred Action and the Discretionary State," 952). I use "legal status precarity" throughout the book, given its emphasis on being a politically induced condition and also because the term would still be applicable in a scenario in which DACA recipients no longer possess DACA status—potentially rendering them even more precarious.

4 Pink, *Situating Everyday Life*, 4; Fish, King, and Almack, "Queerying Activism," 1195–96.

5 Scott, *Domination and the Arts of Resistance*, 118; Scott, *Weapons of the Weak*, 137.

6 Harris, Wyn, and Younes, "Beyond Apathetic or Activist Youth."

7 Batalova, Hooker, and Capps, "DACA at the Two-Year Mark."

8 Chacón, Coutin, and Lee, *Legal Phantoms*.

9 U.S. Citizenship and Immigration Services (USCIS), "Consideration of Deferred Action for Childhood Arrivals (DACA)."

10 USCIS, "Number of Form I-821D."

11 Horton and Heyman, *Paper Trails*, 1.

12 Quesada, Hart, and Bourgois, "Structural Vulnerability and Health"; Carruth et al., "Structural Vulnerability."

13 Obatuase, "DACA's Rollercoaster Ride of Legal Battles." Using a different metaphor, Elizabeth Hanna Rubio has referred to it as "legislative and judicial ping-pong" in "'We Need to Redefine What We Mean by Winning,'" 161.

14 Migration Policy Institute, "U.S. Immigrant Population."

15 Cox and Rodríguez, *President and Immigration Law*.

16 Migration Policy Institute, "Trump Completed 472 Executive Actions on Immigration."

17 Nicholls, *The DREAMers*, 9–10.

18 Wong, García, and Valdivia, "Political Incorporation of Undocumented Youth."

19 Fiorito, "Learning to be Legal," 1104.

20 Batalova, Hooker, and Capps, "DACA at the Two-Year Mark." It is important to note that not all members of the 1.5 generation are undocumented; some are lawful permanent residents or have naturalized and become citizens.

21 Abrego and Gonzales, "Blocked Paths, Uncertain Futures."

22 Gonzales et al., "DACA at Year Three"; Gonzales, Murillo, and Lacomba, "Taking Giant Leaps Forward"; Gonzales et al., "Long-Term Impact of DACA"; and Gonzales, Brant, and Roth, "DACAmented in the Age of Deportation."

23 Sacchetti, "As DACA Immigrant Program Turns 10, Legal Challenges Persist."

24 Wong, Martinez Rosas, and Reyna, "New Study of DACA Beneficiaries"; Wong et al., "DACA Recipients' Livelihoods"; Wong, Flores, and Rodriguez Kmec, "2021 Survey of DACA Recipients."

25 Gonzales, Terriquez, and Ruszczyk, "Becoming DACAmented."

26 Capps, Fix, and Zong, "Education and Work Profiles."

27 Gonzales, Terriquez, and Ruszczyk, "Becoming DACAmented."

28 Enriquez, *Of Love and Papers*. See also Gonzales, Terriquez, and Ruszczyk, "Becoming DACAmented."

29 Hamilton, Patler, and Langer, "Life-Course Timing of Legalization"; Patler, Hamilton, and Savinar, "Limits of Gaining Rights." See also Gonzales et al., "(Un)authorized Transitions."

30 Gonzales, Terriquez, and Ruszczyk, "Becoming DACAmented."

31 Cebulko and Silver, "Navigating DACA in Hospitable and Hostile States"; Flores, Escudero, and Burciaga, "Legal-Spatial Consciousness"; Golash-Boza and Valdez, "Nested Contexts of Reception; Gonzales and Burciaga, "Segmented Pathways of Illegality."

32 Coleman, "'Local' Migration State."

33 National Conference of State Legislatures, "Immigration Laws and Current State Immigration Legislation."

34 Cebulko and Silver, "Navigating DACA in Hospitable and Hostile States"; García, *Legal Passing*; Gonzales, Brant, and Roth, "DACAmented in the Age of Deportation"; Roth, "Double Bind of DACA."

35 Burciaga and Malone, "Intensified Liminal Legality"; Gonzales and Burciaga, "Segmented Pathways of Illegality"; Marrow, "Hope Turned Sour"; Perez, "Nested Contexts of Reception"; Silver, *Shifting Boundaries*.

36 Armenta, *Protect, Serve, and Deport*; Gonzales, Brant, and Roth, "DACAmented in the Age of Deportation"; Maldonado, "Latino Incorporation and Racialized Border Politics"; and Perez, "Nested Contexts of Reception."

37 Varsanyi et al., "Multilayered Jurisdictional Patchwork."

38 Golash-Boza and Valdez, "Nested Contexts of Reception," 536.

39 Silver, *Shifting Boundaries*, 9–11.

40 Jones, "From Open Doors to Closed Gates." See also Aranda et al., "Undocumented Again?"

41 In "Undocumented Critical Theory," Carlos Aguilar uses the term "DACAdemic" to acknowledge a new school of thought articulated by DACA recipient scholars theorizing about undocumented life.

42 Sati, "How DACA Pits 'Good Immigrants' Against Millions of Others."

43 Sati, "'Other' Borders."

44 In "Noncitizenship and the Case for Illegalized Persons," legal studies scholar Joel Sati makes a compelling case for the use of the term "illegalized" to discuss noncitizens without authorization instead of the more commonly used "undocumented," which is predicated on the notion that Western documents should be desirable. He notes that "being illegalized is the product of a historical, social, and epistemic process" that has resulted in the exclusion of noncitizens (as a transnational phenomenon extending beyond the United States) and that its usage better facilitates intersectional discussions about marginalization and other axes of oppression. While scholars are increasingly following Sati's lead (e.g., Martínez, *Illegalized*,

Rubio, "'We Need to Redefine What We Mean by Winning'"; Rubio and Alvarez Almendariz, "Refusing 'Undocumented'"), I continue to use the term "undocumented" because it is the term most commonly used my research participants.

45 Sati, "Noncitizenship and the Case for Illegalized Persons."
46 Alvarez Almendariz, "Whiteness of DACA."
47 Alvarez Almendariz, "Whiteness of DACA." See also Rubio and Alvarez Almendariz, "Refusing 'Undocumented.'"
48 Dunbar-Ortiz, *Not "a Nation of Immigrants."*
49 Gomberg-Muñoz, *Becoming Legal*, 21.
50 Golash-Boza, Duenas, and Xiong, "White Supremacy, Patriarchy, and Global Capitalism."
51 Elsewhere, I provide a much more comprehensive history of immigration policymaking in the twentieth and twenty-first centuries (see Getrich, *Border Brokers*).
52 Massey and Sánchez, *Brokered Boundaries*, 2.
53 Chavez, *Latino Threat*; Dowling and Inda, *Governing Immigration through Crime*.
54 Castañeda, *Borders of Belonging*; Eskenazi et al., "Association of Perceived Immigration Policy Vulnerability"; Getrich, *Border Brokers*; Hardy et al., "Call for Further Research"; Kline, *Pathogenic Policing*; Lopez, *Separated*; Philbin et al., "State-Level Immigration."
55 Castañeda, *Borders of Belonging*; De León, *Land of Open Graves*; Getrich, *Border Brokers*; Slack, *Deported to Death*. Though border policing has intensified during the past three decades, Lytle Hernández's *Migra!* demonstrates that the aggressive policing of immigrants in the U.S.-Mexico borderlands has been a key feature of migration control since the beginnings of the U.S. Border Patrol in 1924.
56 Coutin, "Confined Within," 201; Dowling and Inda, *Governing Immigration through Crime*, 10.
57 Horton, *They Leave Their Kidneys on the Field*; Stuesse and Coleman, "Automobility, Immobility, Altermobility," 51.
58 Coutin, "Confined Within."
59 Lopez, *Separated*.
60 Scheper-Hughes and Bourgois, *Violence in War and Peace*.
61 Menjívar and Abrego, "Legal Violence."
62 Roth, "Double Bind of DACA," 2549–50.
63 García, Diaz-Strong, and Rodriguez Rodriguez, "Matter of Time," 1; Haas, *Suspended Lives*; Haas, "Citizens-in-Waiting, Deportees-in-Waiting," Isaac, "Temporal Dispossession"; Ramsay, "Time and the Other in Crisis."
64 Grace, Bais, and Roth, "Violence of Uncertainty"; Phillimore and Cheung, "Violence of Uncertainty."
65 Heckert, "Bureaucratic Violence of the Health Care System."
66 Scheper-Hughes and Bourgois, *Violence in War and Peace*.
67 Alvarez Almendariz, "Whiteness of DACA."
68 Alvarez Almendariz, "Whiteness of DACA"; Rubio and Alvarez Almendariz, "Refusing 'Undocumented.'" In *Border Thinking*, education scholar Andrea Dyr-

ness and ethnic studies scholar Enrique Sepúlveda likewise subvert hegemonic discourses about immigrant integration by focusing instead on Latinx young adults' critiques of nation-state citizenship and their more radical articulations of belonging (25).

69 Alvarez Almendariz, "Whiteness of DACA"; Rubio and Alvarez Almendariz, "Refusing 'Undocumented.'"

70 Former DACA recipients have forged an organization—onwardreamers.org—and solidarity network to offer mutual support to those who decide to leave the United States and relocate elsewhere.

71 In "The Limits of Gaining Rights while Remaining Marginalized," Patler, Hamilton, and Savinar have similarly examined distinct periods within the DACA program that they have labeled as Stability, Threats, and Election & Beyond.

72 Tsing, "Getting By in Terrifying Times."

73 Willen et al., "Flourishing"; Willen et al., "Rethinking Flourishing."

74 Batalova, Hooker, and Capps, "DACA at the Two-Year Mark."

75 Gonzales, Brant, and Roth, "DACAmented in the Age of Deportation"; Cebulko and Silver, "Navigating DACA in Hospitable and Hostile States."

76 Graauw and Gleeson, "Metropolitan Context and Immigrant Rights Experiences."

77 Migration Policy Institute, "U.S. Immigrant Population."

78 USCIS, "Number of Form I-821D."

79 Enriquez, Of Love and Papers, 17; see also Cebulko, "Becoming White in a White Supremacist State"; Enriquez, "Border Hopping Mexicans"; Enriquez and Millán, "Situational Triggers and Protective Locations"; Escudero, Organizing while Undocumented; and García, "Racializing 'Illegality.'"

80 Abrego and Negrón-Gonzales, We Are Not Dreamers, 8, 16; Aguilar, "Undocumented Critical Theory," 158.

81 Nicholls, "Uneven Geographies of Politicisation," 465.

82 Abrego, "Legitimacy, Social Identity, and the Mobilization of Law"; Abrego and Negrón-Gonzales, We Are Not Dreamers; Escudero, Organizing while Undocumented; Negrón-Gonzales, "Undocumented, Unafraid and Unapologetic"; Nicholls, The DREAMers; Terriquez, "Intersectional Mobilization."

83 Escudero, Organizing while Undocumented; Marquez-Benitez and Pallares, "Not One More"; Mena Robles and Gomberg-Muñoz, "Activism after DACA"; Rubio, "'We Need to Redefine What We Mean by Winning'"; Seif, "'Coming Out of the Shadows'"; Unzueta Carrasco and Seif, "Disrupting the Dream."

84 Escudero, Organizing while Undocumented.

85 Patler, Hamilton, and Savinar, "Limits of Gaining Rights," 257.

86 Gálvez, "I Won't Tell My Story," 124.

87 Erikson, Childhood and Society.

88 Gonzales, Lives In Limbo; Waters et al., Coming of Age in America.

89 Getrich, Border Brokers.

90 Arnett, Emerging Adulthood.

91 Gálvez, "I Won't Tell My Story," 124.

92 Aguilar, "Undocumented Critical Theory," 153; Chang, Mendes, and Salazar, "Qualitative Methodological Considerations"; Ramirez, "Beyond Identity," 149.
93 Harrison, *Decolonizing Anthropology*; Harrison, "Anthropology as an Agent of Transformation"; Lamphere, "Unofficial Histories."
94 See, for example, Allen and Jobson, "Decolonizing Generation," and Tuhiwai Smith, *Decolonizing Methodologies*.
95 Rosa and Bonilla, "Deprovincializing Trump," 205–6. See also Jobson, "Case for Letting Anthropology Burn."
96 Rosa and Bonilla, "Deprovincializing Trump," 206.
97 Abrego and Negrón-Gonzales, *We Are Not Dreamers*, 1.
98 Aguilar, "Undocumented Critical Theory"; Alvarez Almendariz, "Whiteness of DACA"; Chang, Mendes, and Salazar, "Qualitative Methodological Considerations"; Hurtado Moreno, "Anthropology about Us"; Martínez, *Illegalized*; Rubio and Alvarez Almendariz, "Refusing 'Undocumented'"; Sati, "On Trumpism and Illegality"; Sati, "Noncitizenship and the Case for Illegalized Persons"; Solorzano and Ruiz, "Saving DACA, Healing Ourselves."
99 Aguilar, "Undocumented Critical Theory."
100 Bejarano et al., *Decolonizing Ethnography*.
101 Bejarano et al., *Decolonizing Ethnography*, 11, 95.
102 See appendix A for more on my positionality and its influence on this project and book.
103 Coutin, "Confined Within"; Coutin, *Legalizing Moves*; De Genova, "Migrant 'Illegality' and Deportability in Everyday Life."
104 Menjívar, "Liminal Legality"; Menjívar and Abrego, "Legal Violence."
105 Menjívar, "Liminal Legality"; Menjívar and Abrego, "Legal Violence."
106 Patler, Hamilton, and Savinar, "Limits of Gaining Rights"; Patler and Pirtle, "From Undocumented to Lawfully Present"; Sudhinaraset et al., "Dreams Deferred"; Venkataramani et al., "Health Consequences."
107 Patler et al., "Uncertainty about DACA"; Velarde Pierce et al., "Evaluating the Effect of Legal Vulnerabilities."
108 Coutin et al., "Deferred Action and the Discretionary State"; Griffiths, "Out of Time."
109 Aranda et al., "Undocumented Again?"; James, "Haiti, Insecurity, and the Politics of Asylum"; Patler, Hamilton, and Savinar, "Limits of Gaining Rights"; Vaquera, Aranda, and Sousa-Rodriguez, "Emotional Challenges of Undocumented Young Adults."
110 Griffiths, "Out of Time," 1999.
111 Patler, Hamilton, and Savinar, "The Limits of Gaining Rights while Remaining Marginalized," 250.
112 Mallet and García Bedolla, "Transitory Legality"; Patler et al., "Uncertainty about DACA."
113 Aranda et al., "Undocumented Again?," 1322.
114 Alvarez Almendariz, "Whiteness of DACA"; Aranda et al., "Undocumented Again?," 1323; Gonzales and Chavez, "'Awakening to a Nightmare.'"

115 Enriquez and Millán, "Situational Triggers and Protective Locations"; Price and Rojas, "Ordinary Lives and Uneven Precarity of the DACAmented," 4761.
116 Eldridge and Reinke, "Introduction"; Heckert, "Bureaucratic Violence of the Health Care System."
117 Flores, "About Time," 42.
118 As I introduce participants initially, I describe their country of origin and age at arrival. Subsequently, I refer to them only by name, though appendix B also provides a table presenting key participant demographics.
119 Alvarez, "Experiential Knowledge as Capital and Resistance"; Ellis, "Psychology of Migrant 'Illegality.'"
120 Alvarez, "Experiential Knowledge as Capital and Resistance"; Macías, "Scheme Game"; Nájera, "Unauthorized Education"; Yosso, "Whose Culture Has Capital?"; Yosso et al., "Critical Race Theory."
121 Abrego, "Renewed Optimism and Spatial Mobility"; Abrego, "Legal Consciousness of Undocumented Latinos"; Flores, Escudero, and Burciaga, "Legal-Spatial Consciousness."
122 Varsanyi et al., "Multilayered Jurisdictional Patchwork."
123 Madden, "Cultural Health Capital on the Margins"; Shim, "Cultural Health Capital."
124 Fernández et al., "Muxeres en Acción."
125 Getrich, Border Brokers; López-Sanders, "Navigating Health Care."
126 Mansbridge, "Everyday Activism," 1.
127 Pink, Situating Everyday Life, 4; Scott, Weapons of the Weak; Vinthagen and Johansson, "'Everyday Resistance,'" 2.
128 Magaña, "Spaces of Resistance"; Soaita, "Everyday Activism"; Tournadre, "'Because We Are the Only Ones in the Community!'"
129 Mendes and Chang, "Undocumented and Afraid."
130 Getrich, Border Brokers; Mora et al., "Immigrant Rights and Social Movements," 7; Nájera, "Unauthorized Education," 36.
131 Abrego and Negrón-Gonzales, We Are Not Dreamers, 13.
132 Fiorito, "Learning to Be Legal," 1106; see also Aranda, Vaquera, and Castañeda, "Shifting Roles," 10; Ellis, Gonzales, and Rendón García, "Power of Inclusion," 168.
133 Abrego and Negrón-Gonzales, We Are Not Dreamers; Aguilar, "Undocumented Critical Theory"; Cebulko, "Becoming White in a White Supremacist State"; Enriquez, "Border Hopping Mexicans"; Enriquez and Millán, "Situational Triggers and Protective Locations"; García, "Racializing 'Illegality.'"

1. "I HAVE A STRONG SENSE OF IDENTITY TIED TO THIS PLACE"

1 Cebulko and Silver, "Navigating DACA in Hospitable and Hostile States"; Gonzales and Burciaga, "Segmented Pathways of Illegality"; Roth, "Double Bind of DACA"; Silver, Shifting Boundaries.
2 Portes and Rumbaut, Immigrant America.
3 Varsanyi et al., "Multilayered Jurisdictional Patchwork."

4 Enriquez, *Of Love and Papers*, 9.
5 Cebulko, "Becoming White in a White Supremacist State"; Cebulko and Silver, "Navigating DACA in Hospitable and Hostile States"; Coleman, "'Local' Migration State"; García, *Legal Passing*; Gonzales, Brant, and Roth, "DACAmented in the Age of Deportation."
6 Graauw and Gleeson, "Metropolitan Context and Immigrant Rights Experiences."
7 I refer to these cities by the U.S. Census Bureau's official Metropolitan Statistical Area (MSA) designations.
8 Tatian et al., "State of Immigrants in the District of Columbia," 2.
9 Migration Policy Institute, "U.S. Immigrant Population."
10 U.S. Census Bureau, "American Community Survey."
11 Singer, "Metropolitan Washington," 15.
12 Singer, "Metropolitan Washington," 14.
13 U.S. Census Bureau, "American Community Survey."
14 Price and Rojas, "Ordinary Lives and Uneven Precarity of the DACAmented," 4763.
15 Migration Policy Institute, "U.S. Immigrant Population."
16 Singer, "Metropolitan Washington," 2.
17 Sánchez-Molina and Cohen, *Latinas Crossing Borders*, 3.
18 Sánchez-Molina and Cohen, *Latinas Crossing Borders*, 1.
19 Singer, "Metropolitan Washington," 17.
20 Population Reference Bureau, "African-Born Blacks."
21 Coutin, *Legalizing Moves*; Rodríguez, *Dividing the Isthmus*, 168.
22 Sánchez-Molina and Cohen, *Latinas Crossing Borders*, 1–2.
23 Rodríguez, *Dividing the Isthmus*, 169, 176.
24 Singer, "Metropolitan Washington," 12.
25 Singer, "Metropolitan Washington," 17–18; Sánchez-Molina and Cohen, *Latinas Crossing Borders*, 17n16.
26 Tam et al., "From Little Saigon to Eden Center"; Esterline and Batalova, "Korean Immigrants in the United States."
27 Sánchez-Molina and Cohen, *Latinas Crossing Borders*, 17n16.
28 Population Reference Bureau, "African-Born Blacks."
29 Singer, "Rise of New Immigrant Gateways."
30 Chishti and Yale-Loehr, "Immigration Act of 1990."
31 Singer, "Metropolitan Washington," 12.
32 Singer, "Metropolitan Washington," 17–18.
33 Population Reference Bureau, "African-Born Blacks."
34 Singer, "Metropolitan Washington," 18; Zong and Batalova, "Sub-Saharan African Immigrants."
35 Institute for Immigration Research, "The Caribbean."
36 Singer, "Metropolitan Washington," 18.
37 Singer, "Metropolitan Washington," 13–14.
38 Singer, "Metropolitan Washington," 7.

39 Price and Singer, "Edge Gateways"; Price and Rojas, "Ordinary Lives and Uneven Precarity of the DACAmented," 4763.

40 Sánchez-Molina and Cohen, *Latinas Crossing Borders*, 6–12.

41 Cohn and Pan, "Asian Population Swelling in D.C."

42 Population Reference Bureau, "African-Born Blacks."

43 Institute for Immigration Research, "The Caribbean."

44 Singer, "Metropolitan Washington," 19–21.

45 Price and Rojas, "Ordinary Lives and Uneven Precarity of the DACAmented," 4775.

46 Singer, "Metropolitan Washington," 24–25.

47 The National Conference of State Legislatures (NCSL) maintains a regularly updated database of "Immigration Laws and Current State Immigration Legislation," from which this section draws.

48 Austermuhle, "D.C. Council Adds Money."

49 Henderson, "Two Years after DACA."

50 Immigrant Legal Resource Center, "National Map of 287(g) Agreements."

51 Immigrant Legal Resource Center, "National Map of 287(g) Agreements."

52 Jones, "From Open Doors to Closed Gates"; Silver, *Shifting Boundaries*.

53 García, *Legal Passing*, 36.

54 Vaquera, Aranda, and Gonzales, "Patterns of Incorporation of Latinos."

55 Silver, *Shifting Boundaries*.

56 Price and Rojas, "Ordinary Lives and Uneven Precarity of the DACAmented."

57 Enriquez and Millán, "Situational Triggers and Protective Locations."

58 Price and Rojas, "Ordinary Lives and Uneven Precarity of the DACAmented," 4760.

59 Abrego and Negrón-Gonzales, *We Are Not Dreamers*, 11.

60 Abrego, "Legitimacy, Social Identity, and the Mobilization of Law"; Negrón-Gonzales, "Undocumented, Unafraid and Unapologetic," 262.

61 Burciaga and Martinez, "How Do Political Contexts Shape Undocumented Youth Movements?," 458–59.

62 Nicholls, *The DREAMers*, 31–32.

63 Bloemraad, Voss, and Lee, "Protests of 2006"; Getrich, *Border Brokers*; Getrich, "Negotiating Boundaries of Social Belonging"; Wong, García, and Valdivia, "Political Incorporation of Undocumented Youth."

64 Nicholls, *The DREAMers*, 60–61.

65 Marquez-Benitez and Pallares, "Not One More"; Mena Robles and Gomberg-Muñoz, "Activism after DACA"; Seif, "'Coming Out of the Shadows'"; Unzueta Carrasco and Seif, "Disrupting the Dream."

66 Nicholls, *The DREAMers*, 64.

67 Nicholls, *The DREAMers*, 74.

68 Nicholls, *The DREAMers*, 80.

69 Negrón-Gonzales, "Undocumented, Unafraid and Unapologetic," 263.

70 Nicholls, *The DREAMers*, 151–53.

71 USCIS, "Number of Form I-821D."
72 USCIS, "Count of Active DACA Recipients."
73 Benenson, "Fact Sheet."
74 USCIS, "Count of Active DACA Recipients."
75 USCIS, "Number of Form I-821D."
76 Singer, "Rise of New Immigrant Gateways."
77 USCIS, "Approximate Active DACA Recipients."
78 Gonzales, Brant, and Roth, "DACAmented in the Age of Deportation"; Bruhn and Gonzales, "Geographies of Belonging."
79 Graauw and Gleeson, "Metropolitan Context and Immigrant Rights Experiences," 1141; García, *Legal Passing*, 8.
80 Bruhn and Gonzales, "Geographies of Belonging," 3.

2. "I HAVE TO CONTINUE WITH MY NORMAL LIFE"

1 Aranda et al., "Undocumented Again?"; Giddens, *Modernity and Self-Identity*; James, "Haiti, Insecurity, and the Politics of Asylum"; Patler, Hamilton, and Savinar, "Limits of Gaining Rights"; Vaquera, Aranda, and Sousa-Rodriguez, "Emotional Challenges of Undocumented Young Adults."
2 Patler, Hamilton, and Savinar, "Limits of Gaining Rights," 249–50.
3 Coutin et al., "Deferred Action and the Discretionary State"; Griffiths, "Out of Time."
4 García, Diaz-Strong, and Rodriguez Rodriguez, "Matter of Time"; Isaac, "Temporal Dispossession"; Ramsay, "Time and the Other in Crisis."
5 Eldridge and Reinke, "Introduction"; Heckert, "Bureaucratic Violence of the Health Care System."
6 Flores, "About Time." In the "Epilogue" to a special issue about temporality, Griffiths similarly argues that migrants assert autonomy by "reclaiming and recalibrating their own timelines and rhythms." I use Flores's concept of temporal control to encapsulate DACA recipients' assertion of autonomy since it aligns with the term—"control"—that they regularly use.
7 Cabral and Cuevas, "Health Inequities among Latinos/Hispanics"; Cavazos-Rehg, Zayas, and Spitznagel, "Legal Status"; Cobb et al., "Perceptions of Legal Status"; Young and Pebley, "Legal Status."
8 Menjívar and Abrego, "Legal Violence."
9 Abrego, "Legal Consciousness of Undocumented Latinos"; Ellis, Gonzales, and Rendón García, "Power of Inclusion"; Gonzales and Burciaga, "Segmented Pathways of Illegality"; Menjívar and Kanstroom, *Constructing Immigrant "Illegality."*
10 Gonzales, *Lives in Limbo*; Gonzales, Suárez-Orozco, and Dedios-Sanguineti, "No Place to Belong."
11 Gonzales and Chavez, "'Awakening to a Nightmare.'"
12 Gonzales, *Lives in Limbo*; Gonzales and Chavez, "'Awakening to a Nightmare'"; Gonzales, Suárez-Orozco, and Dedios-Sanguineti, "No Place to Belong"; Raymond-Flesch et al., "'There Is No Help Out There'"; Stacciarini et al., "'I Didn't

Ask to Come'"; Vaquera, Aranda, and Sousa-Rodriguez, "Emotional Challenges of Undocumented Young Adults."

13 Negrón-Gonzales, "Navigating 'Illegality'"; Vaquera, Aranda, and Sousa-Rodriguez, "Emotional Challenges of Undocumented Young Adults."

14 Patler, Hamilton, and Savinar, "Limits of Gaining Rights"; Patler and Pirtle, "From Undocumented to Lawfully Present"; Sudhinaraset et al., "Influence of Deferred Action for Childhood Arrivals"; Venkataramani et al., "Health Consequences."

15 Patler, Hamilton, and Savinar, "Limits of Gaining Rights," 254.

16 Ellis, Gonzales, and Rendón García, "Power of Inclusion," 166; Fiorito, "Learning to Be Legal," 1101.

17 Abrego, "Renewed Optimism and Spatial Mobility," 192, 202–4.

18 Hainmueller et al., "Protecting Unauthorized Immigrant Mothers."

19 Ellis, Gonzales, and Rendón García, "Power of Inclusion"; Raymond-Flesch et al., "'There Is No Help Out There.'"

20 Patler, Hamilton, and Savinar, "Limits of Gaining Rights"; Velarde Pierce et al., "Evaluating the Effect of Legal Vulnerabilities."

21 Patler and Pirtle, "From Undocumented to Lawfully Present," 41.

22 Castañeda and Melo, "Health Care Access"; Raymond-Flesch et al., "'There Is No Help Out There.'" DACA recipients were prohibited from seeking health care coverage through the Affordable Care Act marketplace until President Biden implemented a rule change to remove the prohibition in May 2024 (see White House, "Fact Sheet"). Starting in November 2024, DACA recipients can apply for coverage through federal and state-based marketplaces and are also eligible for financial assistance. The rule change is projected to expand coverage to more than 100,000 DACA recipients.

23 Velarde Pierce et al., "Evaluating the Effect of Legal Vulnerabilities," 249.

24 Abrego, "Renewed Optimism and Spatial Mobility"; Aranda, Vaquera, and Castañeda, "Shifting Roles"; Castañeda, Borders of Belonging; Fiorito, "Learning to Be Legal"; Getrich, Border Brokers; Patler and Pirtle, "From Undocumented to Lawfully Present"; Sudhinaraset et al., "Influence of Deferred Action for Childhood Arrivals."

25 Fiorito, "Learning to Be Legal," 1100; Abrego, "Renewed Optimism and Spatial Mobility," 203.

26 Fiorito, "Learning to Be Legal," 1108.

27 Menjívar and Abrego, "Legal Violence"; Fiorito, "Learning to Be Legal," 1097.

28 Horton and Heyman, Paper Trails, 3.

29 Asad, "On the Radar," 135.

30 Patler, Hamilton, and Savinar, "Limits of Gaining Rights," 249–50.

31 Velarde Pierce et al., "Evaluating the Effect of Legal Vulnerabilities," 248.

32 Patler, Hamilton, and Savinar, "Limits of Gaining Rights," 248–49.

33 Valdivia, "Undocumented Young Adults' Heightened Vulnerability," 132.

34 Mallet and García Bedolla, "Transitory Legality"; Patler et al., "Uncertainty about DACA."

35 Mallet and García Bedolla, "Transitory Legality," 11–14.
36 Aranda et al., "Undocumented Again?," 1322.
37 Patler et al., "Uncertainty about DACA."
38 Menjívar, "Liminal Legality," 1001, 1007.
39 Coutin et al., "Deferred Action and the Discretionary State"; Griffiths, "Out of Time."
40 García, Diaz-Strong, and Rodriguez Rodriguez, "Matter of Time," 1; Griffiths, "Epilogue"; Haas, *Suspended Lives*; Haas, "Citizens-in-Waiting, Deportees-in-Waiting."
41 Isaac, "Temporal Dispossession"; Ramsay, "Time and the Other in Crisis."
42 Grace, Bais, and Roth, "Violence of Uncertainty." See also Phillimore and Cheung, "Violence of Uncertainty."
43 Heidbrink, "'How Can I Have a Future?,'" 481.
44 Haas, *Suspended Lives*.
45 Eldridge and Reinke, "Introduction"; Heckert, "Bureaucratic Violence of the Health Care System."
46 Aranda et al., "Undocumented Again?"; Giddens, *Modernity and Self-Identity*; James, "Haiti, Insecurity, and the Politics of Asylum"; Patler, Hamilton, and Savinar, "Limits of Gaining Rights"; Vaquera, Aranda, and Sousa-Rodriguez, "Emotional Challenges of Undocumented Young Adults."
47 Griffiths, "Out of Time," 1999.
48 Patler, Hamilton, and Savinar, "Limits of Gaining Rights," 250.
49 James, "Haiti, Insecurity, and the Politics of Asylum," 357, 362.
50 Suerbaum, "Embodying Legal Precarity"; Willen, "Toward a Critical Phenomenology of 'Illegality.'"
51 Valdivia, "Undocumented Young Adults' Heightened Vulnerability," 132.
52 García, Diaz-Strong, and Rodriguez Rodriguez, "Matter of Time," 29.
53 Ellis, Gonzales, and Rendón García, "Power of Inclusion"; Getrich, *Border Brokers*; Gonzales, *Lives in Limbo*; Hardy et al., "Call for Further Research"; Valdivia, "Undocumented Young Adults' Heightened Vulnerability."
54 Flores, "About Time," 48.
55 Abrego, "Renewed Optimism and Spatial Mobility"; Getrich and Ortez-Rivera, "ICE Was Like an Urban Legend."
56 Flores, "About Time," 42.
57 Gonzales, Suárez-Orozco, and Dedios-Sanguineti, "No Place to Belong"; Negrón-Gonzales, "Navigating 'Illegality'"; Suárez-Orozco and Yoshikawa, "Undocumented Status"; Vaquera, Aranda, and Sousa-Rodriguez, "Emotional Challenges of Undocumented Young Adults."
58 Abarca and Coutin, "Sovereign Intimacies"; Coutin, *Legalizing Moves*; Suárez-Navaz, *Rebordering the Mediterranean*.
59 Regulations for issuing driver's licenses to DACA recipients vary by state. As anthropologist Heide Castañeda points out in *Borders of Belonging* (107–8), many states issue undocumented immigrants alternative licenses that may be stamped

with phrases like "legal presence no lawful status" or are a distinct color to indicate that they are intended solely for driving, not for a broader range of identification purposes. DACA recipients are able to access unmarked driver's licenses in each state, typically by providing proof in the form of an employment authorization or Social Security card. However, in Maryland, their license expiration dates are synched with their employment authorization end dates and must be renewed every two years upon receiving subsequent approval for DACA.

60   Abrego, "Renewed Optimism and Spatial Mobility."

61   To assess participants' psychological health, I included a brief screening scale—the Patient Health Questionnaire (PHQ-4), validated by Kroenke et al. ("Ultra-Brief Screening Scale")—in the questionnaire included in phases I and II. In 2016, more than a third of participants (11/30; 37 percent) registered mild to moderate psychological distress. Beyond these numbers, several participants got quite emotional during interviews—even when their PHQ-4 scores did not indicate psychological distress—suggesting an even higher prevalence.

62   Laura was not the only participant who experienced lapses in their employment when their renewal documents did not arrive on time. At least five other individuals had similar experiences, including Nancy the first time I conducted an interview with her.

63   Giuntella et al., "Immigration Policy and Immigrants' Sleep"; Valdivia, "Undocumented Young Adults' Heightened Vulnerability."

64   Valdivia, "Undocumented Young Adults' Heightened Vulnerability," 141.

65   See Getrich et al., "Navigating a Fragmented Health Care Landscape."

66   Unsurprisingly, in 2017–18 a larger proportion of participants (13/25; 52 percent) reported experiencing psychological distress on the PHQ-4.

67   In "Beyond Access," Cha, Enriquez, and Ro likewise found that some immigrant young adults concluded that therapy could not resolve underlying immigration-related stressors.

68   Vaquera, Aranda, and Sousa-Rodriguez, "Emotional Challenges of Undocumented Young Adults," 298.

69   Suárez-Orozco and Yoshikawa, "Undocumented Status." See also Flores Morales and Garcia, "Beyond Undocumented"; Gonzales, Lives in Limbo; Siemons et al., "Coming of Age on the Margins."

70   Interestingly, Marcela uses a common idiom of distress—"thinking too much"—that anthropologist Bonnie Kaiser and her colleagues in global health, psychiatry, and medicine describe as having surprisingly broad cross-cultural salience in their article "'Thinking Too Much.'"

71   See also Patler, Hamilton, and Savinar, "Limits of Gaining Rights," 263.

72   Enriquez et al., "Mental Health and COVID-19," 282.

73   Aranda et al., "Normalized Expendability"; Clark et al., "Disproportionate Impact of the COVID-19 Pandemic"; Đoàn et al., "Immigrant Communities and COVID-19"; Duncan and Horton, "Serious Challenges and Potential Solutions"; Wilson and Stimpson, "Letter to the Editor."

74 In "Normalized Expendability," Aranda et al. describe how the pandemic hit multigenerational immigrant households like Camila's particularly hard and made managing exposure to COVID-19 challenging for many, which I also found to be true among my participants.

75 These are just a brief sampling of participants' pandemic circumstances. Needless to say, these individuals faced additional challenges not described here and others confronted their own particular pandemic-related challenges.

76 In "Normalized Expendability," Aranda et al. also describe how COVID-era bureaucratic delays in status renewals resulting in expired work permits negatively impacted DACA recipients' well-being.

77 See, for example, Angel, Kirkevold, and Pedersen, "Getting on with Life"; Cartwright, "'Getting on with Life'"; Ferguson and Walker, "'Getting on with Life.'"

78 Price and Rojas, "Ordinary Lives and Uneven Precarity of the DACAmented."

79 Willen et al., "Flourishing"; Willen et al., "Rethinking Flourishing."

3. "D.C. HAS MORE BENEFITS FOR IMMIGRANTS THAN MARYLAND"

1 Abrego "Renewed Optimism and Spatial Mobility"; Abrego, "Legal Consciousness of Undocumented Latinos"; Ewick and Silbey, *Common Place of Law*.

2 Flores, Escudero, and Burciaga, "Legal-Spatial Consciousness."

3 Portes and Rumbaut, *Immigrant America*.

4 Content in this chapter draws from and updates discussions that first appeared in "Manoeuvering through the Multilayered Jurisdictional Policy Patchwork" and "Navigating a Fragmented Health Care Landscape." Reprinted with permission from Taylor & Francis Group and Elsevier.

5 Yosso, "Whose Culture Has Capital?"; Yosso et al., "Critical Race Theory."

6 Cebulko and Silver, "Navigating DACA in Hospitable and Hostile States"; Gonzales and Burciaga, "Segmented Pathways of Illegality"; Menjívar and Kanstroom, *Constructing Immigrant "Illegality"*; Roth, "Double Bind of DACA"; Silver, *Shifting Boundaries*.

7 Burciaga and Malone, "Intensified Liminal Legality"; Coleman, "'Local' Migration State."

8 Cebulko and Silver, "Navigating DACA in Hospitable and Hostile States"; Coleman, "'Local' Migration State"; García, *Legal Passing*; Gonzales, Brant, and Roth, "DACAmented in the Age of Deportation."

9 Abrego and Negrón-Gonzales, *We Are Not Dreamers*, 10–11; Golash-Boza and Valdez, "Nested Contexts of Reception," 540.

10 Golash-Boza and Valdez, "Nested Contexts of Reception."

11 Golash-Boza and Valdez, "Nested Contexts of Reception," 536.

12 García, *Legal Passing*, 36.

13 Jones, "From Open Doors to Closed Gates"; Silver, *Shifting Boundaries*.

14 Burciaga and Malone, "Intensified Liminal Legality"; Maldonado, "Latino Incorporation and Racialized Border Politics"; Marrow, "Hope Turned Sour"; Perez,

"Nested Contexts of Reception"; Roth, "Double Bind of DACA"; Silver, *Shifting Boundaries*.

15 Cebulko and Silver, "Navigating DACA in Hospitable and Hostile States."
16 García, *Legal Passing*, 29.
17 García, *Legal Passing*, 191; see also Gonzales, Brant, and Roth, "DACAmented in the Age of Deportation," 66.
18 Flores, Escudero, and Burciaga, "Legal-Spatial Consciousness," 26.
19 Graauw and Gleeson, "Metropolitan Context and Immigrant Rights Experiences," 1141.
20 Golash-Boza and Valdez, "Nested Contexts of Reception"; Perez, "Nested Contexts of Reception."
21 Bruhn and Gonzales, "Geographies of Belonging."
22 Enriquez and Millán, "Situational Triggers and Protective Locations."
23 Gonzales, Brant, and Roth, "DACAmented in the Age of Deportation," 62, 66.
24 García, *Legal Passing*; Getrich, *Border Brokers*; Gonzales, *Lives in Limbo*; Hardy et al., "Call for Further Research"; Valdivia, "Undocumented Young Adults' Heightened Vulnerability."
25 Hardy et al., "Call for Further Research"; Maldonado, "Latino Incorporation and Racialized Border Politics"; Valdivia, "Undocumented Young Adults' Heightened Vulnerability."
26 García, *Legal Passing*, 29.
27 Cebulko, "Becoming White in a White Supremacist State"; Enriquez, "Border Hopping Mexicans"; Enriquez and Millán, "Situational Triggers and Protective Locations"; García, "Racializing 'Illegality.'"
28 Enriquez, "Border Hopping Mexicans"; García, "Racializing 'Illegality'"; Herrera, "Racialized Illegality"; Patler, "Racialized 'Illegality.'"
29 Cebulko, "Becoming White in a White Supremacist State."
30 Herrera, "Racialized Illegality."
31 Enriquez, "Border Hopping Mexicans," 260; Patler, "Racialized 'Illegality.'"
32 García, "Racializing 'Illegality'"; Herrera, "Racialized Illegality," 322.
33 Abrego, "Legal Consciousness of Undocumented Latinos"; Ewick and Silbey, *Common Place of Law*.
34 Abrego, "Legal Consciousness of Undocumented Latinos," 337, 340–41.
35 Abrego, "Renewed Optimism and Spatial Mobility," 194.
36 León, "Legalization through Marriage."
37 Flores, Escudero, and Burciaga, "Legal-Spatial Consciousness," 13.
38 Flores, Escudero, and Burciaga, "Legal-Spatial Consciousness," 26.
39 Cebulko and Silver, "Navigating DACA in Hospitable and Hostile States," 1570.
40 Abrego, "Renewed Optimism and Spatial Mobility," 199; Castañeda and Melo, "Geographies of Confinement for Immigrant Youth," 94; Getrich and Ortez-Rivera, "ICE Was Like an Urban Legend."
41 Flores, Escudero, and Burciaga, "Legal-Spatial Consciousness," 26.

42 Yosso, "Whose Culture Has Capital?," 80.
43 Alvarez, "Experiential Knowledge as Capital and Resistance"; Macías, "Scheme Game"; Nájera, "Unauthorized Education"; Yosso et al., "Critical Race Theory"; Yosso, "Whose Culture Has Capital?"
44 Varsanyi et al., "Multilayered Jurisdictional Patchwork."
45 Portes and Rumbaut, *Immigrant America*.
46 Aranda and Vaquera, "Racism, the Immigration Enforcement Regime"; Vaquera, Aranda, and Gonzales, "Patterns of Incorporation of Latinos."
47 Enriquez and Millán, "Situational Triggers and Protective Locations," 2103–4.
48 Enriquez and Millán, "Situational Triggers and Protective Locations," 2103–4; García, *Legal Passing*, 29.
49 Alter, "Theory of Workarounds."
50 Alvarez, "Experiential Knowledge as Capital and Resistance"; Yosso, "Whose Culture Has Capital?"; Yosso et al., "Critical Race Theory."
51 National Conference of State Legislatures, "Deferred Action for Childhood Arrivals."
52 As described below, Nancy is included in all of these categories (making it so the total numbers do not add up). During phase I, she had lived in multiple Maryland counties. By phase II she had moved out of state to Massachusetts, and by phase III she had moved back to the area in Virginia.
53 Cho, "Revisiting Ethnic Niches."
54 Asad and Rosen, "Hiding within Racial Hierarchies," 1857.
55 Abrego, "Renewed Optimism and Spatial Mobility," 199; Castañeda and Melo, "Geographies of Confinement for Immigrant Youth," 94.

4. "PEOPLE SHOW UP IN DIFFERENT WAYS"

1 Content in this chapter draws from and updates discussions that first appeared in "'People Show Up in Different Ways.'" Reproduced by permission of the Society for Applied Anthropology.
2 Nicholls, *The DREAMers*, 2.
3 Gomberg-Muñoz and Nussbaum-Barberena, "Everyday Enforcement"; Wong, García, and Valdivia, "Political Incorporation of Undocumented Youth."
4 Mansbridge, "Everyday Activism."
5 Fish, King, and Almack, "Queerying Activism."
6 Pink, *Situating Everyday Life*, 4; Fish, King, and Almack, "Queerying Activism," 1195–96.
7 Mena Robles and Gomberg-Muñoz, "Activism after DACA," 53.
8 Mendes and Chang, "Undocumented and Afraid."
9 Guttman, "Rituals of Resistance."
10 Nicholls *The DREAMers*, 9–10; see also Abrego, "Legitimacy, Social Identity, and the Mobilization of Law," and Patler, "'Citizens but for Papers,'" 99.
11 Nicholls, *The DREAMers*, 9.
12 Dowling and Inda, *Governing Immigration through Crime*, 27.

13 Bloemraad, Voss, and Lee, "Protests of 2006"; Pallares and Flores-González, "Regarding Family," 170; Terriquez, "Legal Status, Civic Organizations, and Political Participation," 315.

14 Nicholls, *The DREAMers*, 8.

15 Nicholls, *The DREAMers*, 1–2.

16 Abrego, "Legitimacy, Social Identity, and the Mobilization of Law"; Negrón-Gonzales, "Undocumented, Unafraid and Unapologetic."

17 Nicholls, *The DREAMers*, 7; Zavella, *I'm Neither Here nor There*, ix.

18 Bloemraad, Voss, and Lee, "Protests of 2006"; Getrich, *Border Brokers*; Getrich, "Negotiating Boundaries of Social Belonging"; Wong, García, and Valdivia, "Political Incorporation of Undocumented Youth"; Zepeda-Millán, *Latino Mass Mobilization*.

19 Abrego, "Renewed Optimism and Spatial Mobility," 193; Nicholls, *The DREAMers*, 7; Sati, "How DACA Pits 'Good Immigrants' Against Millions of Others"; Unzueta Carrasco and Seif, "Disrupting the Dream."

20 Abrego, "Renewed Optimism and Spatial Mobility," 193; Marquez-Benitez and Pallares, "Not One More," 14; Nicholls, *The DREAMers*, 7; Unzueta Carrasco and Seif, "Disrupting the Dream," 288.

21 Nicholls, *The DREAMers*, 153.

22 Wong, García, and Valdivia, "Political Incorporation of Undocumented Youth."

23 Mora et al., "Immigrant Rights and Social Movements"; Terriquez, "Legal Status, Civic Organizations, and Political Participation," 317; Wong, García, and Valdivia, "Political Incorporation of Undocumented Youth," 3.

24 Abrego, "'I Can't Go to College'"; Abrego and Negrón-Gonzales, *We Are Not Dreamers*; Escudero, *Organizing while Undocumented*; Negrón-Gonzales, "Undocumented, Unafraid and Unapologetic"; Nicholls, *The DREAMers*; Terriquez, Brenes, and Lopez, "Intersectionality as a Multipurpose Collective Action Frame."

25 Escudero, *Organizing while Undocumented*; Marquez-Benitez and Pallares, "Not One More"; Mena Robles and Gomberg-Muñoz, "Activism after DACA"; Rubio, "'We Need to Redefine What We Mean by Winning'"; Seif, "'Coming Out of the Shadows'"; Unzueta Carrasco and Seif, "Disrupting the Dream."

26 Nicholls, "Uneven Geography of Politicisation," 465.

27 Marquez-Benitez and Pallares, "Not One More"; Nicholls, *The DREAMers*, 107.

28 Price and Rojas, "Ordinary Lives and Uneven Precarity of the DACAmented"; Rubio, "'We Need to Redefine What We Mean by Winning'"; Solorzano and Ruiz, "Saving DACA, Healing Ourselves."

29 Mora et al., "Immigrant Rights and Social Movements"; Valdivia, "Youth Activism"; Wong, García, and Valdivia, "Political Incorporation of Undocumented Youth."

30 Marquez-Benitez and Pallares, "Not One More," 19, 22; Nájera, "Unauthorized Education."

31 Abrego and Negrón-Gonzales, *We Are Not Dreamers*.

32 Bloemraad and Voss, "Movement or Moment?"; Unzueta Carrasco and Seif, "Disrupting the Dream"; Terriquez, Brenes, and Lopez, "Intersectionality as a Multipurpose Collective Action Frame."

33 Dao, "Out and Asian"; Escudero, *Organizing while Undocumented*, 15; Fiorito, "Learning to Be Legal," 1105; Rubio, "'We Need to Redefine What We Mean by Winning'"; Seif, "'Coming Out of the Shadows'"; Terriquez, "Legal Status, Civic Organizations, and Political Participation"; Terriquez, Brenes, and Lopez, "Intersectionality as a Multipurpose Collective Action Frame."

34 Gomberg-Muñoz and Nussbaum-Barberena, "Everyday Enforcement"; Heredia, "Of Radicals and DREAMers."

35 Gomberg-Muñoz and Nussbaum-Barberena, "Everyday Enforcement"; Mena Robles and Gomberg-Muñoz, "Activism after DACA."

36 Burciaga and Martinez, "How Do Political Contexts Shape Undocumented Youth Movements?," 454; Negrón-Gonzales, "Undocumented, Unafraid and Unapologetic," 262.

37 Marquez-Benitez and Pallares, "Not One More," 16–17.

38 Negrón-Gonzales, "Undocumented, Unafraid and Unapologetic," 263; Unzueta Carrasco and Seif, "Disrupting the Dream"; Wong, García, and Valdivia, "Political Incorporation of Undocumented Youth," 3.

39 Rubio and Alvarez Almendariz, "Refusing 'Undocumented.'"

40 Bloemraad and Voss, "Movement or Moment?," 14; Heredia, "Of Radicals and DREAMers"; Marquez-Benitez and Pallares, "Not One More," 17; Mora et al., "Immigrant Rights and Social Movements," 4.

41 Rosales, Enriquez, and Nájera, "Politically Excluded, Undocu-Engaged," 271.

42 Martinez et al., *Eclipse of Dreams*, 28.

43 Fiorito, "Learning to Be Legal," 1105; Rubio, "'We Need to Redefine What We Mean by Winning'"; Rubio and Alvarez Almendariz, "Refusing 'Undocumented.'"

44 Rubio, "'We Need to Redefine What We Mean by Winning,'" 158.

45 Gálvez, "I Won't Tell My Story"; Martinez et al., *Eclipse of Dreams*; Silvestre, "Me Vestí De Reina."

46 Mendes and Chang, "Undocumented and Afraid," 60, 73.

47 Mendes and Chang, "Undocumented and Afraid," 61; Nuñez-Janes and Ovalle, "Organic Activists," 190.

48 Scott, *Weapons of the Weak*.

49 Vinthagen and Johansson, "'Everyday Resistance,'" 2.

50 Scott, *Domination and the Arts of Resistance*, 118; Scott, *Weapons of the Weak*, 137.

51 Zepeda-Millán, "Weapons of the (Not So) Weak," 277.

52 Pink, *Situating Everyday Life*, 4; Fish, King, and Almack, "Queerying Activism," 1195–96.

53 Mansbridge, "Everyday Activism," 1.

54 Price and Rojas, "Ordinary Lives and Uneven Precarity of the DACAmented," 4762.

55 Lefebvre, *Production of Space*.

56 Tournadre, "'Because We Are the Only Ones in the Community!'"
57 Soaita, "Everyday Activism."
58 Lefebvre, *Production of Space.*
59 Magaña, "Spaces of Resistance."
60 Harris and Roose, "Young Muslims and Everyday Political Practice."
61 Harris and Roose, "Young Muslims and Everyday Political Practice"; Vega, "Politics of Everyday Life."
62 Harris and Roose, "Young Muslims and Everyday Political Practice," 237.
63 Nájera, "Creating Safe Space for Undocumented Students"; Valdivia, "Youth Activism."
64 Nájera, "Creating Safe Space for Undocumented Students," 355.
65 Nuñez-Janes and Ovalle, "Organic Activists," 191.
66 Gonzales, "Left Out but Not Shut Down"; Nájera, "Creating Safe Space for Undocumented Students," 342; Nájera, "Unauthorized Education," 37; Negrón-Gonzales, "Navigating 'Illegality'"; Rosales, Enriquez, and Nájera, "Politically Excluded, Undocu-Engaged," 263.
67 Nájera, "Unauthorized Education," 36.
68 Nuñez-Janes and Ovalle, "Organic Activists," 197; Nájera, "Creating Safe Space for Undocumented Students," 352.
69 Getrich, *Border Brokers*; Mendes and Chang, "Undocumented and Afraid."
70 Fish, King, and Almack, "Queerying Activism."
71 Nájera, "Unauthorized Education," 36.
72 Bloemraad and Voss, "Movement or Moment?," 6; Mora et al., "Immigrant Rights and Social Movements," 11.
73 Fish, King, and Almack, "Queerying Activism," 1204.
74 Heredia, "Of Radicals and DREAMers"; Mora et al., "Immigrant Rights and Social Movements," 4.
75 Gutmann, "Rituals of Resistance," 77.
76 Roberto G. Gonzales captures this phenomenon in his seminal ethnography of undocumented young adults, *Lives in Limbo.*
77 In writing about young activists' practices of refusal, both anthropologist Alyshia Gálvez, in "I Won't Tell My Story," and anthropologists Elizabeth Hanna Rubio and Xitlalli Alvarez Almendariz, in "Refusing 'Undocumented,'" build on longer-standing theorizations of the concept, including anthropologist Audra Simpson's *Mohawk Interruptus*, anthropologist Carole McGranahan's "Refusal as Political Practice," and Indigenous studies and education scholar Eve Tuck and ethnic studies scholar K. Wayne Yang's "Unbecoming Claims."
78 Gomberg-Muñoz, "Hardship Politics," 759.
79 Gálvez, "I Won't Tell My Story."
80 Lavariega Monforti and Michelson, "Firme," 96.
81 Getrich, "'People Show Up in Different Ways'"; Lavariega Monforti and Michelson, "Firme," 96.
82 Harris, Wyn, and Younes, "Beyond Apathetic or Activist Youth," 22.

83 Mena Robles and Gomberg-Muñoz, "Activism after DACA," 53.
84 Gomberg-Muñoz, "Hardship Politics."
85 Nájera, "Unauthorized Education," 36–37.
86 Abrego, "Legal Consciousness of Undocumented Latinos."
87 Pink, *Situating Everyday Life*, 3.
88 Vivienne and Burgess, "Digital Storyteller's Stage."

5. "I'M IN A GOOD POSITION TO ADVOCATE NOW"

1 Content in this chapter draws from and updates discussions that first appeared in "DACA Recipient Health Care Workers' Barriers to Professionalization and Deployment of Navigational Capital in Pursuit of Health Equity for Immigrants" and "I'm in a Good Position to Advocate Now." Reprinted with permission from SpringerNature and Sage Publications.
2 Abrego, "Relational Legal Consciousness of U.S. Citizenship."
3 Alvarez, "Experiential Knowledge as Capital and Resistance"; Nájera, "Unauthorized Education"; Yosso, "Whose Culture Has Capital?"
4 Svajlenka and Truong, "Demographic and Economic Impacts of DACA Recipients."
5 Getrich, *Border Brokers*; López-Sanders, "Navigating Health Care."
6 García-Sánchez, "Children as Interactional Brokers of Care," 168.
7 Lamphere, "Providers and Staff Respond"; Ticktin, "Care and the Commons."
8 Han, *Life in Debt*, 23; Ticktin, "Care and the Commons," 916.
9 Thelen, "Care as Belonging, Difference, and Inequality."
10 Getrich, *Border Brokers*; López-Sanders, "Navigating Health Care."
11 García-Sánchez, "Children as Interactional Brokers of Care"; Katz, *Kids in the Middle*; Menjívar, "Immigrants, Immigration, and Sociology"; Orellana, *Translating Childhoods*; Orellana, Dorner, and Pulido, "Accessing Assets."
12 Dorner, Orellana, and Jiménez, "'It's One of Those Things That You Do to Help the Family.'"
13 Katz, *Kids in the Middle*, 6.
14 Dorner, Orellana, and Jiménez, "'It's One of Those Things That You Do to Help the Family'"; Orellana, Dorner, and Pulido, "Accessing Assets."
15 Orellana, Dorner, and Pulido, "Accessing Assets," 505.
16 Orellana, *Translating Childhoods*, 2.
17 García-Sánchez, "Children as Interactional Brokers of Care," 175; Katz, *Kids in the Middle*, 12; Menjívar, "Immigrants, Immigration, and Sociology"; Orellana, *Translating Childhoods*; Orellana, "The Work Kids Do."
18 Yosso, "Whose Culture Has Capital?," 80.
19 Alvarez, "Experiential Knowledge as Capital and Resistance"; Macías, "Scheme Game"; Nájera, "Unauthorized Education"; Yosso et al., "Critical Race Theory"; Yosso, "Whose Culture Has Capital?"
20 Yosso, "Whose Culture Has Capital?," 80.
21 Madden, "Cultural Health Capital on the Margins"; Shim, "Cultural Health Capital."
22 Fernández et al., "Muxeres en Acción."

23 Castañeda, *Borders of Belonging*; Delgado, "Children of Immigrants"; Getrich, *Border Brokers*.

24 Delgado, "Children of Immigrants," 5.

25 Campbell-Montalvo and Castañeda, "School Employees as Health Care Brokers"; Sosa, Roth, and Rodriguez, "Crossing Borders," 198.

26 Getrich et al., "Buffering the Uneven Impact of the Affordable Care Act"; Getrich et al., "Effective Strategies for Affordable Care Act"; López-Sanders, "Changing the Navigator's Course"; López-Sanders, "Navigating Health Care."

27 Logan, *Boundaries of Care*, 8.

28 Lamphere, "Providers and Staff Respond." See also Getrich et al., "Buffering the Uneven Impact of the Affordable Care Act"; Getrich et al., "Effective Strategies for Affordable Care Act."

29 López-Sanders, "Navigating Health Care," 2075.

30 Logan, *Boundaries of Care*, 17; Campbell-Montalvo and Castañeda, "School Employees as Health Care Brokers," 740.

31 Campbell-Montalvo and Castañeda, "School Employees as Health Care Brokers," 735.

32 López-Sanders, "Navigating Health Care," 2072.

33 López-Sanders, "Navigating Health Care," 2072.

34 López-Sanders, "Changing the Navigator's Course."

35 Logan, *Boundaries of Care*; Campbell-Montalvo and Castañeda, "School Employees as Health Care Brokers."

36 Lamphere, "Providers and Staff Respond," 13.

37 Cook and Trundle, "Unsettled Care," 179; Han, *Life in Debt*; Milligan and Wiles, "Landscapes of Care," 738; Smith-Morris, "Care as Virtue"; Thelen, "Care as Belonging, Difference, and Inequality," 2; Yarris, *Care Across Generations*, 23.

38 Ticktin, "Care and the Commons," 916.

39 Cook and Trundle, "Unsettled Care," 179; Mol, *Logic of Care*.

40 Thelen, "Care as Belonging, Difference, and Inequality," 12.

41 Livingston, *Improvising Medicine*, 96; Ticktin, *Casualties of Care*, 2.

42 Fassin, "Children as Victims," 112.

43 García-Sánchez, "Children as Interactional Brokers of Care," 168.

44 McKearney and Amrith, "Care," 8–9.

45 Finch, "Introduction"; García-Sánchez, "Children as Interactional Brokers of Care," 168; Held, *Ethics of Care*; McKearney and Amrith, "Care," 7; Milligan and Wiles, "Landscapes of Care," 737; Ticktin, "Care and the Commons," 918.

46 Held, *Ethics of Care*; Livingston, *Improvising Medicine*, 96; Thelen, "Care as Belonging, Difference, and Inequality," 2.

47 Coe, *New American Servitude*, 11; McKearney and Amrith, "Care," 2; Campbell-Montalvo and Castañeda, "School Employees as Health Care Brokers"; Milligan and Wiles, "Landscapes of Care," 742.

48 Alber and Drotbohm, *Anthropological Perspectives on Care*, 10; McKearney and Amrit, "Care," 10; Thelen, "Care as Belonging, Difference, and Inequality," 11.

49 Alber and Drotbohm, *Anthropological Perspectives on Care*, 11.

50 Coe, *Scattered Family*; Ehrenreich and Hochschild, *Global Woman*; Parreñas, *Servants of Globalization*; Yarris, *Care Across Generations*.

51 García-Sánchez, "Children as Interactional Brokers of Care," 172.

52 Thelen, "Care as Belonging, Difference, and Inequality, 12–13.

53 Thelen and Coe, "Political Belonging through Elderly Care"; Hobart and Kneese, "Radical Care," 7.

54 Cook and Trundle, "Unsettled Care," 179.

55 Hobart and Kneese, "Radical Care," 2.

56 Hobart and Kneese, "Radical Care," 8.

57 Coe, *New American Servitude*, 245.

58 Yarris, *Care Across Generations*, 25.

59 Hobart and Kneese, "Radical Care," 2; Logan, *Boundaries of Care*, 25; Ticktin, *Casualties of Care*, 3.

60 Anzaldúa, *Borderlands / La Frontera*; Collins, *Black Feminist Thought*; Hobart and Kneese, "Radical Care," 2; hooks, *Feminist Theory*; Moraga and Anzaldúa, *This Bridge Called My Back*.

61 Cook and Trundle, "Unsettled Care," 179; Logan, *Boundaries of Care*; McKearney and Amrith, "Care," 12; Yarris, *Care Across Generations*, 22.

62 Hobart and Kneese, "Radical Care," 10; Ticktin, "Care and the Commons," 916.

63 Finch, "Introduction," 2.

64 Hobart and Kneese, "Radical Care," 2.

65 Ticktin, "Care and the Commons."

66 Han, *Life in Debt*, 23; Ticktin, "Care and the Commons," 916.

67 Coe, *New American Servitude*, 8.

68 McKearney and Amrith, "Care," 21.

69 Thelen and Coe, "Political Belonging through Elderly Care."

70 Ticktin, "Care and the Commons."

71 Nvé Díaz San Francisco, "Care during Pandemic Times," 340.

72 McKearney and Amrith, "Care," 10.

73 Getrich, *Border Brokers*, 177; Katz, *Kids in the Middle*, 32.

74 McKearney and Amrith, "Care," 10; Thelen, "Care as Belonging, Difference, and Inequality," 11.

75 Falicov, Niño, and D'Urso, "Expanding Possibilities."

76 Duncan and Nabor Vazquez, "'I Don't Feel That We Are a Burden,'" 2.

77 Price and Rojas, "Ordinary Lives and Uneven Precarity of the DACAmented," 4762. Price and Rojas draw here from Fians's formulation of the concept outlined in "Prefigurative Politics."

78 Woodly, "Politics of Care."

79 Ticktin, "Care and the Commons," 916–17.

CONCLUSION

1 Quesada, Hart, and Bourgois, "Structural Vulnerability and Health"; Carruth et al., "Structural Vulnerability."

2 Castañeda, *Borders of Belonging*; Getrich, *Border Brokers*; Lopez and Castañeda, "Mixed-Status Community."

3 Hamilton, Patler, and Langer, "Life-Course Timing of Legalization"; Patler, Hale, and Hamilton, "Paths to Mobility"; see also Gonzales et al., "(Un)authorized Transitions."

4 Alvarez Almendariz, "Whiteness of DACA"; Rubio and Alvarez Almendariz, "Refusing 'Undocumented'"; Rubio, "'We Need to Redefine What We Mean by Winning.'"

5 Abrego and Negrón-Gonzales, *We Are Not Dreamers*, 12–15.

6 Willen et al., "Flourishing."

7 Bloemraad and Voss, "Movement or Moment?," 6; Fish, King, and Almack, "Queerying Activism"; Mora et al., "Immigrant Rights and Social Movements," 11; Nájera, "Unauthorized Education."

8 Shange, "Abolition in the Clutch."

9 Hispanic Engineer and Information Technology, "DACA Gets Major Support."

10 In the conclusion to *Accompaniment with Im/migrant Communities*, Yarris and Duncan similarly describe "showing up" as a key principle in working alongside immigrant communities, underscoring that it is a frame that has resonance beyond my participants' use of it.

11 Smith, "Doing Community and Institutionally Engaged Work."

12 Given that these examples do not derive from research data (i.e., questionnaires, interviews) but rather are rooted in my experiences, I do not identify individuals by their pseudonyms.

13 Nájera, "Creating Safe Space for Undocumented Students."

14 Golash-Boza and Valdez, "Nested Contexts of Reception," 547; Nájera, "Creating Safe Space for Undocumented Students."

15 Nájera, "Creating Safe Space for Undocumented Students"; Nájera, "Unauthorized Education"; Nuñez-Janes and Ovalle, "Organic Activists."

16 Nájera, "Unauthorized Education," 36.

17 Gomberg-Muñoz, "Complicit Anthropologist," 36.

18 Gomberg-Muñoz, "Complicit Anthropologist," 36; Schuller, *Humanity's Last Stand.*

19 Ultimately, my colleague pursued another opportunity, which is why she is not one of my "official" collaborators for this project, though I have unofficially sought her input on my findings and this book specifically many times over the years.

20 Abrego and Negrón-Gonzales, *We Are Not Dreamers.*

21 Alvarez Almendariz, "Whiteness of DACA"; Rubio, "'We Need to Redefine What We Mean by Winning'"; Martinez et al., *Eclipse of Dreams.*

22 Fish, King, and Almack, "Queerying Activism," 1204.

23 Cabot and Ramsay, "Deexceptionalizing Displacement," 286.
24 See the website for Showing Up for Racial Justice, available at https://surj.org.
25 Martinez HoSang, *Wider Type of Freedom*.
26 Schuller, *Humanity's Last Stand*.
27 Tsing, *Mushroom at the End of the World*, 20.
28 Tsing, *Mushroom at the End of the World*.
29 Cabot and Ramsay, "Deexceptionalizing Displacement," 287.
30 Allison, "Precarity"; Chacón, Bibler Coutin, and Lee, *Legal Phantoms*.
31 Schuller, *Humanity's Last Stand*, 9–10.
32 Schuller, *Humanity's Last Stand*, 10.
33 Liu and Shange, "Toward Thick Solidarity," 195.
34 López, "Ethnography and Community Based Methods."
35 Harris, Wyn, and Younes, "Beyond Apathetic or Activist Youth."

APPENDIX A

1 Content in this appendix draws from and updates discussions that first appeared in "We've Been There Alongside Each Other Right from the Beginning." Reprinted with permission of the University of Arizona Press.
2 Singer, "Studying Hidden and Hard-to-Reach Populations," 259.
3 Singer, "Studying Hidden and Hard-to-Reach Populations," 259.
4 National Cancer Institute, "Survey Instruments."
5 Kroenke et al., "Ultra-Brief Screening Scale."
6 Charmaz, "Grounded Theory."
7 Emerson, Fretz, and Shaw, *Writing Ethnographic Fieldnotes*.
8 Newman et al., "Community Advisory Boards."
9 Hacker, *Community-Based Participatory Research*.
10 Thomson, "Qualitative Longitudinal Case History."
11 In *Laboring for Justice*, Galemba (26) describes the value of a research design that unfolds iteratively, particularly for long-term, collaborative research.
12 Abrego and Negrón-Gonzales, *We Are Not Dreamers*; Bejarano et al., *Decolonizing Ethnography*; Martinez et al., *Eclipse of Dreams*.
13 Rylko-Bauer, Singer, and Van Willigen, "Reclaiming Applied Anthropology."
14 Lamphere, "Convergence of Applied, Practicing, and Public Anthropology"; Rylko-Bauer, Singer, and Van Willigen, "Reclaiming Applied Anthropology."
15 Hacker, *Community-Based Participatory Research*; Hardy et al., "Hiring the Experts"; Israel et al., *Methods in Community-Based Participatory Research for Health*; Wallerstein et al., *Community-Based Participatory Research for Health*.
16 Stuesse, *Scratching Out a Living*, 235.
17 Low and Merry, "Engaged Anthropology."
18 Low, "Claiming Space for an Engaged Anthropology," 390.
19 Reese, *Black Food Geographies*, 136.
20 Speed, "At the Crossroads of Human Rights and Anthropology."
21 Hale, *Engaging Contradictions*; Stuesse, *Scratching Out a Living*, 17, 235.

22 Pine, "Revolution as a Care Plan"; Scheper-Hughes, "Primacy of the Ethical"; Saxton, *Devil's Fruit*.

23 Scheper-Hughes, "Primacy of the Ethical"; Rylko-Bauer, Singer, and Van Willigen, "Reclaiming Applied Anthropology."

24 Jacobson and Mustafa, "Social Identity Map," 1.

25 In *They Leave Their Kidneys in the Fields*, Horton (188) also advocates chronicling participants' lives over time as a beneficial approach that allows readers to acquaint themselves with immigrants as individuals and better understand how their lives unfold.

26 See, for example, Coutin, *Legalizing Moves*; Galemba, *Laboring for Justice*; Kline, *Pathogenic Policing*; Saxton, *Devil's Fruit*; Stuesse, *Scratching Out a Living*; Unterberger, "The Blur."

27 Unterberger, "The Blur."

28 Unterberger, "The Blur."

29 Stuesse, *Scratching Out a Living*, 233.

30 Lopez, *Separated*, 12–13, 159.

31 Abrego and Negrón-Gonzales, *We Are Not Dreamers*, 1–2.

32 Galemba, *Laboring for Justice*, 22–24.

33 Bejarano et al., *Decolonizing Ethnography*.

34 Hacker, *Community-Based Participatory Research*; Miller et al., "Developing Advisory Boards"; Ortega et al., "Perspectives of Community Advisory Board Members"; Rustage et al., "Participatory Approaches."

35 Miller et al., "Developing Advisory Boards"; Stacciarini et al., "'I Didn't Ask to Come.'"

36 Raymond-Flesch et al., "'There Is No Help Out There'"; Stacciarini et al., "'I Didn't Ask to Come'"; Sudhinaraset et al., "Dreams Deferred"; Sudhinaraset et al., "Influence of Deferred Action for Childhood Arrivals."

37 Nájera, "Creating Safe Space for Undocumented Students"; Nuñez-Janes, Ovalle, and Plancarte, "Creating Sanctuary."

38 See Getrich et al., "'We've Been There Alongside Each Other.'"

39 Yarris and Duncan, *Accompaniment with Im/migrant Communities*.

40 Martinez et al., *Eclipse of Dreams*, 23. See also Sepúlveda, "Toward a Pedagogy of Acompañamiento," 558–59. In *Laboring for Justice*, Galemba similarly describes the centrality of *convivir*, or standing, listening, and learning alongside, to her engaged research approach (25).

41 Yarris and Duncan, *Accompaniment with Im/migrant Communities*.

42 Nuñez-Janes, Ovalle, and Plancarte, "Creating Sanctuary"; Unterberger, "The Blur."

43 Long, "Lockdown Anthropology and Online Surveys."

44 Long, "From Social Distancing to Social Containment."

45 Long, "From Social Distancing to Social Containment."

46 Saxton, *Devil's Fruit*, 24.

47 Saxton, *Devil's Fruit*, 24.

48 Horton, "On Pandemic Privilege."
49 Aguilar, "Undocumented Critical Theory," 153; Chang, Mendes, and Salazar, "Qualitative Methodological Considerations"; Ramirez, "Beyond Identity," 149.
50 Günel, Varma, and Watanabe, "Manifesto for Patchwork Ethnography." I am grateful to Sammy Primiano—whose commendable patchwork dissertation project will surely make an important contribution to the field—for introducing me to this genre of ethnography.

BIBLIOGRAPHY

Abarca, Gray Albert, and Susan Bibler Coutin. 2018. "Sovereign Intimacies: The Lives of Documents within US State-Noncitizen Relationships." *American Ethnologist* 45 (1): 7–19.

Abrego, Leisy J. 2006. "'I Can't Go to College Because I Don't Have Papers': Incorporation Patterns of Latino Undocumented Youth." *Latino Studies* 4 (3): 212–31.

———. 2008. "Legitimacy, Social Identity, and the Mobilization of Law: The Effects of Assembly Bill 540 on Undocumented Students in California." *Law & Social Inquiry* 33 (3): 709–34.

———. 2011. "Legal Consciousness of Undocumented Latinos: Fear and Stigma as Barriers to Claims-Making for First- and 1.5-Generation Immigrants." *Law & Society Review* 45 (2): 337–70.

———. 2018. "Renewed Optimism and Spatial Mobility: Legal Consciousness of Latino Deferred Action for Childhood Arrivals Recipients and Their Families in Los Angeles." *Ethnicities* 18 (2): 192–207.

———. 2019. "Relational Legal Consciousness of U.S. Citizenship: Privilege, Responsibility, Guilt, and Love in Latino Mixed-Status Families." *Law & Society Review* 53 (3): 641–70.

Abrego, Leisy J., and Roberto G. Gonzales. 2010. "Blocked Paths, Uncertain Futures: The Postsecondary Education and Labor Market Prospects of Undocumented Latino Youth." *Journal of Education for Students Placed at Risk* 15 (1–2): 144–57.

Abrego, Leisy J., and Genevieve Negrón-Gonzales, eds. 2020. *We Are Not Dreamers: Undocumented Scholars Theorize Undocumented Life in the United States.* Durham, NC: Duke University Press.

Aguilar, Carlos. 2019. "Undocumented Critical Theory." *Cultural Studies ↔ Critical Methodologies* 19 (3): 152–60.

Alber, Erdmute, and Heike Drotbohm, eds. 2015. *Anthropological Perspectives on Care: Work, Kinship, and the Life Course.* New York: Palgrave Macmillan.

Allen, Jafari Sinclaire, and Ryan Cecil Jobson. 2016. "The Decolonizing Generation: (Race and) Theory in Anthropology Since the Eighties." *Current Anthropology* 57 (2): 129–48.

Allison, Anne. 2016. "Precarity: Commentary by Anne Allison." *Cultural Anthropology.* https://journal.culanth.org.

Alter, Steven. 2014. "Theory of Workarounds." *Communications of the Association for Information Systems* 34 (55): 1041–66.

Alvarez, Adriana. 2020. "Experiential Knowledge as Capital and Resistance among Families from Mexican Immigrant Backgrounds." *Equity & Excellence in Education* 53 (4): 482–503.

Alvarez Almendariz, Xitlalli. 2021. "The Whiteness of DACA." *Fieldsights*, October 19, 2021. https://culanth.org.

American Immigration Council (AIC). 2021. "The Dream Act: An Overview." March 16, 2021. www.americanimmigrationcouncil.org.

Angel, Sanne, Marit Kirkevold, and Birthe D. Pedersen. 2009. "Getting on with Life Following a Spinal Cord Injury: Regaining Meaning through Six Phases." *International Journal of Qualitative Studies on Health and Well-Being* 4 (1): 39–50.

Anzaldúa, Gloria. 1987. *Borderlands / La Frontera: The New Mestiza*. San Francisco: Aunt Lute.

Aranda, Elizabeth, and Elizabeth Vaquera. 2015. "Racism, the Immigration Enforcement Regime, and the Implications for Racial Inequality in the Lives of Undocumented Young Adults." *Sociology of Race and Ethnicity* 1 (1): 88–104.

Aranda, Elizabeth, Elizabeth Vaquera, and Heide Castañeda. 2021. "Shifting Roles in Families of Deferred Action for Childhood Arrivals (DACA) Recipients and Implications for the Transition to Adulthood." *Journal of Family Issues* 42 (9): 2111–32.

Aranda, Elizabeth, Elizabeth Vaquera, Heide Castañeda, and Melanie Escue. 2024. "Normalized Expendability: Navigating Immigrant Legal Status during a Global Pandemic." *American Behavioral Scientist.* https://doi.org/10.1177/00027642241229538.

Aranda, Elizabeth, Elizabeth Vaquera, Heide Castañeda, and Girsea Martinez Rosas. 2023. "Undocumented Again? DACA Rescission, Emotions, and Incorporation Outcomes among Young Adults." *Social Forces* 101 (3): 1321–42.

Armenta, Amada. 2017. *Protect, Serve, and Deport: The Rise of Policing as Immigration Enforcement*. Berkeley: University of California Press.

Arnett, Jeffrey Jensen. 2006. *Emerging Adulthood: The Winding Road from the Late Teens through the Twenties*. New York: Oxford University Press.

Asad, Asad L. 2020. "On the Radar: System Embeddedness and Latin American Immigrants' Perceived Risk of Deportation." *Law & Society Review* 54 (1): 133–67.

Asad, Asad L., and Eva Rosen. 2019. "Hiding within Racial Hierarchies: How Undocumented Immigrants Make Residential Decisions in an American City." *Journal of Ethnic and Migration Studies* 45 (11): 1857–82.

Austermuhle, Martin. 2022. "D.C. Council Adds Money for Excluded Workers to Budget, Votes Against Moving Up Paid Leave Expansion." *DCist* (blog), May 25, 2022. https://dcist.com.

Batalova, Jeanne, Sarah Hooker, and Randy Capps. 2014. "DACA at the Two-Year Mark: A National and State Profile of Youth Eligible and Applying for Deferred Action." Migration Policy Institute, August 4, 2014. www.migrationpolicy.org.

Bejarano, Carolina Alonso, Lucia López Juárez, Mirian A. Mijangos García, and Daniel M. Goldstein. 2019. *Decolonizing Ethnography: Undocumented Immigrants and New Directions in Social Science*. Durham, NC: Duke University Press.

Benenson, Laurence. 2020. "Fact Sheet: Deferred Action for Childhood Arrivals (DACA)." *National Immigration Forum*, October 16, 2020. https://immigrationforum.org.

Bloemraad, Irene, and Kim Voss. 2020. "Movement or Moment? Lessons from the Pro-Immigrant Movement in the United States and Contemporary Challenges." *Journal of Ethnic and Migration Studies* 46 (4): 683–704.

Bloemraad, Irene, Kim Voss, and Taeku Lee. 2011. "The Protests of 2006: What Were They, How Do We Understand Them, Where Do We Go?" In *Rallying for Immigrants: The Fight for Inclusion in the 21st Century Rights*, edited by Kim Voss and Irene Bloemraad, 3–43. Berkeley: University of California Press.

Boehm, Deborah A., and Susan J. Terrio, eds. 2019. *Illegal Encounters: The Effect of Detention and Deportation on Young People*. New York: New York University Press.

Bolter, Jessica, Emma Israel, and Sarah Pierce. 2022. "Four Years of Profound Change: Immigration Policy during the Trump Presidency." Migration Policy Institute, January 25, 2022. www.migrationpolicy.org.

Bruhn, Sarah, and Roberto G. Gonzales. 2023. "Geographies of Belonging: Migrant Youth and Relational, Community, and National Opportunities for Inclusion." *Social Sciences* 12 (3): 167.

Burciaga, Edelina M., and Aaron Malone. 2021. "Intensified Liminal Legality: The Impact of the DACA Rescission for Undocumented Young Adults in Colorado." *Law & Social Inquiry* 46 (4): 1092–114.

Burciaga, Edelina M., and Lisa M. Martinez. 2017. "How Do Political Contexts Shape Undocumented Youth Movements? Evidence from Three Immigrant Destinations." *Mobilization: An International Quarterly* 22 (4): 451–71.

Butler, Judith. 2009. "Performativity, Precarity and Sexual Politics." *AIBR—Revista de Antropología Iberoamericana* 4 (3): i–xiii.

Cabot, Heath. 2012. "The Governance of Things: Documenting Limbo in the Greek Asylum Procedure." *PoLAR: Political and Legal Anthropology Review* 35 (1): 11–29.

Cabot, Heath, and Georgina Ramsay. 2021. "Deexceptionalizing Displacement: An Introduction." *Humanity* 12 (3): 286–99.

Cabral, Jacqueline, and Adolfo G. Cuevas. 2020. "Health Inequities among Latinos/Hispanics: Documentation Status as a Determinant of Health." *Journal of Racial and Ethnic Health Disparities* 7 (5): 874–79.

Campbell-Montalvo, Rebecca, and Heide Castañeda. 2019. "School Employees as Health Care Brokers for Multiply-Marginalized Migrant Families." *Medical Anthropology* 38 (8): 733–46.

Capps, Randy, Michael Fix, and Jie Zong. 2017. "The Education and Work Profiles of the DACA Population." Migration Policy Institute, August 14, 2017. www.migrationpolicy.org.

Carruth, Lauren, Carlos Martinez, Lahra Smith, Katharine Donato, Carlos Piñones-Rivera, and James Quesada. 2021. "Structural Vulnerability: Migration and Health in Social Context." *BMJ Global Health* 6 (suppl. 1): e005109.

Cartwright, Tina. 2007. "'Getting on with Life': The Experiences of Older People Using Complementary Health Care." *Social Science & Medicine* 64 (8): 1692–703.

Castañeda, Heide. 2019. *Borders of Belonging: Struggle and Solidarity in Mixed-Status Immigrant Families*. Stanford, CA: Stanford University Press.

Castañeda, Heide, and Milena Andrea Melo. 2014. "Health Care Access for Latino Mixed-Status Families: Barriers, Strategies, and Implications for Reform." *American Behavioral Scientist* 58 (14): 1891–909.

———. 2019. "Geographies of Confinement for Immigrant Youth: Checkpoints and Immobilities along the US/Mexico Border." *Law & Policy* 41 (1): 80–102.

Cavazos-Rehg, Patricia A., Luis H. Zayas, and Edward L. Spitznagel. 2007. "Legal Status, Emotional Well-Being and Subjective Health Status of Latino Immigrants." *Journal of the National Medical Association* 99 (10): 1126–31.

Cebulko, Kara. 2018. "Privilege Without Papers: Intersecting Inequalities among 1.5-Generation Brazilians in Massachusetts." *Ethnicities* 18 (2): 225–41.

———. 2021. "Becoming White in a White Supremacist State: The Public and Psychological Wages of Whiteness for Undocumented 1.5-Generation Brazilians." *Social Sciences* 10 (5): 184.

Cebulko, Kara, and Alexis Silver. 2016. "Navigating DACA in Hospitable and Hostile States: State Responses and Access to Membership in the Wake of Deferred Action for Childhood Arrivals." *American Behavioral Scientist* 60 (13): 1553–74.

Cha, Biblia S., Laura E. Enriquez, and Annie Ro. 2019. "Beyond Access: Psychosocial Barriers to Undocumented Students' Use of Mental Health Services." *Social Science & Medicine* 233 (July): 193–200.

Chacón, Jennifer M., Susan Bibler Coutin, and Stephen Lee. 2024. *Legal Phantoms: Executive Action and the Haunting Failures of Immigration Law*. Stanford, CA: Stanford University Press.

Chang, Aurora, Júlia Mendes, and Cinthya Salazar. 2019. "Qualitative Methodological Considerations for Studying Undocumented Students in the United States." In *Oxford Research Encyclopedia of Education*, edited by George W. Noblit. https://oxfordre.com.

Charmaz, Kathy. 2011. "Grounded Theory: Objectivist and Constructivist Methods." In *Sage Handbook of Qualitative Research*, 2nd ed., edited by Norman K. Denzin and Yvonna S. Lincoln, 509–36. Thousand Oaks, CA: Sage.

Chavez, Leo. 2008. *The Latino Threat: Constructing Immigrants, Citizens, and the Nation*. 2nd ed. Stanford, CA: Stanford University Press.

Chishti, Muzaffar, and Stephen Yale-Loehr. 2016. "The Immigration Act of 1990: Unfinished Business a Quarter-Century Later." Migration Policy Institute, July 2016. www.migrationpolicy.org.

Cho, Esther Yoona. 2017. "Revisiting Ethnic Niches: A Comparative Analysis of the Labor Market Experiences of Asian and Latino Undocumented Young Adults." *RSF* 3 (4): 97–115.

Clark, Eva, Karla Fredricks, Laila Woc-Colburn, Maria Elena Bottazzi, and Jill Weatherhead. 2020. "Disproportionate Impact of the COVID-19 Pandemic on Immigrant Communities in the United States." *PLOS Neglected Tropical Diseases* 14 (7): e0008484.

Cobb, Cory L., Alan Meca, Dong Xie, Seth J. Schwartz, and Rhoda K. Moise. 2017. "Perceptions of Legal Status: Associations with Psychosocial Experiences among Undocumented Latino/a Immigrants." *Journal of Counseling Psychology* 64 (2): 167–78.

Coe, Cati. 2013. *The Scattered Family: Parenting, African Migrants, and Global Inequality*. Chicago: University of Chicago Press.

———. 2019. *The New American Servitude: Political Belonging among African Immigrant Home Care Workers*. New York: New York University Press.

Cohn, D'Vera, and Philip P. Pan. 1999. "Asian Population Swelling in D.C." *Washington Post*, September 15, 1999, A1. www.washingtonpost.com.

Coleman, Mathew. 2012. "The 'Local' Migration State: The Site-Specific Devolution of Immigration Enforcement in the U.S. South." *Law & Policy* 34 (2): 159–90.

Collins, Patricia Hill. 1990. *Black Feminist Thought: Knowledge, Consciousness, and the Politics of Empowerment*. Philadelphia: Routledge.

Conron, Kerith J., Winston Luhur, and Taylor N. T. Brown. 2020. "LGBT Dreamers and Deferred Action for Childhood Arrivals (DACA)." Williams Institute, June 2020. https://williamsinstitute.law.ucla.edu.

Cook, Joanna, and Catherine Trundle. 2020. "Unsettled Care: Temporality, Subjectivity, and the Uneasy Ethics of Care." *Anthropology and Humanism* 45 (2): 178–83.

Coutin, Susan Bibler. 2000. *Legalizing Moves: Salvadoran Immigrants' Struggle for U.S. Residency*. Ann Arbor: University of Michigan Press.

———. 2010. "Confined Within: National Territories as Zones of Confinement." *Political Geography* 29 (4): 200–208.

Coutin, Susan Bibler, Sameer M. Ashar, Jennifer M. Chacón, and Stephen Lee. 2017. "Deferred Action and the Discretionary State: Migration, Precarity and Resistance." *Citizenship Studies* 21 (8): 951–68.

Cox, Adam B., and Cristina M. Rodríguez. 2020. *The President and Immigration Law*. New York: Oxford University Press.

Dao, Loan Thi. 2017. "Out and Asian: How Undocu/DACAmented Asian Americans and Pacific Islander Youth Navigate Dual Liminality in the Immigrant Rights Movement." *Societies* 7 (3): 1–15.

Das, Veena, and Deborah Poole, eds. 2004. *Anthropology in the Margins of the State*. Advanced Seminar Series. Santa Fe, NM: School of American Research Press.

De Genova, Nicholas. 2002. "Migrant 'Illegality' and Deportability in Everyday Life." *Annual Review of Anthropology* 31 (1): 419–47.

De León, Jason. 2015. *The Land of Open Graves: Living and Dying on the Migrant Trail*. Berkeley: University of California Press.

Delgado, Vanessa. 2020a. "Children of Immigrants as 'Brokers' in an Era of Exclusion." *Sociology Compass* 14 (10): e12832.

———. 2020b. "'They Think I'm a Lawyer': Undocumented College Students as Legal Brokers for Their Undocumented Parents." *Law & Policy* 42 (3): 261–83.

———. 2022. "Leveraging Protections, Navigating Punishments: How Adult Children of Undocumented Immigrants Mediate Illegality in Latinx Families." *Journal of Marriage and Family* 84 (5): 1427–45.

Đoàn, Lan N., Stella K. Chong, Supriya Misra, Simona C. Kwon, and Stella S. Yi. 2021. "Immigrant Communities and Covid-19: Strengthening the Public Health Response." *American Journal of Public Health* 111 (S3): S224–31.

Dorner, Lisa M., Marjorie Faulstich Orellana, and Rosa Jiménez. 2008. "'It's One of Those Things That You Do to Help the Family': Language Brokering and the Development of Immigrant Adolescents." *Journal of Adolescent Research* 23 (5): 515–43.

Dowling, Julie A., and Jonathan Xavier Inda, eds. 2013. *Governing Immigration through Crime: A Reader*. Stanford, CA: Stanford University Press.

Dunbar-Ortiz, Roxanne. 2021. *Not "a Nation of Immigrants": Settler Colonialism, White Supremacy, and a History of Erasure and Exclusion*. Boston: Beacon.

Duncan, Whitney L., and Sarah B. Horton. 2020. "Serious Challenges and Potential Solutions for Immigrant Health during COVID-19." *Health Affairs Forefront*, April 18, 2020. www.healthaffairs.org.

Duncan, Whitney L., and Lupita Nabor Vazquez. 2023. "'I Don't Feel That We Are a Burden': Latinx Immigrants and Deservingness during the COVID-19 Pandemic." *Social Science and Medicine* 333:116125.

Dyrness, Andrea, and Enrique Sepúlveda. 2020. *Border Thinking: Latinx Youth Decolonizing Citizenship*. Minneapolis: University of Minnesota Press.

Ehrenreich, Barbara, and Arlie Russell Hochschild, eds. 2004. *Global Woman: Nannies, Maids, and Sex Workers in the New Economy*. New York: Henry Holt.

Eldridge, Erin R., and Amanda J. Reinke. 2018. "Introduction: Ethnographic Engagement with Bureaucratic Violence." *Conflict and Society* 4 (1): 94–98.

Ellis, Basia D. 2021. "The Psychology of Migrant 'Illegality': A General Theory." *Law & Social Inquiry* 46 (4): 1236–71.

Ellis, Basia D., Roberto G. Gonzales, and Sarah A. Rendón García. 2019. "The Power of Inclusion: Theorizing 'Abjectivity' and Agency under DACA." *Cultural Studies ↔ Critical Methodologies* 19 (3): 161–72.

Ellison, Susan Helen. 2017. "'You Have to Comply with Paper': Debt, Documents, and Legal Consciousness in Bolivia." *Journal of the Royal Anthropological Institute* 23 (3): 523–42.

Emerson, Robert M., Rachel I. Fretz, and Linda L. Shaw. 2011. *Writing Ethnographic Fieldnotes*. 2nd ed. Chicago Guides to Writing, Editing, and Publishing. Chicago: University of Chicago Press.

Enriquez, Laura E. 2019. "Border Hopping Mexicans, Law-Abiding Asians, and Racialized Illegality: Analyzing Undocumented College Students' Experiences Through a Relational Lens." In *Relational Formations of Race: Theory, Method and Practice*, edited by Natalia Molina, Daniel HoSang, and Ramón A. Gutiérrez, 257–77. Berkeley: University of California Press.

———. 2020. *Of Love and Papers: How Immigration Policy Affects Romance and Family*. Berkeley: University of California Press.

Enriquez, Laura E., and Daniel Millán. 2021. "Situational Triggers and Protective Locations: Conceptualising the Salience of Deportability in Everyday Life." *Journal of Ethnic and Migration Studies* 47 (9): 2089–108.

Enriquez, Laura E., Alberto Eduardo Morales, Victoria E. Rodríguez, Karina Chavarría, and Annie Ro. 2023. "Mental Health and COVID-19 Pandemic Stressors among Latina/o/x College Students with Varying Self and Parental Immigration Status." *Journal of Racial and Ethnic Health Disparities* 10 (1): 282–95.

Erikson, Erik H. 1950. *Childhood and Society*. New York: Norton.

Escudero, Kevin. 2020. *Organizing while Undocumented: Immigrant Youth's Political Activism under the Law*. New York: New York University Press.

Eskenazi, Brenda, Carolyn A. Fahey, Katherine Kogut, Robert Gunier, Jacqueline Torres, Nancy A. Gonzales, Nina Holland, and Julianna Deardorff. 2019. "Association of Perceived Immigration Policy Vulnerability with Mental and Physical Health among US-Born Latino Adolescents in California." *JAMA Pediatrics* 173 (8): 744–53.

Esterline, Cecilia, and Jeanne Batalova. 2022. "Korean Immigrants in the United States." Migration Policy Institute, April 13, 2022. www.migrationpolicy.org.

Ewick, Patricia, and Susan S. Silbey. 1998. *The Common Place of Law: Stories from Everyday Life*. Chicago Series in Law and Society. Chicago: University of Chicago Press.

Falicov, Celia, Alba Niño, and Sol D'Urso. 2020. "Expanding Possibilities: Flexibility and Solidarity with Under-Resourced Immigrant Families during the COVID-19 Pandemic." *Family Process* 59 (3): 865–82.

Fassin, Didier. 2005. "Compassion and Repression: The Moral Economy of Immigration Policies in France." *Cultural Anthropology* 20 (3): 362–87.

———. 2013. "Children as Victims: The Moral Economy of Childhood in the Times of AIDS." In *When People Come First: Critical Studies in Global Health*, edited by João Biehl and Adriana Petryna, 109–30. Princeton, NJ: Princeton University Press.

Ferguson, Peter, and Hannah Walker. 2014. "'Getting on with Life': Resilience and Normalcy in Adolescents Living with Chronic Illness." *International Journal of Inclusive Education* 18 (3): 227–40.

Fernández, Jesica Siham, Bianca L. Guzmán, Ireri Bernal, and Yvette G. Flores. 2020. "Muxeres en Acción: The Power of Community Cultural Wealth in Latinas Organizing for Health Equity." *American Journal of Community Psychology* 66 (3–4): 314–24.

Fians, Guilherme. 2022. "Prefigurative Politics." In *The Open Encyclopedia of Anthropology*, edited by Felix Stein. https://anthroencyclopedia.com.

Finch, Aisha K. 2022. "Introduction: Black Feminism and the Practice of Care." *Palimpsest* 11 (1): 1–41.

Fiorito, Tara. 2021. "Learning to Be Legal: Transition Narratives of Joy and Survivor Guilt of Previously Undocumented 1.5-Generation Latinx Immigrants in the United States." *Citizenship Studies* 25 (8): 1096–111.

Fish, Julie, Andrew King, and Kathryn Almack. 2018. "Queerying Activism through the Lens of the Sociology of Everyday Life." *Sociological Review* 66 (6): 1194–208.

Flores, Andrea. 2016. "Forms of Exclusion: Undocumented Students Navigating Financial Aid and Inclusion in the United States." *American Ethnologist* 43 (3): 540–54.

——. 2023. "About Time: Temporal Control and Illegality in Nashville, Tennessee." *PoLAR: Political and Legal Anthropology Review* 46 (1): 39–52.

Flores, Andrea, Kevin Escudero, and Edelina Burciaga. 2019. "Legal-Spatial Consciousness: A Legal Geography Framework for Examining Migrant Illegality." *Law & Policy* 41 (1): 12–33.

Flores Morales, Josefina, and Yuliana Garcia. 2021. "Beyond Undocumented: Differences in the Mental Health of Latinx Undocumented College Students." *Latino Studies* 19 (3): 374–99.

Galemba, Rebecca Berke. 2023. *Laboring for Justice: The Fight Against Wage Theft in an American City.* Stanford, CA: Stanford University Press.

Gálvez, Alyshia. 2021. "I Won't Tell My Story: Narrative Capital and Refusal among Undocumented Activists in the Trump Era." In Gonzales, Rosaldo, and Pratt, *Trumpism, Mexican America, and the Struggle for Latinx Citizenship*, 111–25.

García, Angela S. 2019a. *Legal Passing: Navigating Undocumented Life and Local Immigration Law.* Berkeley: University of California Press.

——. 2019b. "Stay or Go? The Settlement Effects of Restrictive Subnational Laws." In García, *Legal Passing*, 58–96.

García, Angela S., Daysi X. Diaz-Strong, and Yunuen Rodriguez Rodriguez. 2022. "A Matter of Time: The Life Course Implications of Deferred Action for Undocumented Latin American Immigrants in the United States." *Social Problems*, August 24, 2022.

García, San Juanita. 2017. "Racializing 'Illegality': An Intersectional Approach to Understanding How Mexican-Origin Women Navigate an Anti-Immigrant Climate." *Sociology of Race and Ethnicity* 3 (4): 474–90.

García-Sánchez, Inmaculada M. 2018. "Children as Interactional Brokers of Care." *Annual Review of Anthropology* 47 (1): 167–84.

Getrich, Christina M. 2008. "Negotiating Boundaries of Social Belonging: Second-Generation Mexican Youth and the Immigrant Rights Protests of 2006." *American Behavioral Scientist* 52 (4): 533–56.

——. 2019. *Border Brokers: Children of Mexican Immigrants Navigating U.S. Society, Laws, and Politics.* Tucson: University of Arizona Press.

——. 2021. "'People Show Up in Different Ways': DACA Recipients' Everyday Activism in a Time of Heightened Immigration-Related Insecurity." *Human Organization* 80 (1): 27–36.

Getrich, Christina M., Alaska Burdette, Ana Ortez-Rivera, and Delmis Umanzor. 2024. "'We've Been There Alongside Each Other Right from the Beginning': Accompaniment as Multivalent and Evolving Practice for the DACA-Mented Dream Team." In Yarris and Duncan, *Accompaniment with Im/migrant Communities*, 31–47.

Getrich, Christina M., Jacqueline M. García, Angélica Solares, and Miria Kano. 2017. "Effective Strategies for Affordable Care Act Enrollment in Immigrant-Serving Safety Net Clinics in New Mexico." *Journal of Health Care for the Poor and Underserved* 28 (2): 626–34.

———. 2018. "Buffering the Uneven Impact of the Affordable Care Act: Immigrant-Serving Safety-Net Providers in New Mexico." *Medical Anthropology Quarterly* 32 (2): 233–53.

Getrich, Christina, and Ana Ortez-Rivera. 2018. "'ICE Was Like an Urban Legend Here in Maryland.'" *Fieldsights*, January 31, 2018. https://culanth.org.

Getrich, Christina M., Ana Ortez-Rivera, Delmis Umanzor, and Alaska Burdette. 2023. "Manoeuvering through the Multilayered Jurisdictional Policy Patchwork: DACA Recipients' Navigational Capital in the Washington, D.C. Metropolitan Region." *Ethnic and Racial Studies* 46 (1): 141–65.

———. 2024. "'I'm in a Good Position to Advocate Now': Deferred Action for Childhood Arrivals Recipients' Deployment of Navigational Capital and Brokerage in the D.C. Metropolitan Region." *American Behavioral Scientist*. httsp://doi.org/10.1177/00027642241229536.

Getrich, Christina M., Kaelin Rapport, Alaska Burdette, Ana Ortez-Rivera, and Delmis Umanzor. 2019. "Navigating a Fragmented Health Care Landscape: DACA Recipients' Shifting Access to Health Care." *Social Science & Medicine* 223 (February): 8–15.

Getrich, Christina M., Delmis Umanzor, Alaska Burdette, and Ana Ortez-Rivera. 2023. "DACA Recipient Health Care Workers' Barriers to Professionalization and Deployment of Navigational Capital in Pursuit of Health Equity for Immigrants." *Journal of Immigrant and Minority Health* 25: 1279–85.

Giddens, Anthony. 1991. *Modernity and Self-Identity: Self and Society in the Late Modern Age.* Stanford, CA: Stanford University Press.

Giuntella, Osea, Jakub Lonsky, Fabrizio Mazzonna, and Luca Stella. 2021. "Immigration Policy and Immigrants' Sleep: Evidence from DACA." *Journal of Economic Behavior & Organization* 182 (February): 1–12.

Golash-Boza, Tanya, Maria D. Duenas, and Chia Xiong. 2019. "White Supremacy, Patriarchy, and Global Capitalism in Migration Studies." *American Behavioral Scientist* 63 (13): 1741–59.

Golash-Boza, Tanya, and Zulema Valdez. 2018. "Nested Contexts of Reception: Undocumented Students at the University of California, Central." *Sociological Perspectives* 61 (4): 535–52.

Gomberg-Muñoz, Ruth. 2016a. *Becoming Legal: Immigration Law and Mixed-Status Families.* New York: Oxford University Press.

———. 2016b. "Hardship Politics: The Strategic Sharing of Migration Stories." *Journal of Contemporary Ethnography* 45 (6): 741–64.

———. 2018. "The Complicit Anthropologist." *Journal for the Anthropology of North America* 21 (1): 36–37.

Gomberg-Muñoz, Ruth, and Laura Nussbaum-Barberena. 2014. "Introduction to Special Issue: Everyday Enforcement: Heightened Immigration Enforcement and Community Responses in the United States." *City & Society* 26 (1): 3–9.

Gonzales, Phillip B., Renato Rosaldo, and Mary Louise Pratt, eds. 2021. *Trumpism, Mexican America, and the Struggle for Latinx Citizenship.* Albuquerque: University of New Mexico Press.

Gonzales, Roberto G. 2008. "Left Out but Not Shut Down: Political Activism and the Undocumented Student Movement." *Northwestern Journal of Law and Social Policy* 3 (2): 219–39.

———. 2016. *Lives in Limbo: Undocumented and Coming of Age in America.* Berkeley: University of California Press.

Gonzales, Roberto G., Kristina Brant, and Benjamin Roth. 2020. "DACAmented in the Age of Deportation: Navigating Spaces of Belonging and Vulnerability in Social and Personal Lives." *Ethnic and Racial Studies* 43 (1): 60–79.

Gonzales, Roberto G., and Edelina M. Burciaga. 2018. "Segmented Pathways of Illegality: Reconciling the Coexistence of Master and Auxiliary Statuses in the Experiences of 1.5-Generation Undocumented Young Adults." *Ethnicities* 18 (2): 178–91.

Gonzales, Roberto G., Sayil Camacho, Kristina Brant, and Carlos Aguilar. 2019. "The Long-Term Impact of DACA: Forging Futures Despite DACA's Uncertainty. Findings from the National UnDACAmented Research Project (NURP)." Special Report 1. Immigration Initiative at Harvard, National UnDACAmented Research Project. www.immigrationresearch.org.

Gonzales, Roberto G., and Leo R. Chavez. 2012. "'Awakening to a Nightmare': Abjectivity and Illegality in the Lives of Undocumented 1.5-Generation Latino Immigrants in the United States." *Current Anthropology* 53 (3): 255–81.

Gonzales, Roberto G., Basia Ellis, Sarah A. Rendón García, and Kristina Brant. 2018. "(Un)Authorized Transitions: Illegality, DACA, and the Life Course." *Research in Human Development* 15 (3–4): 345–59.

Gonzales, Roberto G., Marco A. Murillo, and Cristina Lacomba. 2017. "Taking Giant Leaps Forward: Experiences of a Range of DACA Beneficiaries at the 5-Year Mark." *Center for American Progress* (blog), June 22, 2017. www.americanprogress.org.

Gonzales, Roberto G., Benjamin Roth, Kristina Brant, Jaein Lee, and Carolina Valdivia. 2016. "DACA at Year Three: Challenges and Opportunities in Accessing Higher Education and Employment: New Evidence from the National UnDACAmented Research Project." Special Report, National UnDACAmented Research Project, American Immigration Council. www.americanimmigrationcouncil.org.

Gonzales, Roberto G., Carola Suárez-Orozco, and Maria Cecilia Dedios-Sanguineti. 2013. "No Place to Belong: Contextualizing Concepts of Mental Health among Undocumented Immigrant Youth in the United States." *American Behavioral Scientist* 57 (8): 1174–99.

Gonzales, Roberto G., Veronica Terriquez, and Stephen P. Ruszczyk. 2014. "Becoming DACAmented: Assessing the Short-Term Benefits of Deferred Action for Childhood Arrivals (DACA)." *American Behavioral Scientist* 58 (14): 1852–72.

Graauw, Els de, and Shannon Gleeson. 2021. "Metropolitan Context and Immigrant Rights Experiences: DACA Awareness and Support in Houston." *Urban Geography* 42 (8): 1119–46.

Grace, Breanne L., Rajeev Bais, and Benjamin J. Roth. 2018. "The Violence of Uncertainty—Undermining Immigrant and Refugee Health." *New England Journal of Medicine* 379 (10): 904–5.

Griffiths, Melanie B. E. 2014. "Out of Time: The Temporal Uncertainties of Refused Asylum Seekers and Immigration Detainees." *Journal of Ethnic and Migration Studies* 40 (12): 1991–2009.

———. 2024. "Epilogue: 'Claiming Time' Special Issue." *International Migration and Integration.* https://doi.org/10.1007/s12134-024-01162-9.

Günel, Gökçe, Saiba Varma, and Chika Watanabe. 2020. "A Manifesto for Patchwork Ethnography." Society for Cultural Anthropology. https://culanth.org.

Gutmann, Matthew C. 1993. "Rituals of Resistance: A Critique of the Theory of Everyday Forms of Resistance." *Latin American Perspectives* 20 (2): 74–92.

Haas, Bridget M. 2017. "Citizens-in-Waiting, Deportees-in-Waiting: Power, Temporality, and Suffering in the U.S. Asylum System." *Ethos* 45 (1): 75–97.

———. 2023. *Suspended Lives: Navigating Everyday Violence in the US Asylum System.* Critical Refugee Studies. Berkeley: University of California Press.

Hacker, Karen. 2013. *Community-Based Participatory Research.* Thousand Oaks, CA: Sage.

Hainmueller, Jens, Duncan Lawrence, Linna Martén, Bernard Black, Lucila Figueroa, Michael Hotard, Tomás R. Jiménez, et al. 2017. "Protecting Unauthorized Immigrant Mothers Improves Their Children's Mental Health." *Science* 357 (6355): 1041–44.

Hale, Charles R., ed. 2008. *Engaging Contradictions: Theory, Politics, and Methods of Activist Scholarship.* Berkeley: University of California Press.

Hamilton, Erin R., Caitlin Patler, and Paola D. Langer. 2021. "The Life-Course Timing of Legalization: Evidence from the DACA Program." *Socius* 7 (January): 23780231211058958.

Han, Clara. 2012. *Life in Debt: Times of Care and Violence in Neoliberal Chile.* Berkeley: University of California Press.

Hardy, Lisa J., Christina M. Getrich, Julio C. Quezada, Amanda Guay, Raymond J. Michalowski, and Eric Henley. 2012. "A Call for Further Research on the Impact of State-Level Immigration Policies on Public Health." *American Journal of Public Health* 102 (7): 1250–53.

Hardy, Lisa J., Amy Hughes, Elizabeth Hulen, Alejandra Figueroa, Coral Evans, and R. Cruz Begay. 2016. "Hiring the Experts: Best Practices for Community-Engaged Research." *Qualitative Research* 16 (5): 592–600.

Harris, Anita, and Joshua Roose. 2018. "Young Muslims and Everyday Political Practice: A DIY Citizenship Approach." In *Young People and the Politics of Outrage and Hope,* edited by Peter Kelly, Perri Campbell, Lyn Harrison, and Chris Hickey, 226–40. Boston: Brill.

Harris, Anita, Johanna Wyn, and Salem Younes. 2010. "Beyond Apathetic or Activist Youth: 'Ordinary' Young People and Contemporary Forms of Participation." *YOUNG* 18 (1): 9–32.

Harrison, Faye. 1997a. "Anthropology as an Agent of Transformation: Introductory Comments and Queries." In *Decolonizing Anthropology: Moving Further toward an Anthropology for Liberation,* 2nd ed., edited by Faye V. Harrison, 1–15. Arlington, VA: American Anthropological Association.

———. 1997b. *Decolonizing Anthropology: Moving Further toward an Anthropology for Liberation*. Arlington, VA: American Anthropological Association.

Heckert, Carina. 2020. "The Bureaucratic Violence of the Health Care System for Pregnant Immigrants on the United States-Mexico Border." *Human Organization* 79 (1): 33–42.

Heidbrink, Lauren. 2022. "'How Can I Have a Future?' The Temporal Violence of Deportation." *Journal of Intercultural Studies* 43 (4): 480–96.

Held, Virginia. 2006. *The Ethics of Care: Personal, Political, and Global*. New York: Oxford University Press, USA.

Henderson, Tim. 2014. "Two Years after DACA, State Responses Vary." *Stateline* (blog), September 1, 2014. https://stateline.org.

Heredia, Luisa Laura. 2015. "Of Radicals and DREAMers: Harnessing Exceptionality to Challenge Immigration Control." *Association of Mexican American Educators Journal* 9 (3). https://amaejournal.utsa.edu.

Herrera, Juan. 2016. "Racialized Illegality: The Regulation of Informal Labor and Space." *Latino Studies* 14 (3): 320–43.

Hispanic Engineer and Information Technology. 2019. "DACA Gets Major Support: Top 25 Companies in Fortune 500 Employ DREAMers." https://hispanicengineer.com.

Hobart, Hiʻilei Julia Kawehipuaakahaopulani, and Tamara Kneese. 2020. "Radical Care: Survival Strategies for Uncertain Times." *Social Text* 38 (1 [142]): 1–16.

hooks, bell. 1984. *Feminist Theory: From Margin to Center*. Cambridge, MA: South End Press.

Horton, Sarah B. 2016. *They Leave Their Kidneys in the Fields: Illness, Injury, and Illegality among U.S. Farmworkers*. Berkeley: University of California Press.

———. 2021. "On Pandemic Privilege: Reflections on a 'Home-Bound Pandemic Ethnography.'" *Journal for the Anthropology of North America* 24 (2): 98–107.

Horton, Sarah B., and Josiah Heyman, eds. 2020. *Paper Trails: Migrants, Documents, and Legal Insecurity*. Durham, NC: Duke University Press.

Hurtado Moreno, Argenis. 2021. "An Anthropology about Us, for Us, by Us." *American Ethnologist*, May 12, 2021. https://americanethnologist.org.

Immigrant Legal Resource Center (ILRC). 2023. "National Map of 287(g) Agreements." June 15, 2023. www.ilrc.org.

Institute for Immigration Research. n.d. "The Caribbean: Caribbean Immigrant Population in the Washington, DC and Baltimore, MD Metro Areas." Institute for Immigration Research. Accessed April 27, 2023. https://iir.gmu.edu.

Isaac, Sara Philipson. 2022. "Temporal Dispossession through Migration Bureaucracy: On Waiting within the Asylum Process in Sweden." *European Journal of Social Work* 25 (6): 945–56.

Israel, Barbara A., Eugenia Eng, Amy J. Schulz, and Edith A. Parker, eds. 2005. *Methods in Community-Based Participatory Research for Health*. San Francisco: Jossey-Bass.

Jacobson, Danielle, and Nida Mustafa. 2019. "Social Identity Map: A Reflexivity Tool for Practicing Explicit Positionality in Critical Qualitative Research." *International Journal of Qualitative Methods* 18: 1–12.

James, Erica Caple. 2011. "Haiti, Insecurity, and the Politics of Asylum." *Medical Anthropology Quarterly* 25 (3): 357–76.

Jobson, Ryan Cecil. 2020. "The Case for Letting Anthropology Burn: Sociocultural Anthropology in 2019." *American Anthropologist* 122 (2): 259–71.

Jones, Jennifer. 2019. "From Open Doors to Closed Gates: Intragenerational Reverse Incorporation in New Immigrant Destinations." *International Migration Review* 53 (4): 1002–31.

Kaiser, Bonnie N., Emily E. Haroz, Brandon A. Kohrt, Paul A. Bolton, Judith K. Bass, and Devon E. Hinton. 2015. "'Thinking Too Much': A Systematic Review of a Common Idiom of Distress." *Social Science & Medicine* 147 (December): 170–83.

Katz, Vikki S. 2014. *Kids in the Middle: How Children of Immigrants Negotiate Community Interactions for Their Families*. New Brunswick, NJ: Rutgers University Press.

Kline, Nolan. 2019. *Pathogenic Policing: Immigration Enforcement and Health in the U.S. South*. New Brunswick, NJ: Rutgers University Press.

Kroenke, Kurt, Robert L. Spitzer, Janet B. W. Williams, and Bernd Löwe. 2009. "An Ultra-Brief Screening Scale for Anxiety and Depression: The PHQ-4." *Psychosomatics* 50 (6): 613–21.

Kubal, Agnieszka. 2013. "Conceptualizing Semi-legality in Migration Research." *Law & Society Review* 47 (3): 555–87.

Lamphere, Louise. 2004. "Unofficial Histories: A Vision of Anthropology from the Margins." *American Anthropologist* 106 (1): 126–39.

———. 2005a. "Providers and Staff Respond to Medicaid Managed Care: The Unintended Consequences of Reform in New Mexico." *Medical Anthropology Quarterly* 19 (1): 3–25.

———. 2005b. "The Convergence of Applied, Practicing, and Public Anthropology in the 21st Century." *Human Organization* 63 (4): 431–43.

Lavariega Monforti, Jessica L., and Melissa R. Michelson. 2021. "Firme: Persistent Activism of Millennial Latino Immigrants in the Trump Era." *Aztlán: A Journal of Chicano Studies* 46 (2): 83–112.

LeBrón, Alana M. W., William D. Lopez, Keta Cowan, Nicole L. Novak, Olivia Temrowski, Maria Ibarra-Frayre, and Jorge Delva. 2018. "Restrictive ID Policies: Implications for Health Equity." *Journal of Immigrant and Minority Health* 20 (2): 255–60.

Le Courant, Stefan. 2019. "Imposture at the Border: Law and the Construction of Identities among Undocumented Migrants." *Social Anthropology / Anthropologie Sociale* 27 (3): 472–85.

Lefebvre, Henri. 1991. *The Production of Space*. Translated by Donald Nicholson-Smith. Oxford: Blackwell.

León, Lucía. 2020. "Legalization through Marriage: When Love and Papers Converge." In Abrego and Negrón-Gonzales, *We Are Not Dreamers*, 190–210.

Liu, Roseann, and Savannah Shange. 2018. "Toward Thick Solidarity: Theorizing Empathy in Social Justice Movements." *Radical History Review* 131: 189–98.

Livingston, Julie. 2012. *Improvising Medicine: An African Oncology Ward in an Emerging Cancer Epidemic*. Durham, NC: Duke University Press.

Logan, Ryan I. 2022. *Boundaries of Care: Community Health Workers in the United States*. Anthropology of Well-Being: Individual, Community, Society. Lanham, MD: Lexington Books.

Long, Nicholas. 2020a. "From Social Distancing to Social Containment." *Medicine Anthropology Theory* 7 (2): 247–60.

———. 2020b. "Lockdown Anthropology and Online Surveys: Unprecedented Methods for Unprecedented Times." *Studies in Indian Politics* 8 (2): 294–97.

López, Andrea M. 2023. "Ethnography and Community Based Methods: In the Meantime." Baltimore: Johns Hopkins University, Bloomberg School of Public Health.

Lopez, William D. 2019. *Separated: Family and Community in the Aftermath of an Immigration Raid*. Baltimore, MD: Johns Hopkins University Press.

Lopez, William D., and Heide Castañeda. 2022. "The Mixed-Status Community as an Analytic Framework to Understand the Impacts of Immigration Enforcement on Health." *Social Science and Medicine* 307: 115180.

Lopez, William D., Nolan Kline, Nicole L. Novak, and Alana M. W. Lebrón. 2024. "A Public Health of Accompaniment." In *Accompaniment as Ethnographic Engagement*, edited by Kristin E. Yarris and Whitney L. Duncan, 119–36. Tucson: University of Arizona Press.

López-Sanders, Laura. 2017a. "Changing the Navigator's Course: How the Increasing Rationalization of Healthcare Influences Access for Undocumented Immigrants under the Affordable Care Act." *Social Science & Medicine* 178 (April): 46–54.

———. 2017b. "Navigating Health Care: Brokerage and Access for Undocumented Latino Immigrants under the 2010 Affordable Care Act." *Journal of Ethnic and Migration Studies* 43 (12): 2072–88.

Low, Setha M. 2011. "Claiming Space for an Engaged Anthropology: Spatial Inequality and Social Exclusion." *American Anthropologist* 113 (3): 389–407.

Low, Setha M., and Sally Engle Merry. 2010. "Engaged Anthropology: Diversity and Dilemmas: An Introduction to Supplement 2." *Current Anthropology* 51 (S2): S203–26.

Lytle Hernández, Kelly. 2010. *Migra! A History of the U.S. Border Patrol*. Berkeley: University of California Press.

Macías, Luis Fernando. 2018. "The Scheme Game: How DACA Recipients Navigate Barriers to Higher Education." *Educational Studies* 54 (6): 609–28.

Madden, Erin Fanning. 2015. "Cultural Health Capital on the Margins: Cultural Resources for Navigating Healthcare in Communities with Limited Access." *Social Science & Medicine* 133 (May): 145–52.

Magaña, Maurice Rafael. 2017. "Spaces of Resistance, Everyday Activism, and Belonging: Youth Reimagining and Reconfiguring the City in Oaxaca, Mexico." *Journal of Latin American and Caribbean Anthropology* 22 (2): 215–34.

Maldonado, Marta Maria. 2014. "Latino Incorporation and Racialized Border Politics in the Heartland: Interior Enforcement and Policeability in an English-Only State." *American Behavioral Scientist* 58 (14): 1927–45.

Mallet, Marie L., and Lisa García Bedolla. 2019. "Transitory Legality: The Health Implication of Ending DACA." *California Journal of Politics and Policy* 11 (2): 1–25.

Mansbridge, Jane. 2022. "Everyday Activism." In *The Wiley-Blackwell Encyclopedia of Social and Political Movements*, edited by David A. Snow, Donatella della Porta, Bert Klandermans, and Doug McAdam, 1–2. New York: Wiley-Blackwell.

Marquez-Benitez, Gabriela, and Amalia Pallares. 2016. "Not One More: Linking Civil Disobediences and Public Anti-deportation Campaigns." *North American Dialogue* 19 (1): 13–22.

Marrow, Helen B. 2020. "Hope Turned Sour: Second-Generation Incorporation and Mobility in U.S. New Immigrant Destinations." *Ethnic and Racial Studies* 43 (1): 99–118.

Martinez, Pedro Santiago, Claudia Muñoz, Mariela Nuñez-Janes, Stephen Pavey, Fidel Castro Rodríguez, and Marco Saavedra, eds. 2020. *Eclipse of Dreams: The Undocumented-Led Struggle for Freedom*. Chico, CA: AK Press.

Martinez HoSang, Daniel. 2023. *A Wider Type of Freedom: How Struggles for Racial Justice Liberate Everyone*. Berkeley: University of California Press.

Martínez, Rafael M. 2024. *Illegalized: Undocumented Youth Movements in the United States*. Tucson, AZ: University of Arizona Press.

Massey, Douglas, and Magaly Sánchez. 2010. *Brokered Boundaries: Immigrant Identity in Anti-immigrant Times*. New York: Russell Sage Foundation.

McGranahan, Carole. 2018. "Refusal as Political Practice: Citizenship, Sovereignty, and Tibetan Refugee Status." *American Ethnologist* 45 (3): 367–79.

McKearney, Patrick, and Megha Amrith. 2021. "Care." In *The Open Encyclopedia of Anthropology*, edited by Felix Stein. https://anthroencyclopedia.com.

Mena Robles, Jorge, and Ruth Gomberg-Muñoz. 2016. "Activism after DACA: Lessons from Chicago's Immigrant Youth Justice League." *North American Dialogue* 19 (1): 46–54.

Mendes, Júlia, and Aurora Chang. 2019. "Undocumented and Afraid: Expanding the Definition of Student Activism." In *Student Activism, Politics, and Campus Climate in Higher Education*, edited by Demetri L. Morgan and Charles H. F. Davis III, 60–76. New York: Routledge.

Menjívar, Cecilia. 2000. *Fragmented Ties: Salvadoran Immigrant Networks in America*. Berkeley: University of California Press.

———. 2006. "Liminal Legality: Salvadoran and Guatemalan Immigrants' Lives in the United States." *American Journal of Sociology* 111 (4): 999–1037.

———. 2010. "Immigrants, Immigration, and Sociology: Reflecting on the State of the Discipline." *Sociological Inquiry* 80 (1): 3–27.

Menjívar, Cecilia, and Leisy J. Abrego. 2012. "Legal Violence: Immigration Law and the Lives of Central American Immigrants." *American Journal of Sociology* 117 (5): 1380–421.

Menjívar, Cecilia, and Daniel Kanstroom, eds. 2014. *Constructing Immigrant "Illegality": Critiques, Experiences, Responses*. New York: Cambridge University Press.

Migration Policy Institute (MPI). 2017. "DACA Recipients and Program Participation Rate, by State." Interactive tool map. www.migrationpolicy.org.

———. 2021. "U.S. Immigrant Population by Metropolitan Area." www.migrationpolicy.org.

———. 2022. "Trump Completed 472 Executive Actions on Immigration during His Presidency, Many That Could Have Lasting Effects on the U.S. Immigration System." February 1, 2022. www.migrationpolicy.org.

Miller, Alisa B., Osob M. Issa, Emily Hahn, Naima Y. Agalab, and Saida M. Abdi. 2021. "Developing Advisory Boards within Community-Based Participatory Approaches to Improve Mental Health among Refugee Communities." *Progress in Community Health Partnerships: Research, Education, and Action* 15 (1): 107–16.

Milligan, Christine, and Janine Wiles. 2010. "Landscapes of Care." *Progress in Human Geography* 34 (6): 736–54.

Mol, Annemarie. 2008. *The Logic of Care: Health and the Problem of Patient Choice.* New York: Routledge.

Mora, Maria De Jesus, Rodolfo Rodriguez, Alejandro Zermeño, and Paul Almeida. 2018. "Immigrant Rights and Social Movements." *Sociology Compass* 12 (8): e12599.

Moraga, Cherríe, and Gloria Anzaldúa. 1981. *This Bridge Called My Back: Writings by Radical Women of Color.* Watertown, MA: Persephone Press.

Nájera, Jennifer R. 2015. "Unauthorized Education: Challenging Borders between Good and Bad Immigrants." *Association of Mexican American Educators Journal* 9 (3): 35–46.

———. 2020. "Creating Safe Space for Undocumented Students: Building on Politically Unstable Ground." *Anthropology & Education Quarterly* 51 (3): 341–58.

National Cancer Institute (NCI). 2018. "Survey Instruments." Online data and survey instrument. Health Information National Trends Survey, NCI. https://hints.cancer.gov.

National Conference of State Legislatures (NCSL). 2020. "Deferred Action for Childhood Arrivals: Federal Policy and Examples of State Actions." Research brief. April 16, 2020. www.ncsl.org.

———. 2022. "Immigration Laws and Current State Immigration Legislation." Database. February 11, 2022. www.ncsl.org.

National Immigration Law Center. 2023. "Basic Facts about In-State Tuition for Undocumented Immigrant Students." August 2023. www.nilc.org.

Navaro-Yashin, Yael. 2007. "Make-Believe Papers, Legal Forms and the Counterfeit: Affective Interactions between Documents and People in Britain and Cyprus." *Anthropological Theory* 7 (1): 79–98.

Negrón-Gonzales, Genevieve. 2013. "Navigating 'Illegality': Undocumented Youth & Oppositional Consciousness." In "Place, Power, and Possibility: Remaking Social Work with Children and Youth," edited by Janet Finn, Lynn Nybell, and Jeffrey Shook. Special issue, *Children and Youth Services Review* 35 (8): 1284–90.

———. 2014. "Undocumented, Unafraid and Unapologetic: Re-articulatory Practices and Migrant Youth 'Illegality.'" *Latino Studies* 12 (2): 259–78.

Newman, Susan D., Jeannette O. Andrews, Gayenell S. Magwood, Carolyn Jenkins, Melissa J. Cox, and Deborah C. Williamson. 2011. "Community Advisory Boards in Community-Based Participatory Research: A Synthesis of Best Processes." *Preventing Chronic Disease* 8 (3): A70.

Ngai, Mae M. 2014. *Impossible Subjects: Illegal Aliens and the Making of Modern America*. Updated ed. Princeton, NJ: Princeton University Press.

Nicholls, Walter J. 2013. *The DREAMers: How the Undocumented Youth Movement Transformed the Immigrant Rights Debate*. Stanford, CA: Stanford University Press.

———. 2021. "The Uneven Geographies of Politicisation: The Case of the Undocumented Immigrant Youth Movement in the United States." *Antipode* 53 (2): 465–85.

Nuñez-Janes, Mariela, and Mario Ovalle. 2016. "Organic Activists: Undocumented Youth Creating Spaces of Acompañamiento." *Diaspora, Indigenous, and Minority Education* 10 (4): 189–200.

Nuñez-Janes, Mariela, Mario Ovalle, and Stephanie Plancarte. 2018. "Creating Sanctuary: Practices of Acompañamiento." *Fieldsights*, January 31, 2018. https://culanth.org.

Nvé Díaz San Francisco, Carolina. 2022. "Care during Pandemic Times: Digital Ethnography with Mental Health Professionals in Equatorial Guinea." *Anthropology and Humanism* 47 (2): 329–45.

Obatuase, Ewaoluwa. 2022. "DACA's Rollercoaster Ride of Legal Battles." New America, March 29, 2022. http://newamerica.org.

Orellana, Marjorie Faulstich. 2009a. *Translating Childhoods: Immigrant Youth, Language, and Culture*. Rutgers Series in Childhood Studies. New Brunswick, NJ: Rutgers University Press.

———. 2009b. "The Work Kids Do: Mexican and Central American Immigrant Children's Contributions to Households and Schools in California." *Harvard Educational Review* 71 (3): 366–90.

Orellana, Marjorie Faulstich, Lisa Dorner, and Lucila Pulido. 2003. "Accessing Assets: Immigrant Youth's Work as Family Translators or 'Para-Phrasers.'" *Social Problems* 50 (4): 505–24.

Ortega, Sigolène, Megan Stamey McAlvain, Katherine J. Briant, Sarah Hohl, and Beti Thompson. 2018. "Perspectives of Community Advisory Board Members in a Community-Academic Partnership." *Journal of Health Care for the Poor and Underserved* 29 (4): 1529–43.

Pallares, Amalia, and Nilda Flores-González. 2011. "Regarding Family: New Actors in the Chicago Protests." In *Rallying for Immigrant Rights: The Fight for Inclusion in the 21st Century*, edited by Kim Voss and Irene Bloemraad, 161–79. Berkeley: University of California Press.

Parreñas, Rhacel. 2015. *Servants of Globalization: Migration and Domestic Work*. 2nd ed. Stanford, CA: Stanford University Press.

Patler, Caitlin. 2014. "Racialized 'Illegality': The Convergence of Race and Legal Status among Black, Latino and Asian-American Undocumented Young Adults." In *Scholars and Southern Californian Immigrants in Dialogue*, edited by Victoria Carty,

Tekle M. Woldemikael, and Rafael Luévano, 93–113. New Conversations in Public Sociology. Lanham, MD: Lexington.

———. 2018. "'Citizens but for Papers': Undocumented Youth Organizations, Anti-deportation Campaigns, and the Reframing of Citizenship." *Social Problems* 65 (1): 96–115.

Patler, Caitlin, Jo Mhairi Hale, and Erin Hamilton. 2021. "Paths to Mobility: A Longitudinal Evaluation of Earnings among Latino/a DACA Recipients in California." *American Behavioral Scientist* 65 (9): 1146–64.

Patler, Caitlin, Erin Hamilton, Kelsey Meagher, and Robin Savinar. 2019. "Uncertainty about DACA May Undermine Its Positive Impact on Health for Recipients and Their Children." *Health Affairs* 38 (5): 738–45.

Patler, Caitlin, Erin R. Hamilton, and Robin L. Savinar. 2021. "The Limits of Gaining Rights while Remaining Marginalized: The Deferred Action for Childhood Arrivals (DACA) Program and the Psychological Wellbeing of Latina/o Undocumented Youth." *Social Forces* 100 (1): 246–72.

Patler, Caitlin, and Whitney Laster Pirtle. 2018. "From Undocumented to Lawfully Present: Do Changes to Legal Status Impact Psychological Wellbeing among Latino Immigrant Young Adults?" In "The Role of Racism in Health Inequalities: Integrating Approaches from across Disciplines," edited by Margaret Hicken, Myles Durkee, Nicole Kravitz-Wurtz, and James Jackson. Special issue, *Social Science & Medicine* 199 (February): 39–48.

Perez, Nicole. 2021. "Nested Contexts of Reception: Latinx Identity Development across a New Immigrant Community." *Ethnic and Racial Studies* 44 (11): 1995–2015.

Philbin, Morgan M., Morgan Flake, Mark L. Hatzenbuehler, and Jennifer S. Hirsch. 2018. "State-Level Immigration and Immigrant-Focused Policies as Drivers of Latino Health Disparities in the United States." In "The Role of Racism in Health Inequalities: Integrating Approaches from across Disciplines," edited by Margaret Hicken, Myles Durkee, Nicole Kravitz-Wurtz, and James Jackson. Special issue, *Social Science & Medicine* 199 (February): 29–38.

Phillimore, Jenny, and Sin Yi Cheung. 2021. "The Violence of Uncertainty: Empirical Evidence on How Asylum Waiting Time Undermines Refugee Health." *Social Science & Medicine* 282 (August): 114–54.

Pierce, Velarde, Alein Y. Haro Sharon, Cecilia Ayón, and Laura E. Enriquez. 2021. "Evaluating the Effect of Legal Vulnerabilities and Social Support on the Mental Health of Undocumented College Students." *Journal of Latinos and Education* 20 (3): 246–59.

Pine, Adrienne. 2013. "Revolution as a Care Plan: Ethnography, Nursing and Somatic Solidarity in Honduras." *Social Science & Medicine* 99 (December): 143–52.

Pink, Sarah. 2012. *Situating Everyday Life: Practices and Places.* London: Sage.

Population Reference Bureau (PRB). 2008. "African-Born Blacks in the Washington, D.C., Metro Area." January 24, 2008. www.prb.org.

Portes, Alejandro, and Rubén G. Rumbaut. 2007. *Immigrant America: A Portrait.* 3rd ed. Berkeley: University of California Press.

Price, Marie, and Giancarla Rojas. 2021. "The Ordinary Lives and Uneven Precarity of the DACAmented: Visualising Migrant Precarity in Metropolitan Washington." *Journal of Ethnic and Migration Studies* 47 (20): 4758–78.

Price, Marie, and Audrey Singer. 2008. "Edge Gateways: Suburbs, Immigrants and the Politics of Reception in Metropolitan Washington." In *Twenty-First Century Immigrant Gateways: Immigrant Incorporation in Suburban America*, edited by Audrey Singer, Susan Hardwick, and Caroline B. Brettell, 137–68. Washington, DC: Brookings Institution Press.

Quesada, James, Laurie K. Hart, and Philippe Bourgois. 2011. "Structural Vulnerability and Health: Latino Migrant Laborers in the United States." *Medical Anthropology* 30 (4): 339–62.

Ramirez, Maria Liliana. 2020. "Beyond Identity: Coming Out as UndocuQueer." In Abrego and Negrón-Gonzales, *We Are Not Dreamers*, 146–67.

Ramsay, Georgina. 2020. "Time and the Other in Crisis: How Anthropology Makes Its Displaced Object." *Anthropological Theory* 20 (4): 385–413.

Raymond-Flesch, Marissa, Rachel Siemons, Nadereh Pourat, Ken Jacobs, and Claire D. Brindis. 2014. "'There Is No Help Out There and if There Is, It's Really Hard to Find': A Qualitative Study of the Health Concerns and Health Care Access of Latino 'DREAMers.'" *Journal of Adolescent Health* 55 (3): 323–28.

Reese, Ashanté M. 2019. *Black Food Geographies: Race, Self-Reliance, and Food Access in Washington, D.C.* Chapel Hill: University of North Carolina Press.

Rodríguez, Ana Patricia. 2009. *Dividing the Isthmus: Central American Transnational Histories, Literatures, and Cultures.* Austin: University of Texas Press.

Rosa, Jonathan, and Yarimar Bonilla. 2017. "Deprovincializing Trump, Decolonizing Diversity, and Unsettling Anthropology." *American Ethnologist* 44 (2): 201–8.

Rosales, William E., Laura E. Enriquez, and Jennifer R. Nájera. 2021. "Politically Excluded, Undocu-Engaged: The Perceived Effect of Hostile Immigration Policies on Undocumented Student Political Engagement." *Journal of Latinos and Education* 20 (3): 260–75.

Roth, Benjamin J. 2019. "The Double Bind of DACA: Exploring the Legal Violence of Liminal Status for Undocumented Youth." *Ethnic and Racial Studies* 42 (15): 2548–65.

Rubio, Elizabeth Hanna. 2019. "'We Need to Redefine What We Mean by Winning': NAKASEC's Immigrant Justice Activism and Thinking Citizenship Otherwise." *Amerasia Journal* 45 (2): 157–72.

Rubio, Elizabeth Hanna, and Xitlalli Alvarez Almendariz. 2019. "Refusing 'Undocumented': Imagining Survival Beyond the Gift of Papers." *Fieldsights*, January 17, 2019. https://culanth.org.

Rustage, Kieran, Alison Crawshaw, Saliha Majeed-Hajaj, Anna Deal, Laura Nellums, Yusuf Ciftci, Sebastian S. Fuller, Lucy Goldsmith, Jon S. Friedland, and Sally Hargreaves. 2021. "Participatory Approaches in the Development of Health Interventions for Migrants: A Systematic Review." *BMJ Open* 11 (10): e053678.

Rylko-Bauer, Barbara, Merrill Singer, and John Van Willigen. 2006. "Reclaiming Applied Anthropology: Its Past, Present, and Future." *American Anthropologist* 108 (1): 178–90.

Sacchetti, Maria. 2022. "As DACA Immigrant Program Turns 10, Legal Challenges Persist." *Washington Post*, June 14, 2022. www.washingtonpost.com.

Salazar, Cinthya. 2021. "We Are Friends? Navigating Relationships with Undocumented College Students as Co-researchers in Participatory Action Research." *International Journal of Qualitative Studies in Education* 34 (8): 715–32.

Sánchez-Molina, Raúl, and Lucy M. Cohen, eds. 2016. *Latinas Crossing Borders and Building Communities in Greater Washington: Applying Anthropology in Multicultural Neighborhoods*. Lanham, MD: Lexington Books.

Sati, Joel. 2017a. "Noncitizenship and the Case for Illegalized Persons." *Berkeley News* (blog), January 24, 2017. https://news.berkeley.edu.

———. 2017b. "How DACA Pits 'Good Immigrants' Against Millions of Others." *Washington Post*, September 7, 2017. www.washingtonpost.com.

———. 2020a. "On Trumpism and Illegality." In *Trumpism and Its Discontents*, edited by Osagie K. Obasogie, 115–29. Berkeley, CA: Berkeley Public Policy Press.

———. 2020b. "'Other' Borders: The Illegal as Normative Metaphor." In Abrego and Negrón-Gonzales, *We Are Not Dreamers*, 23–44.

Saxton, Dvera I. 2021. *The Devil's Fruit: Farmworkers, Health, and Environmental Justice*. New Brunswick, NJ: Rutgers University Press.

Scheper-Hughes, Nancy. 1995. "The Primacy of the Ethical: Propositions for a Militant Anthropology." *Current Anthropology* 36 (3): 409–40.

Scheper-Hughes, Nancy, and Philippe Bourgois, eds. 2003. *Violence in War and Peace: An Anthology*. Wiley Blackwell Readers in Anthropology. New York: Wiley-Blackwell.

Schuller, Mark. 2021. *Humanity's Last Stand: Confronting Global Catastrophe*. Rutgers, NJ: Rutgers University Press.

Scott, James C. 1985. *Weapons of the Weak: Everyday Forms of Peasant Resistance*. New Haven, CT: Yale University Press.

———. 1990. *Domination and the Arts of Resistance: Hidden Transcripts*. New Haven, CT: Yale University Press.

Seif, Hinda. 2014. "'Coming Out of the Shadows' and 'Undocuqueer': Undocumented Immigrants Transforming Sexuality Discourse and Activism." *Journal of Language and Sexuality* 3 (1): 87–120.

Sepúlveda, Enrique, III. 2011. "Toward a Pedagogy of Acompañamiento: Mexican Migrant Youth Writing from the Underside of Modernity." *Harvard Educational Review* 81 (3): 550–73.

Shange, Savannah. 2022. "Abolition in the Clutch: Shifting through the Gears with Anthropology." *Feminist Anthropology* 3:187–97.

Shim, Janet K. 2010. "Cultural Health Capital: A Theoretical Approach to Understanding Health Care Interactions and the Dynamics of Unequal Treatment." *Journal of Health and Social Behavior* 51 (1): 1–15.

Siemons, Rachel, Marissa Raymond-Flesh, Colette L. Auerswald, and Claire D. Brindis. 2017. "Coming of Age on the Margins: Mental Health and Wellbeing among Latino Immigrant Young Adults Eligible for Deferred Action for Childhood Arrivals (DACA)." *Journal of Immigrant and Minority Health* 19 (3): 543–51.

Silver, Alexis M. 2018. *Shifting Boundaries: Immigrant Youth Negotiating National, State, and Small-Town Politics.* Stanford, CA: Stanford University Press.

Silvestre, Audrey. 2020. "Me Vestí De Reina: Trans and Queer Sonic Spatial Entitlement." In Abrego and Negrón-Gonzales, *We Are Not Dreamers*, 168–89.

Simpson, Audra. 2014. *Mohawk Interruptus: Political Life across the Borders of Settler States.* Durham, NC: Duke University Press.

Singer, Audrey. 2004. "The Rise of New Immigrant Gateways." Living Cities Census Series, Center on Urban and Metropolitan Policy. Washington, DC: Brookings Institution.

———. 2012. "Metropolitan Washington: A New Immigrant Gateway." In *Research in Race and Ethnic Relations*, edited by Enrique S. Pumar, 17:3–24. Washington, DC: Emerald.

Singer, Merrill. 2013. "Studying Hidden and Hard-to-Reach Populations." In *Specialized Ethnographic Methods: A Mixed Methods Approach*, edited by Jean J. Schensul and Margaret D. LeCompte, 255–317. Walnut Creek, CA: AltaMira Press.

Slack, Jeremy. 2019. *Deported to Death: How Drug Violence Is Changing Migration on the U.S.-Mexico Border.* Berkeley: University of California Press.

Smith, Robert Courtney. 2024. "Doing Community and Institutionally Engaged Work and Promoting Immigrant Well-Being while Building a Research Career." *American Behavioral Scientist.* https://doi.org/10.1177/00027642241229539.

Smith-Morris, Carolyn. 2018. "Care as Virtue, Care as Critical Frame: A Discussion of Four Recent Ethnographies." *Medical Anthropology* 37 (5): 426–32.

Soaita, Adriana Mihaela. 2024. "Everyday Activism: Private Tenants Demand Right to Home." *Housing Studies* 39 (6): 1422–43.

Solorzano, Lizette, and Paulina Ruiz. 2021. "Saving DACA, Healing Ourselves: Aggressions and Healing Experiences during the Course of DACA Activism in Washington, DC." *Latino Studies* 19 (2): 269–75.

Sosa, Leticia Villarreal, Benjamin Roth, and Sophia Rodriguez. 2021. "Crossing Borders: Exploring the Role of School Social Workers in Immigrant-Serving Schools." *Social Work Research* 45 (3): 198–206.

Speed, Shannon. 2006. "At the Crossroads of Human Rights and Anthropology: Toward a Critically Engaged Activist Research." *American Anthropologist* 108 (1): 66–76.

Stacciarini, Jeanne-Marie R., Rebekah Felicia Smith, Brenda Wiens, Awilda Pérez, Barbara Locke, and Melody LaFlam. 2015. "I Didn't Ask to Come to This Country . . . I Was a Child: The Mental Health Implications of Growing Up Undocumented." *Journal of Immigrant and Minority Health* 17 (4): 1225–30.

Stuesse, Angela. 2016. *Scratching Out a Living: Latinos, Race, and Work in the Deep South.* Berkeley: University of California Press.

Stuesse, Angela, and Mathew Coleman. 2014. "Automobility, Immobility, Altermobility: Surviving and Resisting the Intensification of Immigrant Policing." *City & Society* 26 (1): 51–72.

Suárez-Navaz, Liliana. 2004. *Rebordering the Mediterranean: Boundaries and Citizenship in Southern Europe*. Oxford: Berghahn Books.

Suárez-Orozco, Carola, Frosso Motti-Stefanidi, Amy Marks, and Dalal Katsiaficas. 2018. "An Integrative Risk and Resilience Model for Understanding the Adaptation of Immigrant-Origin Children and Youth." *American Psychologist* 73 (6): 781–96.

Suárez-Orozco, Carola, and Hirokazu Yoshikawa. 2013. "Undocumented Status: Implications for Child Development, Policy, and Ethical Research." *New Directions for Child and Adolescent Development*, no. 141 (Fall): 61–78.

Substance Abuse and Mental Health Services Administration (SAMHSA). 2017. "Key Substance Use and Mental Health Indicators in the United States: Results from the 2016 National Survey on Drug Use and Health." HHS Pub. No. SMA 17-5044, NSDUH Series H-52. Rockville, MD: Center for Behavioral Health Statistics and Quality, SAMHSA.

Sudhinaraset, May, Irving Ling, Tu My To, Jason Melo, and Thu Quach. 2017. "Dreams Deferred: Contextualizing the Health and Psychosocial Needs of Undocumented Asian and Pacific Islander Young Adults in Northern California." *Social Science & Medicine*, no. 184 (July): 144–52.

Sudhinaraset, May, Tu My To, Irving Ling, Jason Melo, and Josue Chavarin. 2017. "The Influence of Deferred Action for Childhood Arrivals on Undocumented Asian and Pacific Islander Young Adults: Through a Social Determinants of Health Lens." *Journal of Adolescent Health* 60 (6): 741–46.

Suerbaum, Magdalena. 2023. "Embodying Legal Precarity: Living with Ongoing Short-Term Protection in Germany." *International Migration* 61 (3): 25–38.

Svajlenka, Nicole Prchal, and Trinh Q. Truong. 2021. "The Demographic and Economic Impacts of DACA Recipients: Fall 2021 Edition." *Center for American Progress* (blog), November 24, 2021. www.americanprogress.org.

Tam, Ruth, Patrick Fort, Shweta Watwe, and Ann Marie Awad. 2022. "From Little Saigon to Eden Center: The Story of Northern Virginia's Vietnamese Community." *WAMU* (blog), June 23, 2022. https://wamu.org.

Tatian, Peter A., Sara McTarnaghan, Olivia Arena, and Yipeng Su. 2018. "State of Immigrants in the District of Columbia: Data Profiles of Immigrants from Latin America, Asia, Africa, and the Caribbean." Urban Institute, December 2018. www.urban.org.

Terriquez, Veronica. 2015. "Intersectional Mobilization, Social Movement Spillover, and Queer Youth Leadership in the Immigrant Rights Movement." *Social Problems* 62 (3): 343–62.

———. 2017. "Legal Status, Civic Organizations, and Political Participation among Latino Young Adults." *Sociological Quarterly* 58 (2): 315–36.

Terriquez, Veronica, Tizoc Brenes, and Abdiel Lopez. 2018. "Intersectionality as a Multipurpose Collective Action Frame: The Case of the Undocumented Youth Movement." *Ethnicities* 18 (2): 260–76.

Thelen, Tatjana. 2021. "Care as Belonging, Difference, and Inequality." In *Oxford Research Encyclopedia of Anthropology*, edited by Mark Aldenderfer. https://oxfordre.com.

Thelen, Tatjana, and Cati Coe. 2019. "Political Belonging through Elderly Care: Temporalities, Representations and Mutuality." *Anthropological Theory* 19 (2): 279–99.

Thomson, Rachel. 2007. "The Qualitative Longitudinal Case History: Practical, Methodological and Ethical Reflections." *Social Policy and Society* 6 (4): 571–82.

Ticktin, Miriam. 2011. *Casualties of Care: Immigration and the Politics of Humanitarianism in France.* Berkeley: University of California Press.

———. 2021. "Care and the Commons." In "The Politics of Care," edited by Deva Woodly and Rachel H. Brown. Special issue, *Contemporary Political Theory* 20 (4): 890–925.

Tournadre, Jérôme. 2017. "'Because We Are the Only Ones in the Community!' Protest and Daily Life in Poor South African Neighborhoods." *Focaal* 2017 (78): 52–64.

Tsing, Anna Lowenhaupt. 2018. "Getting By in Terrifying Times." *Dialogues in Human Geography* 8 (1): 73–76.

———. 2021. *The Mushroom at the End of the World: On the Possibility of Life in Capitalist Ruins.* Princeton, NJ: Princeton University Press.

Tuck, Eve, and K. Wayne Yang. 2014. "Unbecoming Claims: Pedagogies of Refusal in Qualitative Research." *Qualitative Inquiry* 20 (6): 811–18.

Tuhiwai Smith, Linda. 2012. *Decolonizing Methodologies: Research and Indigenous Peoples.* 2nd ed. London: Zed Books.

Unterberger, Alayne. 2009. "The Blur: Balancing Applied Anthropology, Activism, and Self vis-à-vis Immigrant Communities." *NAPA Bulletin* 31 (1): 1–12.

Unzueta Carrasco, Tania A., and Hinda Seif. 2014. "Disrupting the Dream: Undocumented Youth Reframe Citizenship and Deportability through Anti-deportation Activism." *Latino Studies* 12 (2): 279–99.

U.S. Census Bureau. 2021. "American Community Survey 5-Year Estimates." Census data, retrieved from Census Reporter profile page for Washington-Arlington-Alexandria, DC-VA-MD-WV metro area. http://censusreporter.org.

U.S. Citizenship and Immigration Services (USCIS). 2020a. "Approximate Active DACA Recipients." www.uscis.gov.

———. 2020b. "Number of Form I-821D, Consideration of Deferred Action for Childhood Arrivals, Status, by Fiscal Year, Quarter, and Case Status: Aug. 15, 2012–Sep. 30, 2020." Data report. www.uscis.gov.

———. 2022. "Count of Active DACA Recipients by Month of Current DACA Expiration." www.uscis.gov.

———. 2023. "Consideration of Deferred Action for Childhood Arrivals (DACA)." September 18, 2023. www.uscis.gov.

Valdivia, Carolina. 2019. "Youth Activism." In Boehm and Terrio, *Illegal Encounters*, 147–58.

———. 2020. "Undocumented Young Adults' Heightened Vulnerability in the Trump Era." In Abrego and Negrón-Gonzales, *We Are Not Dreamers*, 127–45.

Vaquera, Elizabeth, Elizabeth Aranda, and Roberto G. Gonzales. 2014. "Patterns of Incorporation of Latinos in Old and New Destinations: From Invisible to Hypervisible." *American Behavioral Scientist* 58 (14): 1823–33.

Vaquera, Elizabeth, Elizabeth Aranda, and Isabel Sousa-Rodriguez. 2017. "Emotional Challenges of Undocumented Young Adults: Ontological Security, Emotional Capital, and Well-Being." *Social Problems* 64 (2): 298–314.

Varsanyi, Monica W., Paul G. Lewis, Doris Marie Provine, and Scott Decker. 2012. "A Multilayered Jurisdictional Patchwork: Immigration Federalism in the United States." *Law & Policy* 34 (2): 138–58.

Vega, Sujey. 2012. "The Politics of Everyday Life: Mexican Hoosiers and Ethnic Belonging at the Crossroads of America." *City & Society* 24 (2): 196–217.

Velarde Pierce, Sharon, Alein Y. Haro, Cecilia Ayón, and Laura E. Enriquez. 2021. "Evaluating the Effect of Legal Vulnerabilities and Social Support on the Mental Health of Undocumented College Students." *Journal of Latinos and Education* 20 (3): 246–59.

Venkataramani, Atheendar S., Sachin J. Shah, Rourke O'Brien, Ichiro Kawachi, and Alexander C. Tsai. 2017. "Health Consequences of the US Deferred Action for Childhood Arrivals (DACA) Immigration Programme: A Quasi-Experimental Study." *Lancet Public Health* 2 (4): e175–81.

Vinthagen, Stellan, and Anna Johansson. 2013. "'Everyday Resistance': Exploration of a Concept and Its Theories." *Resistance Studies Magazine*, no. 1. https://resistance-journal.org.

Vivienne, Sonja, and Jean Burgess. 2012. "The Digital Storyteller's Stage: Queer Everyday Activists Negotiating Privacy and Publicness." *Journal of Broadcasting & Electronic Media* 56 (3): 362–77.

Wallerstein, Nina, Bonnie Duran, John G. Oetzel, and Meredith Minkler, eds. 2017. *Community-Based Participatory Research for Health: Advancing Social and Health Equity*. Newark, NJ: John Wiley.

Waters, Mary C., Patrick J. Carr, Maia J. Kefalas, and Jennifer Holdaway. 2011. *Coming of Age in America: The Transition to Adulthood in the Twenty-First Century*. Berkeley: University of California Press.

White House. 2024. "Fact Sheet: Biden-Harris Administration Expands Health Care Coverage to DACA Recipients." May 3, 2024. www.whitehouse.gov.

Willen, Sarah S. 2007. "Toward a Critical Phenomenology of 'Illegality': State Power, Criminalization, and Abjectivity among Undocumented Migrant Workers in Tel Aviv, Israel." *International Migration* 45 (3): 8–38.

———. 2014. "Plotting a Moral Trajectory, Sans Papiers: Outlaw Motherhood as Inhabitable Space of Welcome." *Ethos* 42 (1): 84–100.

Willen, Sarah S., Nasima Selim, Emily Mendenhall, Miriam Magaña Lopez, Shahanoor Akter Chowdhury, and Hansjörg Dilger. 2021. "Flourishing: Migration and Health in Social Context." *BMJ Global Health* 6 (suppl. 1): e005108.

Willen, Sarah S., Abigail Fisher Williamson, Colleen C. Walsh, Mikayla Hyman, William Tootle Jr. 2022. "Rethinking Flourishing: Critical Insights and Qualitative

Perspectives from the U.S. Midwest." *Social Science and Medicine—Mental Health* 2:100057.

Wilson, Fernando A., and Jim P. Stimpson. 2020. "Letter to the Editor: US Policies Increase Vulnerability of Immigrant Communities to the COVID-19 Pandemic." *Annals of Global Health* 86 (57): 1–2.

Wong, Tom K., Sanaa Abrar, Claudia Flores, Tom Jawetz, Ignacia Rodriguez Kmec, Girsea Martinez Rosas, Holly Straut-Eppsteiner, and Philip E. Wolgin. 2019. "DACA Recipients' Livelihoods, Families, and Sense of Security Are at Stake This November." *Center for American Progress* (blog), September 19, 2019. www.americanprogress.org.

Wong, Tom K., Claudia Flores, and Ignacia Rodriguez Kmec. 2022. "2021 Survey of DACA Recipients Underscores the Importance of a Pathway to Citizenship." *Center for American Progress* (blog), February 3, 2022. www.americanprogress.org.

Wong, Tom K., Angela S. García, and Carolina Valdivia. 2019. "The Political Incorporation of Undocumented Youth." *Social Problems* 66 (3): 356–72.

Wong, Tom K., Greisa Martinez Rosas, and Adrian Reyna. 2016. "New Study of DACA Beneficiaries Shows Positive Economic and Educational Outcomes." *Center for American Progress* (blog), October 18, 2016. www.americanprogress.org.

Woodly, Deva. 2020. "The Politics of Care with Deva Woodly | The New School." YouTube, June 30, 2020. https://www.youtube.com/watch?v=ih6F6N9pg-A.

Woodly, Deva, Rachel H. Brown, Mara Marin, Shatema Threadcraft, Christopher Paul Harris, Jasmine Syedullah, and Miriam Ticktin. 2021. "The Politics of Care." *Contemporary Political Theory* 20 (4): 890–925.

Yarris, Kristin E. 2017. *Care Across Generations: Solidarity and Sacrifice in Transnational Families.* Stanford, CA: Stanford University Press.

Yarris, Kristin E., and Whitney L. Duncan, eds. 2024. *Accompaniment with Im/migrant Communities: Ethnographic Engagements.* Tucson: University of Arizona Press.

Yosso, Tara J. 2005. "Whose Culture Has Capital? A Critical Race Theory Discussion of Community Cultural Wealth." *Race Ethnicity and Education* 8 (1): 69–91.

Yosso, Tara, William Smith, Miguel Ceja, and Daniel Solórzano. 2010. "Critical Race Theory, Racial Microaggressions, and Campus Racial Climate for Latina/o Undergraduates." *Harvard Educational Review* 79 (4): 659–91.

Young, Maria-Elena De Trinidad, and Anne R. Pebley. 2017. "Legal Status, Time in the USA, and the Well-Being of Latinos in Los Angeles." *Journal of Urban Health* 94 (6): 764–75.

Zavella, Patricia. 2011. *I'm Neither Here nor There: Mexicans' Quotidian Struggles with Migration and Poverty.* Durham, NC: Duke University Press.

Zepeda-Millán, Chris. 2016. "Weapons of the (Not So) Weak: Immigrant Mass Mobilization in the US South." *Critical Sociology* 42 (2): 269–87.

———. 2017. *Latino Mass Mobilization: Immigration, Racialization, and Activism.* New York: Cambridge University Press.

Zong, Jie, and Jeanne Batalova. 2017. "Sub-Saharan African Immigrants in the United States." Migration Policy Institute, May 3, 2017. www.migrationpolicy.org.

INDEX

Page numbers in italics indicate Figures and Tables.

tan regions and, 93–94; policies and, 14–15; racism and, 50, 95; as socio-legal contexts, 52; well-being and, 168
executive powers, orders and, 7–8, 52–53, 171
existential fatigue, 22, 26–27, 69, 77, 80–81, 83

failure, of DACA, 15–17; success compared to, 13–14, 18–19
faith, 79–80
families, 122, 180; brokers and, 145–46, 152–53, 155–56; care and, 151, 161–63; COVID-19 pandemic and, 82, 234n74; deportation of, 74–75; homeownership and, 158–60, 162; ICE and, 61; immigration status and, 57–58, 66, 70, 144, 171; labor and, 159; mixed status of, 58, 139, 144, 171, 181, 183; precarity and, 157; relocation and, 112; risk and, 133–34; support from, 104–8
fear, 68, 94, 137–38; of deportation, 65–66, 71, 134, 153; mental health and, 71, 82; stigma compared to, 95; Trump and, 74
federal immigration policy reform, 9, 12, 51–52, 171–72, 188–89; local policies and, 48–49; precarity and, 94
Fiorito, Tara, 66
Flores, Andrea, 68, 90, 93, 96, 230n6
Florida, 52, 97–98
former DACA recipients, 17, 24, 225n70
futures, 35; DACA rescission and, 154; security and, 26, 63–64, 68

Galemba, Rebecca Berke, 207, 244n11, 245n40
Gálvez, Alyshia, 21–22, 132, 239n77
García, Angela S., 93–94
gateway cities, 51–52; DACA recipients and, 54; D.C. Metro region as, 40–44
gendered expectations, 12, 147–49; labor and, 41

geography, 12–13, 92; belonging and, 94; identity and, 37–39; immigration enforcement and, 93–94; metropolitan regions and, 20; navigational capital and, 96–97, 109, 142–44, 150–56, 162, 165; policies and, 110–11; precarity and, 90–91; racism and, 113; security and, 50, 111; uncertainty and, 114
Golash-Boza, Tanya, 13
Gomberg-Muñoz, Ruth, 185–86
Gonzales, Roberto G., 11–12, 60, 65–66, 94, 225n88
Great Migration, 40
guilt, activism and, 134–35
Gutmann, Matthew C., 120

health and well-being, 12, 35, 65–69, 75, 171, 199. See also mental health
health care, 37, 45–48, 88–90, 146, 158–59; careers in, 150, 162–66; COVID-19 pandemic and, 155, 166; navigational capital and, 29
health insurance, 2, 66, 155, 178, 231n22; anxiety and, 76; CHCs and, 151–52; relocation and, 98–100; social support and, 153–54; stress and, 73–74
higher education, 103–7; advocacy and, 183–88; careers and, 157–60, 179–80; exclusion in, 186–87; inclusion and, 180–81, 186; participants and, 59, 176–78; policies on, 50–51; resources and, 154, 185, 188
Hobart, Hiʻilei Julia Kawehipuaakahaopulani, 148–49
homeownership, 85, 108, 142–43, 163; communities and, 161; families and, 158–60, 162; phase III and, 157
Horton, Sarah B., 215, 245n25

ICE. See Immigration and Customs Enforcement
identity, 25, 203; DACA recipients and, 82, 129; geography and, 37–39

ABOUT THE AUTHOR

CHRISTINA M. GETRICH is an anthropologist whose research, teaching, and advocacy are focused on the health, well-being, and incorporation of immigrants in the United States. She is the author of *Border Brokers: Children of Mexican Immigrants Navigating U.S. Society, Laws, and Politics* and more than thirty peer-reviewed articles.